T0247557

TRIGGERS

TRIGGERS

A LIFE IN MUSIC

GLEN
MATLOCK

WITH PETER STONEMAN

weldon**owen**

weldon**owen**

an imprint of Insight Editions
P.O. Box 3088
San Rafael, CA 94912
www.weldonowen.com

CEO Raoul Goff
VP Publisher Roger Shaw
Editorial Director Katie Killebrew
Executive Editor Edward Ash-Milby
Art Director Allister Fein
VP Manufacturing Alix Nicholaeff
Sr Production Manager Joshua Smith
Sr Production Manager, Subsidiary Rights Lina s Palma-Temena

This edition first published in 2023 by
Bonnier Books UK Limited
4th Floor, Victoria House
Bloomsbury Square
London, WC1B 4DA
www.bonnierbooks.co.uk

Text © 2023 Glen Matlock

Design and layout © 2023 Bonnier Books UK Limited

All rights reserved. No part of this book may be reproduced in any form without
written permission from the publisher.

ISBN: 979-8-88674-181-0

Manufactured in China by Insight Editions

10 9 8 7 6 5 4 3 2 1

ROOTS of PEACE   REPLANTED PAPER

Insight Editions, in association with Roots of Peace, will plant two trees for each
tree used in the manufacturing of this book. Roots of Peace is an internationally
renowned humanitarian organization dedicated to eradicating land mines
worldwide and converting war-torn lands into productive farms and wildlife
habitats. Roots of Peace will plant two million fruit and nut trees in Afghanistan and
provide farmers there with the skills and support necessary for sustainable land use.

CONTENTS

PROLOGUE

It's early 1995 and, for want of something better to do, and with-out anybody being particularly interested in what I was up to, I found myself at a crossroads. If not a crossroads, then at the very least I was at a junction. Twenty years in the game and I wasn't getting any younger. I was pushing forty, but I still felt just as restless as I had when I started out on this road. Still, I hadn't been idle. Hopefully that's not something you could ever accuse me of. I was still chipping away at my craft. Over the past year or so, I'd put pen to paper on a bunch of songs that I thought were pretty good. It's not an earth-shattering observation to make, but if you're a fisherman, you'd better get that boat out to sea and catch some fish. If you're a centre-forward, you'd better get down the pitch and score a few goals. By the same token, if you call yourself a songwriter and don't write any songs, you're full of shit. Writing songs is item number one on the songwriter's job description. What you do with them afterwards, well, that's up to you. Usually you record them yourself, or occasionally you might pitch them to other artists, depending on how they come out. In this case, I had the songs earmarked for myself. Possibly this new batch of songs wasn't suited to anyone else anyway. I don't know. Looking back, maybe they were a bit too much like me, too personal, for somebody else to record a cover. Whatever the case, I had all these songs knocking around in my head and they didn't have a home. I laid down a rough batch of demos, but, despite all of that, I couldn't really think straight. The only way to clear out the wardrobe of your mind, as the great Vivian Stanshall put it, for me at least, is to start recording. Decluttering, they call it these days. So that's what I did. I made a start clearing out the proverbial wardrobe. I gathered up all the songs and the demos, and I set about making a new record. Writing songs is like a kind of therapy for me. Something's on your mind, you work on it. All the blood, sweat and artistic angst go into the pot and then it's out there in the world. It can be quite healthy to clear the decks. In terms of percentage, my guess is there are probably far fewer songwriters going into therapy than the rest of the population. Having said that, I didn't really know how or when the record was going to come out, or even if anybody would be bothered, but I got underway nonetheless. Fortunately, I didn't have to wait too long for the record to find a home. As always, I was looking forward, but I had no idea that the past was about to come a-knocking. But we'll come to that.

I'm friends with a guy called Tony Barber. Tony was playing bass with the Buzzcocks around that time in the 1990s. He played with, and was a fan of, the band the Creation, the legendary British Mod band from the 1960s. The Creation had a minor hit with the song 'Painter Man' back in the day, but it went on to be a smash hit for Boney M. a few years later. Tony called and told me he had a couple of tickets to see a Creation show at the Mean Fiddler in Harlesden, so I tagged along. It was a good night. While we were milling about, we had a chance meeting with Alan McGee, the head of Creation Records. Alan had named his record label after the band, so of course he was there. When the band were persuaded to re-form in the mid-1990s, he even signed them to his label. That led to the Creation releasing a single called 'Creation' on the label Creation the year before. Make of that what you will. This was at a time when Creation Records were riding high and everything they touched turned to gold, so they could do those kinds of pet-projects without getting any flak. The whole Cool Britannia thing was just starting to take off and Tony Blair and New Labour were waiting in the wings, as John Major's government was being kept on life support. Oasis were literally everywhere and shifting a lot of records, and generally making bank for Creation Records. Fair play to Alan. Despite all that glory, he was still an A&R guy at heart, and he always kept his ear to the ground. He struck me as someone who never rested on his laurels. Tony introduced Alan to me and, Alan being an old punk, we got to talking. He loved the Pistols, so he was keen to hear a few old war stories from the horse's mouth, so to speak. Eventually, he asked what I was up to now, and I told him about the new record I was working on and that I didn't have a home for it yet. Right on the spot, Alan said he'd put the record out on Creation. So, from that point on, Alan took over. I signed a deal with Creation, and I finished recording the album. It's a good record. If I'm going to be self-critical, maybe my singing wasn't so great back then, but I'm proud of that album, *Who's He Think He Is When He's at Home.*

Towards the end of the year, when I had the album in the can, a friend of mine, Calvin Hayes, called me up from out of the blue. Calvin was the son of music producer Mickie Most and he'd been the drummer in the 1980s pop band Johnny Hates Jazz. He asked what I was up to, and I explained where I was at: we'd finished the album and were just waiting for it to be mastered. Calvin was living in Los Angeles with his wife and daughter, and he told me he'd discovered this fantastic singer and maybe we could do something with them. Because I was just hanging around, waiting on Creation to schedule the album, he told me to jump on a flight and come over. Maybe bring Steve New along for the ride, he suggested. Steve New from the Rich Kids was always my 'go-to' guitarist, so that seemed a no-brainer. He was unheralded, a fantastically inventive player and a good friend. *What the hell*, I thought. I made a call to Steve, and we flew out to LA to meet Calvin.

On arrival, Steve was immediately pulled aside and quizzed by immigration for two hours, having overstayed his visa on his last visit. It wasn't the most auspicious start to the trip, to be honest. Two hours later, despite keeping me hanging on, Steve scampered up to me like butter wouldn't melt and we made our way out of the terminal. I'd pre-booked a rental car, so, after a long thirteen-hour flight into LAX, passport checks, the two-hour wait for Steve, plus the usual baggage claim rigmarole, we eventually rolled up at the car pick-up place to find an enormous, winding queue. Half an hour later, we'd wound our way to the front and the guy at the desk started giving me this big spiel about an upgrade to the rental car I'd booked. I said I didn't need the upgrade, but once he'd explained it was free, I figured why not? I asked what car we were getting, but he just grinned and tossed me the keys. So we headed out to the rental car lot and there, shimmering in the California sunshine, we found a brand-new gold Lexus 400. *Looks kind of cool,* I thought, so Steve and I jumped in, thinking we were going to look the bee's knees cruising down Sunset in this beast. Naturally we didn't. We drove out of the lot, immediately drove in the wrong direction for a while, and before too long we were hopelessly lost. In my defence, LA's a confusing place if you don't know your way around. All the roads seem like they're 30 miles long and every couple of miles there's an intersection and the road names suddenly change for a mile or two before reverting to the previous name. Somehow, we eventually made it into south Los Angeles and found our way to Calvin's place just east of Sunset Boulevard, where Steve and I were both staying. When we pulled up outside, it was already quite late, but I banged on the horn a few times to let him know we'd arrived. Eventually, a crumpled Calvin came out with Cindy, his missus.

'Is that your car?' he said, scratching his head.

'Yeah.'

'You're gonna get carjacked in that,' he told me, and I immediately felt paranoid about the gold Lexus and the free upgrade.

We knocked around LA for a few days, and I caught up with a few faces I hadn't seen in a while. Everywhere we parked up, someone shuffled over to tell me that the car was almost certainly going to get jacked. It was a daily occurrence. I got used to it, in fact. One day, I arranged to meet up with Anita Camarata for lunch in Santa Monica, where she had an office. Anita used to look after the Sex Pistols residuals after the split and she also managed Steve Jones's career. She'd been looking after him for a long time and had taken him on as a client when he was really on his heels. He was spending his days walking up and down Hollywood Boulevard without a cent to his name. One day, by pure luck, he found Anita at the side of the road, where her Porsche had broken down. Steve helped her hotwire the car and, when they got talking, he discovered she was working for Danny DeVito and that she was a big wheel in the music business. She took Steve under her wing and attempted to start sorting out his affairs. I like Anita, but even she shook her head when she caught sight of the gold Lexus parked up outside.

'You'll get carjacked in that,' she told me.

After our lunch and we'd said our goodbyes, I headed back to Calvin's and – of course – I found myself heading in the wrong direction. I could feel the paranoia creeping up on me. The further I went, the worse my situation became. The surroundings were becoming less and less opulent with every block and there was no way for me to turn the beast around. The gold Lexus was now the only car on this long, long four-lane road heading into the heart of Compton. My palms sweating, I pulled up at a stop sign, and a patrol car, a proper *Car 54, Where Are You?* prowler, pulled up in the lane beside me and the officer motioned for me to wind my window down.

'Hey, mac, are you lost?'

I told him yes and he shook his head and asked me to follow him. I gratefully did so as he performed an elaborate U-turn across the four lanes. *Jeez*, I thought, even the cop was thinking I was going to get carjacked.

Safely back in the studio, we tried out the singer Calvin was talking about. He was a great guy, very interesting, but he wasn't the right fit for me to work with, so that was that, I thought. I was stuck in LA not really doing much, just taking up real estate, and Calvin asked what I was planning to do. And this was when the past came knocking.

'You should call Steve Jones while you're here,' he suggested.

I mulled the idea over for a while. At this point, I hadn't spoken to Steve Jones in seventeen years. I said I wouldn't mind saying hello. See how that goes. The next day at breakfast, Calvin handed me a scrap of paper with Steve's LA number written on it.

'Call him up,' he said.

Steve had been in Los Angeles probably since I last saw him. He hadn't returned to England in all that time because, like Steve New, he'd overstayed his visa. Having a few convictions from his small-time criminal career, he was concerned that he wouldn't be allowed back in the country if he left, so he stayed put. I thought about all the water under the bridge, all the shit that had been said down the years, so I didn't make the call and put the idea out of my mind. The next day, when I saw Calvin, he said the same thing.

'Call him up,' he said.

This went on for about five days – Calvin telling me to give him a call, me thinking about all the shit. Then, eventually, on the sixth day, I summoned up the nerve and called Steve.

'Hello, mate,' Steve said, picking up the phone. If *he* was thinking about all the water that had passed under the bridge, all the shit, he wasn't showing it. He sounded as if we'd just spoken the day before. Before I knew what to say, he invited me over. 'I heard you was in town. I just didn't have your number,' he said. 'Come over.'

What the hell, I thought. I jumped in the car and drove over to his place in the Hollywood Hills and Steve was standing outside waiting for me. To be honest, he didn't look much different. A bit older, maybe. More tanned. He was carrying a bit more timber, but he seemed like someone who had been living his best life in the West Coast sunshine.

'Is that your car?' he said by way of a hello. 'You're gonna get carjacked in that.'

I would probably have rolled my eyes but, in a flash, he clapped his hands together and said, 'Let's go and see John.'

Before I had a chance to think, we were heading over to Venice to meet John. Now, I hadn't seen John Lydon for more than seventeen years and probably even *more* shit had been said in that time. I was curious to see if anything had changed between us in the intervening years. In terms of character, we were always like chalk and cheese. I couldn't help but wonder: *what were we going to say to one another?*

On arriving, we were ushered inside. John was upstairs, we were told, so we stood in the hall gawping at the interior for a couple of minutes and making polite chitchat. It was a nice place, with a kind of minstrel gallery-type affair, leading to the bedrooms. It wasn't the best timing, but suddenly I could feel nature calling. I was bursting, so I excused myself and went upstairs to take a leak, still wondering what the hell I was going to say to him. I didn't have to wonder for long because, as I stepped out of the bathroom, I literally bumped into John as he walked past on the landing. It was a kind of funny moment, like 'fancy meeting you here', and we both laughed on our way downstairs.

So there we were – three Sex Pistols in the same room for the first time in almost twenty years. This particular three, in any case. It was a surreal moment. We stood around exchanging pleasantries for a few minutes, then Steve suggested we call Paul. Paul was in London at the time and because of the time difference it was probably the middle of the night when we rang, so he either wasn't home or was tucked up in bed. Steve just left a message while John and I stood around laughing.

'Hello, you old cunt. Guess who I'm with?'

We laughed at what he would think when he played back his messages in the morning, then we headed out into Venice for a spot of lunch. It was alright. Quite nice. A bit of chat. Nothing too heavy. John was still a bit tricky, but it was affable enough. There isn't much to say about a lunch in LA, unless you need to know who ordered the chicken and who had the shrimp on their Caesar salad. We didn't dwell too much on the old days. As ever, John and Steve both took the coward's way out and blamed Malcolm for everything that went down. Then the bill arrived and there was that awkward moment, that game of Russian roulette, wondering who was going to blink first. It's always been a pet peeve of mine, so I picked up the check and paid the bill.

'I was going to get that,' John said, like he was the soul of innocence.

'Yeah, right,' I said, and that was that. The ice was broken between us.

We travelled back to Steve's place after lunch and Steve pressed play on his answering machine. Paul Cook had called back and left a frantic message. The seeds had been sown, I suppose. That was late November, heading towards December. I remember because Calvin and Cindy and I went to pick out a Christmas tree from one of those vast lots in Los Angeles. It was strange, but LA was more Christmassy than back home. No subtlety. Kitsch as you like. All the big mansions in Hollywood and Beverly Hills were decked out like Harrods' Christmas department. In Beverly Hills, they don't do things by halves. Everywhere had fake snow on the grass, even though the temperature was still 75 degrees all day long. One afternoon before we left, Calvin and Cindy took me along to their daughter's school Christmas concert. It was pretty far removed from a nativity back home. This being LA, all these kids aged nine or ten were coming out and doing their party pieces, hoping to catch the eye of a casting director.

Shortly after, I said goodbye to the gold Lexus. It didn't get jacked on my watch, although I realise now that would have made for a better ending to this story, but life is rarely so neat and tidy that it comes with its own punchlines. Steve New and I flew home and were back in London in time for Christmas. I put in a call to Alan McGee. My album on Creation was scheduled for release in early 1996 but, because of some hiccough with the pressing, he told me it wasn't going to be ready in time. As I said, life isn't always neat and tidy. A January release became February and, in the interim period, Steve Jones had spoken with Anita and John, and I started hearing talk of a reunion: the Sex Pistols Filthy Lucre tour. I wasn't sure how that was going to sit with me. I like to live in the moment, keep an eye on the future with maybe just a nod to what's come before. Don't get me wrong, I love the old songs, but I also like to concentrate on the new ones, too. In some ways, it's grounding to have a foot in the past, but maybe not both feet. However, events quickly overtook us all when it became clear that a reunion was going to be a big deal. Whatever misgivings I might have had, I agreed to sign on the dotted line. They're our songs and, ultimately, it wasn't called the Filthy Lucre tour for nothing. There was a big pay cheque in the offing for us and a man's got to eat, after all.

After that, I was caught up in a whirlwind. We held a press conference at the 100 Club, the scene of many of our past glories. There was no Malcolm this time, but the press conference was almost as purposely shambolic as if he'd had a hand in organising it. We hadn't played any shows and I don't think we'd even started rehearsing at that stage. There was a little hostility from some sectors of the press, saying that punk bands shouldn't get back together, but the way I saw it, whatever your view on the Pistols, we always made our own rules. The only way I saw us maybe having egg on our faces would have been if no one had turned up for the shows, but the people turned up in droves. Seventy-eight dates in six months. I think that was more dates than I'd played with the Pistols the first time around and, in those days, we played in front of hundreds of people, not tens of thousands. I was a little bemused by the whole reunion hullabaloo, to be honest. But then, I don't think any of us was 100 per cent sure it was the right thing to be doing.

Come spring 1996, I was back in Los Angeles rehearsing with the Sex Pistols full tilt. We found a way to make it work. I think it was John who said, 'We're not the best of friends, but we're not worst enemies either,' and I kind of agree with that sentiment. It was the first time the original four Pistols had played together in almost two decades. Naturally, I did the decent thing and told McGee that the Pistols thing was looming on the horizon, and he thought it would make sense to push my album back further to coincide with the publicity around the tour. Personally, I didn't think it was a good idea, but Alan was the boss, so I went along with his decision. Ultimately the album came out when Creation decided and subsequently kind of got lost in all the Pistols reunion hoopla. I imagine some people thought the timing was cynical, as if I was trying to cash in on the reunion, but the songs were written and the album was recorded long before I knew anything about the Sex Pistols ever getting back together. I don't have any regrets. The deal I struck with Alan at Creation may not have been the biggest deal in the history of recorded music, but it felt as if some of my confidence was restored. It didn't help pay the bills, but there were a couple of years during Britpop when suddenly all these kids who grew up listening to the Pistols and the Clash found themselves at the top of the tree with the bands they'd formed. In a small way, that helped to cement our legacy. Through the Creation link, I played with Primal Scream on their *Vanishing Point* LP, and I even had a conversation about touring with Oasis after they fell out with their bass player. It was kind of cool that we were getting a little recognition at last. I've always thought of music as being like a relay race. The 1960s bands passed the baton to bands like the Faces, and then Bowie, and that generation passed the baton to the Sex Pistols, and we'd now passed the baton on to people like Bobby Gillespie from the Primals and Noel Gallagher. I'd worked with my idols from the generation before mine – Mick Ronson, Iggy Pop and Ian Hunter – and I was now rubbing shoulders with the generation that came after. It was a nice place to be. Ultimately, though, that album got me back on track. And it's the track I'm on to this very day.

1

DEAD END STREET

I was born in London in 1956, a mere two years after the end of rationing and almost bang on time for the Great British Empire's last choking breath. A couple of months after Stanley and Barbara Matlock welcomed me, their only son, into the world, Tory PM Anthony Eden would oversee the Suez Crisis. Eden was forced to resign in the aftermath and for a while there, our nation became a bit of a joke. Suez was going to be our nation's last great embarrassment on the international stage. Or so we thought, at least.

When I was a kid, we lived in Kensal Green, a little north-west London hamlet, situated halfway up the Harrow Road. Money was always tight, but I don't remember ever minding that much. Accommodations were modest but homely. My folks rented the top half of an old two-up, two-down house with a small backyard and no bathroom. On bath nights, once a week, whether you needed one or not, we just had a tin bath that was dragged out into the middle of the room. In the winter, when the house got so cold you could see your breath in front of your face, there were heaters on the landing to keep the frostbite at bay. They ran on pink paraffin, which was the cheapest paraffin you could get in those days. I'd always hoped my parents might stump up the extra cash to buy the more prestigious Esso Blue paraffin, which seemed a lot more glamourous, chiefly because it was advertised everywhere, and the ad campaign featured Bing Crosby, the beloved American crooner and movie star. In the sitting room there was a plug-in three-bar electric fire but, because things were always tight, we were never allowed to have more than two bars going at any one time. My dad was always concerned about the electric bill, and used to watch it like a hawk to make sure the third bar was never switched on. In January and February, when the cold used to get in your bones and you needed fresh underwear from the washing line, it would be frozen solid, and we'd have to thaw it out over the fire before putting it on. That was more than half a century ago, but I suppose in respect to heating bills, nothing much has changed in this country since those days. I remember we had a pet cat called Jenny, and I don't know if she was in heat or something, but one day she attracted a randy tomcat in from out in the street. The tomcat chased her all around the house and, on his way back out, he sprayed whatever it is that tomcats spray, all over the electric fire. After that day, whenever you turned on the second bar of the fire, the heat reacted with the dried cat piss and the whole house stank to high heaven of tomcat musk. Because of the subsequent odour, we were only ever allowed to light one bar after that, so the winters were twice as cold. There are some old photographs of the Sex Pistols rehearsing in the room we had on Denmark Street, and if you look closely, you can just make out that three-bar fire in the pictures. You can't tell from the photos of course, but it still stank whenever you lit more than a single bar.

As upbringings go, it wasn't exactly Dickensian, but I didn't feel as if I was living the high life as a kid. As people say these days, we didn't know we were poor, because everyone around us lived their lives just the same as we did. Day to day. Pay packet to pay packet. I didn't have any brothers or sisters, but I had my mum and dad around me, and we seemed okay. We lived at number 18 Ravensworth Road, and my nan and my uncle lived just up the road at number 28, so we were a tight family unit, and the street was a friendly place. Everyone knew you and you knew them. Everyone's doors were left open, as the cliché goes. But you could probably argue that the doors were always open because no one had anything worth nicking.

In those days, if I wasn't at school or in bed, I was playing outside in the street. Nearly all my mates lived one street over, so that's where you'd find me most of the time. Usually, kicking a football about in the autumn and winter, then when May and Wimbledon came around, we'd switch to tennis. When tennis season started, we'd stretch a length of string from one side of the street to the other and tie it to a lamppost or a tree. That would be our tennis net and the road would act as our Centre Court. There were fewer cars on the roads back then, but every forty-five minutes or so, one of the other kids would spot an Austin or an Anglia and shout, 'Car!' and we'd have to temporarily untie the string and wind it back until the car had passed before carrying on. After Wimbledon and with the onset of summer, we'd switch to cricket, and then the cycle would begin again with football in the autumn. Occasionally one of us would mistime a shot and put a window through and all the housewives would be out on their stoops muttering about the world going to pot. If it was me, my usual ploy was to get on the number 18 bus, travel up the Harrow Road and sneak into the powder puff factory where my mum and my nan worked and lie low there for a few hours.

'What have you done now, Glen?' my mum would ask, shaking her head sadly.

When I was around eleven and I'd put through my umpteenth window, my dad had become so used to the breakages that he'd give me a bit of money and a tape measure and send me to apologise and then measure up the broken pane. My dad always told me to measure up carefully because the windows down our way were never plumb. You know that old tailor's adage, measure twice, cut once? Well, he drummed that into me from an early age. All the houses were crooked and bent out of shape after the war, so you could never assume that the straight line at the top would be parallel with the line at the bottom. And even if the Luftwaffe hadn't hit the house directly, all the vibrations caused by the falling bombs had left all the windows a slightly off-kilter trapezoid shape. So, once I'd checked the measurements twice, my dad would lend me his tools and I'd go down to Pocock's hardware store. There, I'd get a pane of glass cut and buy some putty and, upon my return, under the supervision of the irritated housewife, I'd install the new window myself. It still strikes me as funny that the housewives on our road didn't mind an eleven-year-old kid repairing their front windows. I didn't have any aspirations to become a glazier, funnily enough, but I still got pretty good at it.

Everything we had growing up was the cheapest version of itself. Even the Action Man I had as a kid wasn't the genuine article. I don't know if he was a Korean knock-off, but he didn't look the same as the other kids' Action Men. It wasn't just cheap Action Men either. We had a set of well-thumbed encyclopaedias from my nan that had pages pasted in where they'd been misprinted, so sometimes there were three different versions of certain pages. On the rare occasions we were lucky enough to have ice cream, I'd be sent up the road for a block of vanilla. I used to fantasise about being allowed to pick something a little more exotic, like strawberry or chocolate, or even Neapolitan, which was three flavours in one block, but no, it was always vanilla. It wasn't until I was a little older that I realised vanilla was a flavour. I'd always assumed it to be blank.

On rainy Sundays, we'd have 'Round the Horne' on the wireless while we ate our Sunday dinner. Julian and Sandy and *Hancock's Half Hour*,[1] which I loved. As an only child, I spent a lot of time learning to amuse myself. I had my own room, so I became quite self-sufficient. I had a little Dansette record player, I made Airfix kits, I read the old adventure story books that my dad had finished with – *Mr Midshipman Easy*, *King Solomon's Mines*,

---

[1] I still have a Tony Hancock poster in my sitting room now, from his movie *The Rebel*. In these post-pandemic times, it's made a great backdrop for Zoom interviews.

all those old swashbucklers. I used to enjoy a bit of a spy caper, too. I've always had a soft spot for *Casino Royale*. It was the first Ian Fleming Bond novel I read as a kid. This is by the by, but I remember it had a fantastic car chase along the Côte d'Azur, but Ian Fleming's Bond didn't drive an Aston Martin like he did in the movies. I remember he drove a Straight-Eight Bentley, which was a bit of an ungainly machine and was easily outmanoeuvred by Bond's enemy's Citroën, which had state-of-the-art suspension.

If I wasn't reading and imagining myself as 007, I wrote, I drew pictures – which probably put me in good stead for getting into art school later – and I waited for the rain to stop so I could go back outside and play football. Musically speaking, these were the days before Radio 1, so you only had the Light Programme on BBC Radio. If you wanted to hear pop music, the only two chances you had were the Brian Matthews show on Saturday morning – where he'd play clips from the past week's comedy shows interspersed with the latest hits from the Dave Clark Five and Freddie and the Dreamers and the like – and on Sunday afternoons you could hear a countdown of that past week's hit parade.

Around this time, transistor radios became all the rage. They weren't too expensive, so all the kids got one for Christmas. I loved it. Every night when I was sent to bed, I'd squirrel my transistor radio under the pillow, and tune in to Radio Luxembourg or the American Forces Network. Then the pirate radio stations started broadcasting, Radio Caroline and Radio London, and that all coincided with the British Beat explosion, so it seemed after years of nothing, you got to hear all these amazing sounds that didn't get played on the BBC: the Stones, the Kinks, the Yardbirds, the Who and the Small Faces, who were all coming through. Hearing the Kinks at that time really resonated with me. 'Dead End Street' especially. That song stood apart from whatever else was happening at the time. It wasn't just pop music. It was social commentary: 'Out of work and got no money / A Sunday joint of bread and honey.'

I don't know about a joint of bread and honey, but we always had a bit of meat to see us through the week. We'd have it hot on Sunday, then cold meat leftovers and chips on Monday and that was probably stretched out to last for cold meat *leftover leftovers* and chips on Tuesday, too. Wednesday, for a change, I'd be sent to Day's, the grocery store around the corner, for a tin of luncheon meat for that day's dinner.

Later, when I was at grammar school, I got a weekend job stacking shelves in Day's and taking grocery deliveries around the neighbourhood. I remember I had a weird fascination with that luncheon meat that had a hard-boiled egg running through its centre, as if there were chickens somewhere that laid these long eggs especially for tins of luncheon meat. I'm jumping ahead a little, but a few years later, after I'd finished school, my mum told me I had to get out from under her feet and get myself down to the labour exchange. I was fifteen years old and too young to sign on, but somehow, I did qualify for these things called butter tokens. When my mum asked how I got on, I showed her the tokens, imagining that she would be pissed off with me. I felt like Jack from 'Jack and the Beanstalk', like I'd just exchanged the prize family cow for a handful of magic beans, but, in fact, my mum was delighted. Butter tokens didn't have any cash value, you could only exchange them for butter, but my mum would take them to up to Day's, flutter her eyelashes at the manager and he'd make an exception and exchange them for ham or luncheon meat or basically anything she needed.

Around this time, my dad had a job in Neasden working for Mickleover Transport, a company that made milk floats out of fibreglass. I remember they were made from fibreglass because sometimes I'd find shards of the stuff in my socks when they came off the washing line. No matter how well or how often they were washed, there was always a stray piece of fibreglass in there. Because I was just a kid, I don't think I paid too much attention, but one day my dad came home from work and suddenly it seemed like everything was changing. He tossed that day's *Daily Mirror* to me, which he always did when he'd finished, but I could sense something was wrong. I looked at the paper for a minute, then back at my old man.

'You alright, Dad?' I asked.

'No,' he told me. 'We had a meeting at work and the guys have voted for me to be their shop steward.'

'Isn't that good?' I asked. 'It must mean they all like you.'

'No.' My dad shook his head. 'It's trouble. You'll see.'

About a month later, there was a lockout at his factory. In contrast to a labour dispute, in which the workers go out on strike, a lockout is a work stoppage initiated by the management of a company. And that's what happened. The workers wanted more money and better conditions. Rather than respond to them, the company simply closed the doors, and no one was allowed to go to work. It was a no-win situation. No one was getting their wages, and because they were locked out, but technically still employed, it meant that no one was entitled to sign on for unemployment benefits either. Ultimately, the workers were forced out on strike, and Mickleover instigated a little coup and made all the shop stewards redundant. After that, my dad was unemployed for a good while. He ended up working a couple of menial jobs just to make ends meet and I barely saw him for about a year and a half. It was a sad situation. Every evening, he'd come home, eat his dinner, and then head straight back out the door to start a nightshift at some widget factory. Looking back, I think that was my first real experience of politics and the unfairness of the world outside my front door. A small glimpse into the trade union world, seeing a group of people band together against the powers that be. It was eye-opening to see them try to make a stand and then to see them come unstuck. In a small way, even at that tender age, I could feel the impact that politics was having on our lives. In my mind, these memories all feed into the tail end of that old post-war Britain: Harold Macmillan,[2] Alec Douglas-Home and then Harold Wilson and

---

[2] Some years later, I was walking along a road near where I live, and I was nearly run over by a Bentley. I had a good look at the driver, and he was the spitting image of Harold Macmillan, the late former PM. Later I learned that it wasn't Macmillan or Macmillan's ghost. It *was* the actor Edward Fox, who was playing him in a West End play, and he was probably driving back from a matinee performance in his big coat and full hair and make-up. The *NME* would have had a field day, I thought, and the headline flashed across my brain: *Sex Pistol killed by Harold Macmillan.*

the white heat of technology – his speech about technological change and the implications for industry – and then suddenly, as if by magic, it was the beginning of Swinging London.

The time that a record is released isn't necessarily the time that you hear it, but it was probably 1965 that I first laid ears on the Kinks. The moment was kind of an epiphany. I can still remember the feeling I had, the first time I heard 'Dead End Street'. I guess everyone has had a similar experience, but when I heard it, I really felt that Ray Davies was singing directly to me about my own experience. Things were tight, but we weren't completely skint. Even with all my dad's employment woes, he always made sure I got a little pocket money every week, and I saved up and bought 'Dead End Street' on 45. I picked it up one Saturday morning when we were out grocery shopping for the week. Radio Rentals used to have a little record department, so while my dad paid the week's rental on our television set, I picked out the Kinks single from the top thirty and paid for it with the pocket money I'd put aside: 'No chance to emigrate / I'm deep in debt and now it's much too late.'

I always think of the Ten Pound Poms when I hear Ray Davies sing the line, 'no chance to emigrate'. The Ten Pound Poms were Brits who applied for assisted passage to up sticks and move their families to Australia or New Zealand to start a new life down under. We missed the boat on that maybe, but would life have been so different? As bleak as post-war Britain was, maybe life on this new frontier wasn't for everyone. I do know someone who was a Ten Pound Pom, although only briefly. That was Mel Herberfield. Mel was one of the founders of fashion brand Swanky Modes in the '70s and wife of Clive Langer, the record producer. She told me that her family took the ten pounds assistance cash and travelled all the way to Australia, stayed for twenty-four hours, before her mum decided she didn't like it down under and they turned around and came straight back to England. I guess the grass is always greener, until it isn't.

Since then, I've learned the song and I've played it live a few times. The words still resonate with me today, the same as they did when I was a kid. Some people grow to love Wordsworth, or they have their favourite authors, but I felt a strong connection with the way Ray Davies could tell a story. I didn't immediately feel I was going to rush off and write my own songs, but it felt so accessible. I don't know if it was some kind of musical osmosis, but even then, something was seeping into my consciousness.

2

BLACK AND WHITE

Following junior school, I naturally assumed I'd be heading to Willesden High School (soon to become Willesden Comprehensive) with all my friends. My dad had other ideas, however, and he pushed for me to go to grammar school. It wasn't exactly *Tom Brown's School Days*, but walking into St Clement Danes Grammar for the first time was a little like going back in time. Back then, the teachers still wore these flowing black capes, and their Oxford brogues squeaked as they paced up and down the halls. The older teachers all wore these impressive three-piece suits that they'd had made before the war and which had gone on to last them a lifetime of prowling the school halls. You could see immediately it was a place where you were best advised to keep your head down.

It was a very academic school, and everything was geared towards getting decent O levels and going on to higher education. I was always more interested in English, art and history. The art teachers seemed cool, but the real focus at Danes was on the sciences and mathematics. To illustrate the point, when I was at Saint Martins on my art foundation course, one of my old art teachers got in touch somehow and asked to come along to my end-of-year show. I walked him around the college and at the end of the tour he thanked me and confessed it had been his first time inside an art college. Even the art teachers hadn't set foot in an art college, it turned out.

While I was at Danes working towards my O levels, it seemed like I was always on the go. I used to play football every Saturday for this local team called the Penguins. They organised maybe six teams of different age groups around the various London leagues, and I played for their youth team. The chap who oversaw the Penguins was a guy called Reg Turner. Reg was a bit of a boy, a massive character. He had this amazing old Humber Super Snipe estate, a monster of a car, that he used to ferry all the young kids in the team around to away fixtures. Every other Saturday when we played away, there was Reg and a tangle of eleven kids all crammed in there in the back, pootling about London and probably breaking every regulation in the Highway Code.

On paper, Reg worked in publishing, but he always had some racket going on. He used to pay me to do odd jobs around the place and do a spot of gardening when the sun was out. One of his regular scams was to reappropriate books from various places, presumably from his work, and then sell them on to local libraries around London. It was my job to take the dustjackets off the books, put them in plastic sleeves, and then put them back on the books. Reg's place was always filled with these teetering stacks of books waiting to be re-covered, so it was obviously a lucrative side-hustle. It was monotonous as all hell, but the pay was okay, and Reg was cool to hang out with. It was regular cash in hand and every year there was a bit of extra money to be earned working at the Penguins annual dinner and dance. Reg used to employ some of us to work as hat-check boys and to serve drinks while the footballers and their wives got legless and danced the night away. It was a popular date on the social calendar and was always well attended. It was also my first real, admittedly minor, brush with celebrity.

I remember one year's do, serving drinks to QPR's Tony Hazell and Peter Bonetti, aka The Cat, the England and Chelsea keeper. We weren't really allowed to, but I managed to get Bonetti's autograph. When I handed the piece of paper to Tony Hazell for him to follow suit, he took a long hard look at Bonetti's signature and turned to him. 'You call that a signature, you pissed cunt?' They were pro footballers, so it wasn't Oscar Wilde exactly, but it made me laugh. The guest of honour speaker that night was Simon Dee, the radio and television personality. Dee had been a huge deal in the '60s, basically the Jonathan Ross of his day, but his star had fallen after he moved from the BBC to ITV following a pay dispute. After his move, his late-night ITV show was a ratings catastrophe and I gather his career never fully recovered after that. By the time Dee gave his keynote speech, the hundreds of people in attendance were all quite well-oiled and spent the entire speech catcalling and barracking him, but he kept them all in their place effortlessly. He had a good line in pithy ripostes, and I think about how well he handled himself that night every time I'm called into action as a public speaker myself.

The times being what they were – homosexuality wasn't decriminalised in the UK until 1967 – I think Reg Turner was aware that he had a bit of a reputation as regards to his sexuality. In my memory, Reg Turner wasn't gay. He was an old-fashioned homosexual. The word 'gay' hadn't found its way into the lexicon at that time, at least not into mine. Still, whatever he was, that was a matter for him. Reg was a straight-looking, slightly thickset bloke. He was a funny guy, all told, with a manner that sometimes reminded me of Jools and Sandy from 'Round the Horne'. He wasn't overtly camp, but he had a great line in withering comebacks.

I was never that great at football, but I played every week. However, if you played badly, rather than tell you that you were going to be dropped for the next game, Reg would simply take your shirt and say, 'I'll wash that for you.' It was his understated way of telling you that you'd had a terrible game without having to hurt your feelings. Reg being gay was never an issue for me, but I suppose at the time it was probably a big elephant in the room for some less enlightened people round our way. I remember, before I started working for him, he made a point of coming around to our house to speak with my mum and dad. I presume that was to allay any fears they might have had about my new job. He didn't have to do that, but I suppose it was a way of saying everything would be okay, without saying it specifically; tap dancing around the subject, the way he probably had to with some people back then. My uncle Colin, who was a pretty good footballer in his day, had played for the Penguins himself, so I can only presume my family already knew Reg was gay by this point and weren't bothered by it. Still, it was sad that he felt he had to do that.

Reg had a place near King Edward's Park in Willesden, and I would go around at the weekends and help him out with whatever jobs he had on that week. Reg's place was just a short walk over the railway bridge from where I lived in Kensal Green, but in terms of wealth, it was a station or two higher than my patch. Once you were over the bridge, before you knew it, the houses started to get a little bigger, until you approached the park, where the homes were grander still. The houses there all had neat green lawns and their own garages, which was unheard of on my road. As for working for Reg, my duties were quite varied. Along with helping him out with whatever scheme he had going, Reg used to have me wash his car every Saturday morning. While I was there with the bucket and sponge, I used to hear a band rehearsing in one of the nearby garages, playing a kind of cheesy reggae version of that Pete Seeger tune, 'Black and White': 'The ink is black, the page is white / Together we learn to read and write.'

It was a song about racial unity, although we all seemed to be getting on fine in our neck of the woods in that regard. That whole part of London was very diverse. In fact, it was probably almost half and half in terms of racial mix. Ska and Blue Beat were everywhere back then. Living on the Harrow Road, we had one of the earliest West Indian immigrant communities in the country. Every summer, practically everyone had their windows wide open playing old Blue Beat and King Tubby records, and those sounds became part of everyone's DNA. When one of my school friends' parents got a divorce, his mum took in boarders to help make ends meet and there was a buzz of excitement when they had an actual member of the Skatalites as a lodger for a time. We used to knock on his door, and if he wasn't shagging one of the neighbours' wives, he'd come out to play football in the street with us in his hipster trousers.

The Willesden Apollo was just up the road from Reg's house, and they had a big reggae night there and would have all the big stars like Max Romeo coming down to play every week. There was a whole Willesden music scene, and everyone was picking up on it. There was a group of kids at my school who were of West Indian extraction, so you'd have all these local lads calling each other 'blood' and saying things like, 'I am a true Trojan' in their Jamaican patois. We didn't call it reggae back then, it was still Blue Beat or ska, but I used to tune into the Mike Raven radio show just to hear all these ace records like Desmond Dekker's 'Israelites'. Raven's show used to go out just before John Peel's *Top Gear* show on Saturday night and it was wall-to-wall blues, with a smattering of R&B and Blue Beat thrown in for good measure. The garage band who practised near Reg's house were Greyhound, and they actually went on to have a few hits in the UK a few years later during that early 1970s reggae boom. I must have heard them practise that song 300 times every Saturday when I was washing Reg's car. Their version of 'Black and White' was cheesy, but the sentiment was right, at least.

3

BAD 'N' RUIN

Beyond what was played on the wireless, my earliest experience of music in the house emanated from the old-fashioned mahogany radiogram that had pride of place in our sitting room. I didn't have any records, but my uncle Colin, who had previously gone through a bit of a Teddy Boy phase at the tail end of the 1950s, gifted us his collection of old 78 records. He was only ten years or so older than me, so it wasn't all naff crooners. He had some great rock 'n' roll records, and those 78s proved to be an early source of excitement for me. Suddenly I had access to all these classic tunes by artists like the Big Bopper, Gene Vincent and Elvis. Besides the music, I also found them to be very aesthetically pleasing just as objects. The records came in these generic card sleeves with ornate Art Deco-style lettering across the front and back. The sleeves were stitched along the sides, with a hole in the centre so you could read the label.

The records themselves were made from shellac and broke like glass if you weren't careful, and they played at breakneck speed compared with an LP (33 rpm) or a single (45 rpm). They whizzed around so fast it felt a bit like lighting the blue touch-paper on a firework whenever you put them on the turntable. It was exciting and nerve-wracking at the same time. Whenever I played 'Great Balls of Fire!' by Jerry Lee Lewis or something equally explosive, I'd drop the needle into the groove and the turntable started spinning like a Catherine wheel, matching the ferocity of the music, beat for beat.

As I headed into my teens, I was starting to hone my own tastes. The 1960s were done and dusted, and you could see everyone was trying to make their mark or carve out their own scene as we started out on the new decade. Everywhere around me, everyone was sliding into a new street culture and setting up as suedeheads or mods or rude boys. Whatever was happening, there was always something else, something more interesting somewhere further up the road. But you had to have your antenna up, otherwise you might get stuck in a rut. When you're thirteen or fourteen, and on the march to young adulthood, you don't want to stagnate. You want to keep pushing forward.

When I was hanging with my mates, kids who were cut from a similar cloth as myself, we tended to gather at the other end of the Harrow Road, in Harlesden. Habitually we'd take the number 18 bus to Harlesden and congregate in the Wimpy Bar under the Jubilee Clock and lark about, whiling away the days until the classified football results, seeing how long we could make a cup of coffee last before being asked to leave, or daring each other to order a Bender Burger. The Bender, for those who need to know, was essentially a loop of frankfurter presented in a toasted burger bun and topped off with a little dollop of tomato relish in the centre. Looking back, I don't know why we used to hang out in Harlesden, because it was Nowheresville, basically. If it was out of habit, I'm glad we broke it eventually. One Saturday, we decided to change things up and caught the bus heading in the opposite direction to see what we could see. The other direction led us to Ladbroke Grove and Portobello Market.

It seemed hard to believe that Ladbroke Grove was on the same bus route as Harlesden. It felt like I was in a different world entirely. By contrast, Harlesden was grey and bleak, but visiting Portobello Road for the first time was like switching from a black and white to a colour TV set. The place was bustling, alive with possibility. A world of hippies, headbands, striped loon pants, cool shades and Afghan coats. Hip and happening people were scuttling about in army surplus jeeps, which were all the rage.[1] And beneath all that multicultural hubbub, that whole area of London was a hotbed of radical politics and communes. Not that I knew that much about any of that at the time. I was aware of the underground paper the *International Times*, and I had seen a mate's copy of the notorious *Oz* 'Schoolkids' issue

---

[1] When I dug deeper into the Faces' catalogue, I got turned on to some of the earlier Rod Stewart stuff. Rod had a gentle dig at those in-vogue hippies, darting around W10 in their jeeps in his tune 'Italian Girls' in 1972, and that always conjures images of Portobello Road in my mind's eye and takes me right back.

a while back. That was the controversial issue that was edited by a group of teenagers and led to the now infamous trial for breaking obscenity laws. Looking back, I realise I was lucky to be coming into my own at such an explosive time, culturally. The old empire was crumbling, and there was a sense that we weren't going to be so malleable as the generation before ours.

Jumping off the number 18 bus at the top of Ladbroke Grove, I remember walking along the Golborne Road for the first time. I kept walking down Golborne Road to where it cuts across Portobello and eventually stumbled upon an emporium, made up of little stalls and shops, a little like Kensington Market. Inside, I found a record stall that immediately took my fancy. Rock On records, Ted Carroll's place. It was a far cry from Radio Rentals and their top-thirty singles selection. Ted Carroll, it turned out, managed Thin Lizzy in their early days. Rock On records even got namechecked in their tune, 'The Rocker', when Phil Lynott sang, 'I get my records at the Rock On stall', so it was immediately a cooler, more magical place than the Harlesden Wimpy Bar. You couldn't swing a cat in there, but even so, Rock On was a really happening place. Jimmy Page regularly shopped there, as did Lemmy from Motorhead and pretty much any cool vinyl fan you could think of. The clientele was like a snapshot of the underground scene, all flicking through the racks, shoulder to shoulder with day-tripper Teddy Boys on the hunt for that rare rock 'n' roll 45. And because it wasn't exactly spacious, I guess if you were ever shopping at the same time as Jimmy Page, you literally would have been rubbing shoulders with him.

Anyway, in Rock On, I began flicking through some of the records and I found this album that looked exactly like the old 78s my uncle Colin had given me when I was a kid. I had no idea who it was or how it sounded, but it had the same Art Deco-style lettering, the same stitching along the sides, so I felt there was a direct correlation between this record and the records we had at home. I figured that everything they had in Rock On was probably cool, so I took a punt and bought it there and then. The album was called *Long Player* and the band was the Faces. I didn't realise at the time, but the Faces had emerged from the Small Faces, after their lead singer, Steve Marriott, left to form Humble Pie with Peter Frampton. The remaining three Small Faces recruited Ronnie Wood on guitar, Rod Stewart on vocals, and would go on to become one of the biggest bands in the world. I had been a fan of the Small Faces since childhood. They always seemed so cool, like they *knew* they were great. They were fellow Londoners too, so I always felt I had a special bond with them when compared with their Merseybeat rivals. Still, at this point, the Faces were an unknown quantity to me. I'd bought the LP based entirely on the elaborate cover artwork. I genuinely had no idea what effect it would have on my life when I finally heard the music.

The first track on side one was 'Bad 'n' Ruin'. It was a funky, Booker T type kind of groove, everyone jamming on the same chord. The playing on the record is fantastic, as you'd expect, but it was so more than that. Lyrically, it told a story about Rod Stewart travelling across Europe and becoming a changed man and then sneaking back to London with no money left to spend and his tail between his legs. The lyrics serve almost as an imaginary phone call back home or a postcard from overseas: 'Mama, you won't recognise me now.'

I must have listened to the record a hundred times. I came to love the whole album, but it was 'Bad 'n' Ruin' that really hit home with me. The lyrics are talking about a change in a young man's life, feeling the need to take some risks, and the shift from childhood into adulthood, which is precisely where I was at the time. I fell in love with the Faces from that moment on. They had a certain jack-the-lad swagger that had real appeal to me, a genuine streetwise kind of style. They were rough-and-ready working-class lads, singing about life as I was seeing it myself. It was laddish, probably not PC, and in a certain light, not too far removed from *Confessions of a Plumber's Mate* kind of storytelling. And when you saw them on TV, I liked the fact they didn't take themselves too seriously. They were acting as if they were having the time of their lives. Which I guess they were. Who wouldn't be? It's worth remembering that there were still traces of the previous decade everywhere, and that kind of hung over into the early part of the 1970s. You'd still see these bands like the Tremeloes dressed in cheap satin trousers, looking like someone had made them get their outfits from the Carnaby Cavern. Without exception, those bands didn't seem authentic. They looked like they were in fancy dress. But the Faces looked like they had just rocked up in the clothes they were wearing. They didn't give a toss what you thought and that triggered something in me. Before too long, I started to take more care about the way I dressed, and I started to learn the guitar. Once I had the rudiments of that instrument down, I bought a cheap bass from someone at school and set about trying to learn that, too. It looked like a Fender Mustang, with a go-faster stripe, and I later learned that it was probably a regular electric guitar that had had the strings replaced, so it was a bit of a Frankenstein's monster. Still, it was only £15 and I got to pretend I was Ronnie Lane in front of my bedroom mirror, playing along to the record.

I loved Ronnie Lane. Even as far back as the Small Faces days, I always thought there was something different about him. So, while there was a laddish quality to a lot of the Faces material, Ronnie's songs stood apart somehow. He had a real tenderness to his songwriting and a kind of romantic poet side that acted as a direct counterpoint to some of the band's other songs. They wouldn't have been the same band without him. When I think back, I realise the whole reason I bought the bass in the first place was so I could emulate Ronnie 'Plonk' Lane. Who would have imagined that, decades later, I'd be taking Lane's role on stage and touring far and wide with Ronnie Wood, Ian McLagan and Kenney Jones in a later version of the Faces? I mean, we played in front of 50,000 people at the Fuji festival. Occasionally I still have to pinch myself that that really happened.[2]

---

[2] In 1978, I went to see Ronnie's Slim Chance play a *Time Out* magazine tenth-anniversary party at the Lyceum. I was on a date with Sheila Rock, the photographer. She wasn't best pleased because I pretty much abandoned her and shot to the front of the stage. It's stretching things a bit to say I met him, but when Ronnie was studying the setlist during a break between songs, I leaned forward and shouted, 'Half a pound of butter, a pint of milk and packet of Daz,' and Ronnie laughed and said, 'I get it. Wrong list!'

At the same time as I discovered there was life outside of Nowheresville, I was tuning in to John Peel's *Top Gear* show and its predecessor, *The Perfumed Garden*, and had my ears opened to bands and artists outside of the chart rundown. Bands like Audience, the Third Ear Band, Soft Machine and Tyrannosaurus Rex. Suddenly, it seemed that there was something outside of the mainstream that I could relate to. The Faces, though – they were the band that led me down that road in the first place.

4

STARMAN

I think I was only vaguely aware of David Bowie as a kid. Back then, it was as if he was just someone out there in the ether somewhere. But, in the mid-'60s, Bowie wasn't the magical, other-worldly human being we remember now. He was just another pop hopeful, plying his trade and hoping he was going to score a number-one hit single and a couple of turns on *Top of the Pops*.

Thinking back, I probably first heard him on *Two-Way Family Favourites*, the request show that used to go out on Sunday lunchtimes on the BBC Light Programme. Bowie was still in his Anthony Newley phase at this point, and he had this novelty record, 'The Laughing Gnome', that they used to play every now and then. I was, and still am, a big fan of Anthony Newley, so for that reason, although it wasn't great, the song was memorable to me.

Tony Newley's records, with their roots in post-war English-ness, formed a bridge between traditional pop and the proto-British rock singers. I was too young to really appreciate that early British take on rock 'n' roll at the time, but looking back, it had a kind of naffness to it that I find quite appealing. I liked Newley and I was also fond of Tommy Steele. Tommy, let's not forget, was really our first bona fide rock 'n' roll star in the UK. In fact, if you look at some of those early photographs of Tommy Steele with his grown-out crew cut and quiff, he literally could be Bowie, the similarity is so great. After 'The Laughing Gnome', I didn't hear of Bowie again until 'Space Oddity' in 1969, then it was radio silence for a couple more years. The next time I was aware of him was one evening round at my girlfriend's house. We used to have kind of record parties there, and her older sister had a decent record collection, including a copy of *Hunky Dory*. So I'd heard him, but I didn't lay eyes on him until one day when I was working at Reg Turner's house. *Lift Off with Ayshea* was on the telly. It was seen as an ITV junior *Top of the Pops*-type show that was on every week after school. It was the usual procession of forgettable pop, one identikit singer or band after another, and a regular dance troupe, until suddenly it wasn't. A full two weeks before Bowie's legendary appearance on *Top of the Pops*, the nation's school kids got an early preview of the performance that would become a *where were you when?* moment. From my perspective, the world of pop music got turned on its head in the blink of an eye. It was the moment Bowie performed his song 'Starman' on TV for the first time. Even Reg looked up from whatever he was doing.

'Oh, he seems interesting,' Reg noted. 'Shame about his teeth.'

I wasn't paying attention to his teeth. The first thing I noticed was Bowie looked like an actual star. Mick Ronson and the Spiders from Mars looked fantastic too, but Bowie as Ziggy was something else. I imagine a million kids across the nation had the same sensation I had when he pointed his finger into the camera and sang the line, 'I had to phone someone, so I picked on you', because it seemed as if nothing was going to be the same again after that. I didn't know it then, but Bowie was going to be a constant in my life from that moment forward.

I think it was the very next day after that *Lift Off with Ayshea* appearance that I went out and bought the album, *The Rise and Fall of Ziggy Stardust and the Spiders from Mars*. From a personal point of view, when I started down that road myself, the whole record would be an object lesson in the craft of good songwriting. And obviously, for the wider world, it was the birth of glam rock. As a moment, it started to tie all these other strands together. Old hippies Tyrannosaurus Rex learned how to write two-minute pop songs and became T-Rex, Roxy Music appeared out of nowhere and made *The Old Grey Whistle Test* a programme worth watching. Suddenly there was this huge cultural sea change and I found myself getting hip to all this wild new music. I wasn't at the Hammersmith Odeon show, where Steve infamously nicked Bowie's gear, but I saw Bowie play at Earl's Court a little later in 1973. In another of those curious moments of interconnectivity in my life, I've seen pictures of John Beverley, latterly Sid Vicious, outside the same show, dressed in a Bowie T-shirt. We were both there.

When Bowie, or rather Ziggy, arrived on the scene, everybody at my school suddenly decided to grow their hair long, into that rooster feather cut Bowie had, but school regulations meant we weren't allowed to have our hair down below our shirt collars. It didn't stop those kids. They just found a compromise solution. All the kids made a pilgrimage to Dimitri's, the hairdresser's on Hammersmith Broadway, and got a customised version of the Bowie cut. To not break the school rules, they all had to get the rooster tail at the back cut short, so the hair didn't fall below their shirt collars. Essentially, it was half a haircut, and to my mind, it looked ridiculous. All these kids had adopted this long hair hairstyle that was too short at the back, long at the front, like a mullet in reverse. At the time, I was mad keen on the Faces, so I was still sporting a Ronnie Lane kind of cut, but even I wasn't immune to Bowie fever. As a concession, one bank holiday weekend, I went to a hairdresser in Wembley. I'd saved a little money from my Saturday job, and I had the barber put a flash of red dye into my hair.

Years later, when I was with the Pistols on the Anarchy in the UK tour, I became friends with this guy, Leee Black Childers. Childers was part of Bowie's MainMan management team and had worked with Bowie on his first tour of the US. He was a renowned photographer, and around the time I met him, he was managing the Heartbreakers. Leee told me he'd met Bowie while he was over in London working on Andy Warhol's *Pork*, which played at the Roundhouse in Camden. *Pork* was a controversial production and had caused quite a scandal, owing to its gratuitous nudity. Geri Miller, one of the actresses in the show, was arrested and caught up in a tabloid storm after she exposed a breast during a photo session in front of Clarence House, the official residence of the Queen Mother. The show had no money basically, so when it came to wardrobe, everyone was naked, but covered in a sheen of glitter. Leee told me that came about because one of the actors who was scheduled to appear in *Pork* died suddenly before the production made it to England. Following the actor's funeral service in New York, all his friends from the Village went around to his place to help clear his effects and they found bags and bags of glitter inside his apartment. All the mourners, who had had a few drinks, started taking handfuls of glitter and throwing it at one another. They were sad, a little drunk and didn't know quite how to express their grief, so why not? Anyway, that's where the idea came from. They didn't have the budget for costumes, so all the performers came out onstage in their birthday suits, with just a light sprinkling of glitter. Bowie came to see the show in London, and according to Leee, that's where Bowie picked up on the whole glitter thing. I really like that. An actor dies in Greenwich Village and his friends mourn his passing by scattering glitter over each other and then, a little down the line, Bowie and Bolan take to wearing glitter on stage. It's a silly thing I guess, but I'm a big fan of those kinds of random connections, the serendipity of the world.

All this exciting stuff was bubbling up to the surface around this time. When I was still at school, I started dating one of the girls from the local girls' school, Jackie Barnet. We used to hang out and go to gigs together, so she invited me along one night to see this guy play a show at Imperial College. It was a Friday night, which meant I had work in the morning and football in the afternoon, so I decided to give it a swerve. She went with her friend Elaine instead. I remember feeling disappointed because although I was dating Jackie, I was quite taken with Elaine. She used to wear this fabulous Ossie Clark chiffon dress.

'Who's this guy you're seeing, anyway?' I asked.

'Lou Reed. He used to be in the Velvet Underground,' Jackie said.

I wasn't aware of Lou Reed or the Velvet Underground at this point. I only discovered him afterwards, with the release of his *Transformer* LP – which was co-produced by Bowie and had Mick Ronson and Herbie Flowers playing on it. I look back some-times, and I'm still disappointed I didn't go. A few months later, I had my own copy of *Transformer* and was playing it to death. It still irks me that I didn't take Jackie up on the invitation.

Flash-forward a few years to late 1980, and I was in NYC to play a gig. I bumped into Tina Weymouth and Chris Frantz from Talking Heads, and they invited me to see them play at Radio City Music Hall, so I went along with Danny Kustow, and we hung around backstage for the show. Danny had played guitar with the Tom Robinson Band, and we were playing together in a short-lived band of mine called the Spectres. Radio City Music Hall is this grand old Art Deco theatre in midtown Manhattan and Talking Heads were a hot ticket. There was a bar backstage, filled out with all of New York's finest, dressed in the high fashion of the age. The New York punks were a bit more polished than their London counterparts, but if you ask me, everyone looked like something the cat had dragged in. I went over to get myself a drink at the bar and spotted Coco Schwab and said hi. Coco was David Bowie's formidable personal assistant. I'd got to know Coco and David during my days working with Iggy Pop, and she was always easy to get along with.

'David's there,' she said and nodded in the direction of the stage. 'Go and say hello.'

On stage, Talking Heads were just starting the show and Bowie was watching from the wings. Adrian Belew, who'd played on a clutch of Bowie's records in the previous couple of years, was Talking Heads' second live guitarist, so I assumed David was there supporting his mate and that he probably didn't need the likes of me crowding him. Thinking that I was maybe feeling a bit shy, Coco walked from the bar to the side of the stage and told David that I was there. My first meeting with Bowie hadn't gone great, if I'm honest – as you will see later in this memoir – but we were on friendly terms now. Even so, I was still a little overawed. It was Bowie, when all's said and done. It turned out I needn't have worried. Instantly, he came over and, without a word, took me by the hand and led me back to the wings. We squatted there in the darkness and watched the whole show together. The thing I most remember is David mouthing the words as they played. He knew every single word to every Talking Heads song and he sang along in his best David Bowie voice. Between each number, we chatted a little.

'Do you like my stuff, Glen?' he asked, and I nodded. He didn't strike me as insecure, but it seemed strange that he wanted to know. 'Do you have a favourite?'

'I really like *Low*,' I told him. '"Be My Wife".'

'Oh, that's interesting,' he said. 'It didn't do very well, though. Not commercially.'

I laughed and told him, 'I think it did okay. All my friends like it.' Bowie thought about that for a second or two.

'Yeah, but "The Laughing Gnome" sold more copies,' he said with a grin. Even if the rest of the world insisted on taking Bowie very seriously indeed, he never did.

I met David several times in subsequent years and, although we had many conversations, it saddens me that we never once talked of our shared fondness for Anthony Newley. Then, a few years ago, after Bowie passed, and in all the sadness that swept through the world, I was listening to that tape of David in the studio that was doing the rounds. In between takes of his song 'Absolute Beginners', David was entertaining the producer and technicians with impersonations of famous singers. He was a great mimic. The final one was his impression of Anthony Newley. It is spot on. Of course it is. Bowie's Anthony Newley phase is often written off, but I loved the fact that Bowie still carried that influence with him. He was into Talking Heads, but he was also of the generation that fell in love with Tommy Steele and *The Strange World of Gurney Slade*.

5

HOLD YOUR HEAD UP

As I became an older hand at Danes, I got more used to the regime, but occasionally I would step out of line. It was still an intimidating environment, but sometimes it was surprisingly relaxed. One day, I got into some trouble and was told to report to Mr Spurgeon in the gym. Spurgeon had a reputation as one of the most feared teachers at the school, but I thought he was kind of cool. When I presented myself, Spurgeon told me to get myself some boxing gloves and to meet him back at the gym at 5 p.m. Classes finished at 3.30 p.m., so I hung around for an hour and a half, absolutely bricking it, wondering what was going to become of me. Was Spurgeon going to fight me?

'What are you doing here?' he said when 5 p.m. rolled around and he found me waiting outside. I reminded him that he'd told me to find some gloves and to meet him at the gym. He laughed. 'Never mind that,' he said. 'Let's go and have a cup of tea.'

He was clever. He hadn't even had to break a sweat to teach me a lesson. He was an all-round good guy, Spurgeon.

Later, when I had my O levels under my belt, I was learning the guitar with a vengeance. We did have music lessons, but they weren't worth the paper they were written on. An hour of singing hymns and watching as the music teacher's dentures got dislodged whenever he hit the high notes. I mean, it was funny, but I didn't learn much. Probably the only teacher who had some insight to offer, musically speaking, was our French teacher, this guy called Bill Ashton. Bill was the leader of the London Youth Jazz Orchestra. He didn't do much in the way of actual teaching as I remember it. He would hand out a paper at the beginning of the lesson or tell us to read quietly and then he'd spend the hour working on his jazz scores while we sat in silence conjugating verbs. I got an O level in French, but he didn't teach me anything about music, sadly. The school didn't have guitar lessons either, so I basically taught myself, with the Bert Weedon *Play in a Day!* book, which was the way everybody did it. Along with some other kids, we'd rehearse in these old Portakabins they had on the school grounds. When we realised we needed a bass player, I made the switch and picked up the rudiments quite quickly. One of the first tunes I learned to play on bass was 'Hold Your Head Up' by Argent. They were a big deal at the time, and the bass part was easy to learn. I'd been a fan of Rod Argent's previous group, the Zombies, so they still had a kind of cool sheen to them. The school Portakabin rehearsals were short-lived, however. They came to an end when our vice headmaster, Don Palmer, told us we were too loud and that we had to stop. I had no idea that in a few short years, I'd have to get used to people telling me I wasn't allowed to play. A few weeks later when he asked if we could play at an upcoming school dance, I told him no.

'We won't be any good,' I said. 'You didn't let us rehearse.'

I was a teenager, so I was starting to go and see bands and having the odd drink, if the opportunity arose. The weight of all the constant homework, combined with trying to apply myself to learning the bass, meant that something eventually had to give. Ultimately, I ended up only doing the homework for the more high-maintenance teachers. When I say high-maintenance, I mean the ones who were going to make my life a misery if I didn't hand in an assignment on time. Those teachers tended to be the science teachers, because the arts teachers were always more of a soft touch.

When it came to selecting the A levels I was going to study in sixth form, I took maths and physics, but the subjects I really wanted to take had been history and English literature. I've always enjoyed history, but unfortunately, because the teachers were more intimidating, I'd applied myself more to the science subjects and my hopes to study history and English fell by the wayside. I was a good student, but over time I was inundated with the pressure of all the academic work. One day, I cracked, and I simply walked out of my maths class. I couldn't take it any more. Later, one of the art teachers found me in one of the art rooms, where I'd gone to seek refuge. Despite being annoyed that I was hiding out in his classroom, he was always encouraging. I don't think I was particularly good at art, but I was enthusiastic about the subject. Whatever the case, he saw something in me and helped me prepare for my foundation interview at Saint Martins. Part of the reason I was looking at going to art college was because I'd read so many interviews with bands who started that way. Chiefly because they didn't want to get 'straight' jobs and didn't know what they wanted to do. They all got a grant from the government and art college gave them a little bit of breathing space while they decided what they were going to do with their lives and to meet some like-minded people. Saint Martins was, as it is now, a highly prestigious college to get into. Gilbert & George were old alumni, Stella McCartney and Alexander McQueen went there after I'd done my stint. When I applied, I had to put together a folder of my work to be assessed by the admissions people, some pictures I'd drawn of some popstars and suchlike. I remember there was a particularly good biro drawing I'd done of Charlie Watts on a scrap of paper that I'd copied from the back pages of the *Daily Mirror*. I submitted it all for consideration and although I got in, after being interviewed by a panel of lecturers, I never saw that folder again. Artwork by a former Sex Pistol can be quite valuable in some circles, so if it's in a cupboard somewhere, I would still like it back. Perhaps they also have Stella McCartney and Gilbert & George's submissions lurking in a safe somewhere? They could be sitting on a small fortune.

Meanwhile, I was still studying for my A levels, and I was struggling with them if I'm honest. I was put in for pure and applied mathematics, physics, and art. Sixth form was two years, and after the first year, I was sacked from physics. The physics exam relied heavily on maths, and the maths classes weren't keeping pace with the physics lessons, and I started to fall behind. Eventually I replaced physics with technical drawing. I only had a year to do the two-year course, but despite that, I still got the A level. Coming off the back of doing physics, technical drawing made a lot of sense to me – seeing how things work and what their structure was, knowing which was the x and which was the y axis – so I felt a real affinity with the subject. It's not a life skill I've called upon too often as a songwriter, but a few years later, before the Rich Kids went into the studio with Mike Thorne, he suggested that I make a drawing of the song before we laid it down. He wanted me to outline the peaks and troughs, the quiet passages, and the changes in tempo before recording. As for art, initially it wasn't my great love. At the time, I saw it as a way out from under the incessant homework of the more academic subjects, which was starting to get on top of me. However, at the end of grammar school, I passed my art A level and, ultimately, I was awarded the school arts and crafts prize. There were half a dozen or so kids who went on to study at Oxbridge, but I was the only kid in my year who went on to be a Sex Pistol.

6

THREE BUTTON HAND ME DOWN

As a musician, I've always been of the view that you need to play if you want to earn your keep. Seeing my dad working two jobs and barely spending a minute in the house, just to keep his family warm and fed, meant the importance of having a strong work ethic was drummed into me from a young age. Since I was a kid, I've always worked for my supper. To fund a trip to France one summer I took a holiday job at a lino factory, humping great 100-foot rolls of lino around, so I've been known to get my hands dirty from time to time. I had a job stacking shelves and doing local deliveries at Day's, the grocery store on the Harrow Road where my mum used to send me to get our tins of luncheon meat. I didn't mind the work, or the few quid I earned, but the job quickly lost its shine for me. I can remember the exact moment, in fact.

It was one Saturday in July 1969 and, 4 miles down the road, the Rolling Stones were set to play their legendary show in Hyde Park. It was the first Stones concert in two years, and although the show was announced long beforehand, it had evolved into a tribute to their former guitarist, Brian Jones, who'd tragically died a couple of days before. I was twelve years old, almost thirteen, and desperate to go. Unfortunately, when I asked for the day off, I got short shrift from the manager, who told me in no uncertain terms that he expected me to work as usual on Saturday. So, while the Stones were playing to a quarter of a million adoring fans, I was dragging a little hand trolley up and down the streets around Kensal Green, delivering Mrs Collins's groceries and Mrs Brown's milk. I wasn't ever going to make this mistake again. When Humble Pie announced they were playing with Grand Funk Railroad at Hyde Park in 1971, I didn't even ask for the day off. I quit Day's and went to the free festival. I have no regrets about my decision. It was one of the greatest gigs I've ever seen.

When I moved up into sixth form, along with a few school friends, I took a job at Whiteleys in Bayswater, working Fridays after school and all day on Saturday. Whiteleys has changed a lot over the years, but it was still an old-school department store back in those days. It was a grand building, with a real Grace Brothers feel. There were hundreds of employees, and me and my friends were taken on as cover. We had general dogsbodies' duties all over the shop. One minute I'd be in the sports department, the next I'd be lending a hand delivering food to the refreshment hall. Back then, the food hall wasn't a Burger King and a McDonald's. It was fine dining and high tea for tired, well-to-do shoppers. In the kitchens, they had rows of deep freezers, stocked up with strange and exotic foods from around the world, things I'd never seen or tasted before. The building originally opened before the First World War and was something of a wonder of the Edwardian age. There was a network of compressed air pipes running all around the store, so when a punter paid for an item, the money or the cheque along with the sales docket would be tucked inside a little aluminium cannister, placed in the pipe, and the compressed air would carry the contents to a different part of the store to be totted up at the end of the day.

It was a good time, but it couldn't last for ever. The writing was on the wall for me after a crowd of us went to a show at the Lyceum in the West End. It was an all-night concert, featuring all these unmemorable bands with three-letter names: Ace, Man, and some others that were consigned to the dustbin of history. What was memorable, though, was the Lyceum had a retractable roof, so when it was opened, you could look up and see the moon and the stars above you while the three-letter bands noodled away. We stayed up all night and then hotfooted it to Whiteleys just in time for our shifts. It was the first time I'd ever stayed up through the whole night, but probably thanks to the exuberance of youth I was fine, if maybe a little tired. Some of my mates, on the other hand, had taken some Blues, so they were probably somewhat wired as they carried out their shifts. I didn't take any myself, so by around

11 a.m. I found myself starting to flag a little. As the morning wore on, I started to feel more and more out of it, and was forgetting to fill out the sales docket before sending the payment off into the compressed air tubes. Within twenty minutes, it was chaos. A volley of metal cannisters were tearing through the system and there was either no docket, or I'd forgotten to write the department number on the paperwork. I don't think they realised I was the root of the commotion, so I somehow managed to make it through the day. I was ragged, paranoid, but also feeling that life was too short for this level of stress. Maybe it was time for a career change. Perhaps something a little less straight.

One of my friends had told me there was a place in west London that was selling cool retro clothes and brothel creeper shoes. I wasn't a skinhead, but it was the end of that mod and skinhead phase, and I was starting to show more of an interest in how I presented myself to the world. I'd started to wear Ben Sherman shirts and we all had Sta Press trousers and the usual accoutrements. On hearing about the boutique with the brothel creepers, I caught a 76 bus from Scrubs Lane, changed for a number 11 from Hammersmith, just by Dimitri's hairdresser's, and stayed on the bus until it terminated at World's End on the King's Road. I hadn't been to the King's Road before, so I wandered around a while, trying to get my bearings, and came across a boutique that had half a 1958 Dodge saloon car sticking out the front. I stuck my head in and asked if this was the place that sold the brothel creepers. The shop was full of stoned hippies, hanging out smoking and generally looking like off-duty members of the Rolling Stones. That place was Granny Takes a Trip, which was a mainstay of swinging London in the 1960s and paved the way for several cool boutiques that opened on the King's Road in subsequent years. Through the smoke and over the sound of psychedelic rock, one of the hippies told me I was at the wrong end of the King's Road. Heavy symbolism.

'You're looking for Let It Rock,' he said, and pointed me in the right direction.

Walking into Let It Rock was like stepping into my gran's living room. The walls were covered in old-fashioned kitsch patterned wallpaper and lined with neat little cabinets littered with all manner of chintzy 1950s artefacts. You couldn't miss the fact that along one wall, there was an old wooden radio-gram playing old rock 'n' roll tunes. The walls were adorned with old drape-style jackets and rockabilly fashions in a variety of colours. I scanned the shelves, looking for the shoes my mate had told me about. When I found the brothel creepers, I turned them over to see the price; £12.50, which was probably a month's wages from my Whiteleys job and more than £100 in today's money. An assistant shuffled over and asked if I needed any help.

'Nice stuff you got here,' I told him. 'I don't suppose you need someone to work here, do you?' Nothing ventured, nothing gained, I figured.

'As it happens, I'm leaving at the weekend,' he said, and he scribbled a phone number on a scrap of paper. 'Why don't you call this guy?'

The next day, I did just that. Malcolm McLaren answered the phone. I said I was looking for work and he told me I could start on Saturday. That was the extent of the interview.

'It's seven quid a week,' he told me, and promptly hung up.

I was earning £3.50 a week for working Friday evenings and all day on Saturday at Whiteleys, so £7 for a Saturday and getting my Friday nights back felt like an easy decision. I had no idea then, but it was a seismic, life-changing moment for me.

I arrived for my first Saturday shift at 11 a.m. to find the shop was still shut. Puzzled, I walked past and then around the block until 11.30. When I returned, the shop still hadn't opened, so I went and found a place to get a cup of tea and circled back again at 12. Still there was nobody there. I started to think I'd made a mistake when I caught sight of a pretty girl with bright, cherry red hair tottering towards me along the King's Road.

'Are you Glen?' she asked, fumbling in her bag for a set of keys. 'I'm Elaine,' she told me. 'No point getting here before one o'clock. I always have a late one on a Friday night,' she told me, matter-of-factly. I realised immediately that this place was going to be more fun than working at Whiteleys. And it was.

As my time there unfolded, I slowly found my feet. The cash register wasn't ringing all day, every day, but at certain times it was a mad rush. Generally, the shop took its delivery of new brothel creepers on a Friday, all different colours, shapes and sizes. At a certain point every Saturday, once word had gotten out, there would be a long, winding queue of Teddy Boys, all eager to get their hands on the latest pair. The line of Teddy Boys used to stretch right out of the shop and onto the King's Road. Then, after the mad Teddy Boy stampede, the shop would quieten down for a while, but even then it was generally buzzing with activity. There'd be dribs and drabs of people coming in, someone asking for a drape suit, and I'd take their measurements, and then there'd be the casual punters coming in off the street to gawp, as well as a procession of pretty happening people. *The Rocky Horror Show* was still playing at the King's Road Theatre, and Malcolm and Vivienne Westwood had created some costumes for that, so we'd see a steady stream of cast members coming along and chatting and trying on the latest trends.

When I first met Malcolm in person, he was decked out entirely in authentic '50s gear: box black half-belted fleck jacket and pegged slacks, looking like Jerry Lee Lewis on a day off. He wasn't a true Teddy Boy, though. The smudge of curls was greased back, but his hair was still an uncontrollable orange wave. He didn't carry himself like a Teddy Boy either. The first time I spoke with him, I'd already started working in the shop. He was quite a contradictory character. All airs and graces one minute if the customer seemed refined, switching to a kind of Cockney persona if the punter was more like one of us. He adapted his character depending on whoever his audience was at any given moment. There again, he was quite contrary, so he might just as easily do the exact opposite: refined and posh for someone who was not, and vice versa. Even from these small initial interactions, it was apparent he was someone who enjoyed throwing a cat among the pigeons, even if it was just for his own amusement. It being a small shop, you always knew when Malcolm was in the room. It was his little kingdom, and he was, for the most part, in his mind at least, a *force majeure*.

One of my duties was to man the phone and make calls, so I was privy to Malcolm's strictly non-alphabetical address book. It was a complicated system, kind of a reflection of Malcolm's mad thought processes. If ever I was asked to put in a call to Mr Green, Malcolm's East End tailor, and pass on the measurements for somebody's custom drape suit, I'd have to wade through pages and pages of contacts before I found him. That address book of Malcolm's had some seriously wild contacts. Yoko Ono, the editor of the *NME*, Malcolm's barrister, someone from the IRA, *Oz* and *IT*, the *International Times*. They were all in there.

One of my main duties in the store was to act as their store detective whenever shoplifters were on the prowl. I was told on my first shift that I had to keep a special eye out for a couple of rascals who came as a double feature and would rob you blind as soon as look at you. They were called Steve Jones and Paul Cook. Now and for ever, Steve and Paul are practically inseparable in my memory. They were a double act. They came as a package deal. At first glance, they could be cartoon characters; Fred Flintstone and Barney Rubble, Steve being Fred to Paul's Barney. I don't say that in a snide way, because I am very fond of Fred and Barney. Who isn't? They were a little older than me, a lot more streetwise, and certainly more self-assured than I, a kid who was studying for his A levels, was at the time.

Steve came across as kind of a shifty character from the outset, but in truth, he is a lot more complex than that. I often say Steve could be a whole chapter in a Jean Genet novel. Whatever was happening on the surface, there was always something else going on that he had half a mind on. Like Reg Turner and his library books, he always seemed like he had some scheme or other going on. As a double act, both Paul and Steve's hair had grown out a bit, but they still had that rough, skinhead kind of look to them. They could easily have passed as extras in the 1970s show *Budgie*, the show Adam Faith made for ITV after he packed up his singing career. Like Budgie, they were likely lads, nice wrong 'uns, if you see what I mean. They were constantly on the rob, but also, they were always trying to get Malcolm interested in this fledgling band they had formed. The band was named the Strand, after the Roxy Music tune 'Do the Strand'. Whenever they came in, Malcolm always liked to humour them about their progress.

'How's the band going, lads?'

'I dunno,' Barney Rubble said. 'We're trying to take it seriously, but the bass player never turns up for rehearsals.' The Strand's bass player was this chap called Del Noones, who was Paul Cook's sister's fiancée at the time. I was walking the shopfloor, keeping an eye out for one of them having it away with some gear, so I couldn't help but overhear. That's when I first met them properly.

'I've got an old bass,' I piped up. I had my £15 bass with the go-faster stripe. It wasn't great, but it played.

'Have ya?' Fred Flintstone chimed in. 'What bands d'you like?'

I reeled off a few bands. When it came up that I was into the Faces, that helped to seal the deal, and not long afterwards, I went for an audition at this council house in East Acton. That was the guitarist's house, a chap called Wally Nightingale. As I recall, I played the Faces' 'Three Button Hand Me Down'. It was one of the only tunes I could play from start to finish. When I was done, I looked up to see their reaction.

'You're in,' they told me.

Steve walked over to inspect my bass guitar and shook his head gravely. I still had the Frankenstein bass with the go-faster stripe. 'That's not a bass,' he said.

'Well, it's not the best bass in the world,' I half-agreed. As I spoke, he pulled a case out from under a bed. He clicked the catches and opened the case to reveal a Fender Precision bass gleaming alluringly inside. It was a beauty.

'Where d'you get that?'

'Don't ask,' he said, and handed me the bass.

It wasn't long after I joined the band that I took my girlfriend at the time, a girl called Julie Billard, to see Ronnie Wood play. He was playing a show in Kilburn with the New Barbarians at the Gaumont State Theatre. Ian McLagan was on keys, with Willie Weeks on bass, Andy Newmark on drums, plus Keith Richards and Rod Stewart. We were in the cheap seats, stuck up on the balcony. The place was pitch black and as we made our way up the stairs to the circle, there was this almighty, loud kerfuffle. When we peered into the darkness, and through this cloud of dust, we could see Steve, Paul and their mate Jim walking down, covered in dust from head to toe. They had just bunked into the show by climbing over the roof and in through the fire escape at the back.[1] Whatever happened with these two characters, I realised, it was going to be memorable.

I had no idea.

---

[1] When I was playing with the Faces some years later, and had become friendly with Ronnie Wood, the DVD of that Barbarians show was released for the first time. I went along to a screening of the film at a private preview theatre in London, on Rupert Street, near Chinatown. I walked into the dark screening room and started scanning the place for a seat when I heard someone shouting after me in the dark. I looked over and it was Ronnie. "Ere, Matlock! There's a seat here,' he said, so I bundled past the people on his row and sat down beside Ronnie. When the lights came up after the movie, I looked around and realised I'd been sitting between Ronnie and the Edge from U2, watching the show that had been so instrumental in my career and my friendship with Steve and Paul. It was a sweet moment. It seemed like I'd travelled a long way in thirty years.

7

BILLY BENTLEY

I was still a kid, but even I could see that the mid-1970s weren't exactly a golden period in this nation's history. In some respects, the music scene had come to reflect that. Progressive dinosaurs were still stalking the earth and taking themselves very seriously indeed. Concept albums and guitar solos were king, and everything seemed to be getting more and more self-indulgent. You don't have to look much further than Rick Wakeman and his *King Arthur on Ice* extravaganza to see what I mean. It felt a little bit like music – just like the nation – seemed a bit full of itself and was trading on its past glories.

In counterpoint to all the extravagance of the progressive rock movement, there was a livelier, rootsier scene springing up across the country and particularly in London. From around 1972, hundreds of bands who'd seen enough of the excess of the era adopted a more back-to-basics approach to making music.

The scene came to be known as pub rock. In contrast to what was happening in prog, pub rock was deliberately nasty, dirty and post-glam. It was a lot of fun, but it also laid some important foundations for what was to follow. By shifting the focus to smaller venues, the pub rock bands reinvigorated a scene that had been on its knees since the '60s when half the beat bands of the time moved over to playing big theatre tours.

I'm not exactly a pub rock purist, but it was a formative time for me musically and I have a lot of great memories. When I went to see my first pub rock gigs, I was still at school, and it was still a while before I ventured onto the King's Road and started working at Malcolm's. While I was in sixth form, some of the local schools had organised a charity walk for the homeless charity Shelter. It was a long old schlep. A bruising 36-mile walk from Shepherd's Bush to Runnymede and back, but because it was held on the weekend, we were allowed to wear what we liked. Even so, I didn't choose my outfit wisely. For some reason, I opted to wear a brand-new pair of Levi's jeans, which was a bit optimistic of me. They were my first ever pair and my pride and joy, fashion-wise, but I had no idea you were supposed to wash them before putting them on for the first time. I don't know what I was thinking because after the first mile, they just felt like cardboard against my skin and my thighs were red raw from chaffing against the fabric. On the plus side, I met a girl on the walk, the aforementioned Jackie Barnet, who was the head girl at one of the local schools, and after the 36-mile walk, we wound up on a sort of date, seeing Brinsley Schwarz at the Greyhound on the Fulham Palace Road. I had to stuff cardboard down my Levi's to guard against the chaffing, and I was aching from the 36-mile yomp, but from that day on, I was a pub rock enthusiast.

My favourite venues were usually the nearest ones, but the Greyhound was always a good spot. The pubs were never quiet and there was some great music being played, and it proved to be a useful way to see bands for not a lot of money. Usually, you'd hand over 50p and they'd let you past, no questions asked about your age. Today, people often comment on the price of a beer in London, but you could buy four pints for a pound back then, so it was never hard on your pocket. You didn't have to spend a fortune to find yourself at close quarters with some really happening musicians. Whatever your take on the scene, in that period prior to punk, particularly in London, it sparked a lot of interest in live music and was the first real antidote to all the bloated Emerson, Lake & Palmer nonsense that was dominating the album charts. Additionally, it became quite a social scene, with a lot of the same faces popping up every week: Mick Jones, Paul Weller and Tony James, all of whom would go on to carve out their own little niches in the punk and new wave world. In some ways, it's become kind of a forgotten scene. Possibly that's because very few of the bands went on to sell a lot of records, but they moved music on more than some people might think. Because they were playing more stripped-back, blues-based rock 'n' roll, the music they were making was cheaper to record and release, so a slew of independent labels sprang up in their wake. They may not have sold in Pink Floyd numbers, but a little label like Chiswick could sell 20,000 copies of a record and the artists involved could make a modest living doing something that they loved.

Most of the bands played old-fashioned R&B, so a lot of the time, you had to put up with a bit too much of that 'I been six days on the road and I'm gonna see my baby tonight' kind of blues jamming, just because the lead singer had been to America once for a week's holiday. It wasn't always that way, however. There were some groups who stood out from the crowd and some faces that would rise to prominence when pub rock kind of fizzled out and punk exploded. I used to see Brinsley Schwarz whenever I could and stood at the front so I could watch Nick Lowe play the bass. Brinsley Schwarz were a really good band and Nick's a terrific bass player. Heavy Metal Kids were great, too. I saw them a couple of times. Gary Holton, who went on to play Wayne in the TV show *Auf Wiedersehen, Pet*, was their frontman at the time, and he was a real showman. He had a kind of *Clockwork Orange* droog thing going on when the Kubrick movie was all the rage. Joe Strummer had his band, the 101ers. They were quite loose, but they had *something* going for them. I'm not sure what it was, so, by process of elimination, I guess it was Joe. The Stranglers were on the pub rock circuit long before they went punk, but it was Dr Feelgood who were the scene's biggest draw. They came on stage looking like a proper gang of hard cases. Lead singer Lee Brilleaux looked like someone you didn't want to cross. He had a great, raw R&B voice, and you always had the idea that if you spilled his pint, you'd be in deep trouble. In Wilko

Johnson, they had one of the most influential guitarists of the era, with more than a few punk guitarists going on to ape his style. On stage, he had a real manic energy. I don't know what he was on – probably some kind of sulphate – but he was mesmerising to watch. Because my family used to go to Canvey Island on our holidays every year, I always felt like I had a kind of kinship with those guys. Looking back, I can see how instrumental pub rock was in feeding into what was going to happen with punk a couple of years down the line.

Of all the bands, Kilburn and the High Roads were my favourite, though. The Kilburns were something special. They had been knocking around for a few years and they'd churned through a lot of members over that time, but Ian Dury was the band's mainstay. They were a gang and Dury stood out as their leader. He was one of the most charismatic, genuinely funny frontmen I've ever seen. Eventually they signed a record deal with Dawn records and released an album, *Handsome*, in 1975, but I don't think it really captured the raucous magic of their live shows. I'm not sure Ian did either, because he split from the Kilburns later that year, before eventually resurfacing with the Blockheads. In terms of production, the Kilburns album wasn't great, but they released a single called 'Rough Kids' produced by future Pistols producer Chris Thomas, and that went some way to making amends for the album.

I think they must have received an advance from the record company, because when they got a little bit of money, their manager, Tommy Roberts, brought them into Malcolm's shop to buy some stage gear. Malcolm made Ian the boxer's robe that he used to wear when he arrived on stage. I can vividly remember the time I measured the whole band up for their suits. In the early 1950s, several years before a vaccine became available, the UK suffered a devastating polio outbreak. Dury contracted polio at the age of seven, most likely from a swimming pool at Southend-on-Sea during the 1949 polio epidemic. My grandad had suffered from polio, so I knew how bad it was. When it came to taking Ian's measurements for his new suit, his leg was withered all along one side, but he took his misfortune with a lot of humour. I recall seeing the Kilburns play a show at the Hope and Anchor in Islington, and as the band took to the stage, Ian found his route to the stage was cut off by the crowd and he had to push his way through, shouting over the crowd.

'Get out the way!' he told them. 'Here comes the raspberry!'[1]

Naturally the crowd parted for him. He really understood the pub rock crowd, but I think he was aware of its limitations even then. Over time, they started to make inroads elsewhere, trying to broaden their appeal beyond the pub scene. I saw them play in front of an art school crowd at Saint Martins around that time, and even if Kilburn and the High Roads weren't going to make it in the long run, it was clear that Ian himself was destined for greater things. I know he had a reputation as a complicated character, but in my experience, he was always a diamond. Later

---

[1] Raspberry is Cockney rhyming slang: raspberry ripple/cripple. I appreciate of course that this might not land so well in 2023, but we were living in a far more unreconstructed age.

in life, I named my band the Philistines, in a kind of tribute to the Blockheads.

Lyrically, Ian was second-to-none. He was still cutting his teeth at this point, but his work with the Kilburns was a blueprint for what he would eventually perfect with the Blockheads. He had this incredible lyrical dexterity, harking back to those pre-beat, post-music-hall numbers like 'Hole in the Ground' and 'Right Said Fred', those old Bernard Cribbins[2] hits that I'd loved as a kid. I don't know if it was a deliberate callback or even if it was something that Ian was aware of, but I saw the parallels straight away. They both had the same common touch, and the sense of humour was evident in every song Ian wrote. It was almost the

---

[2] A lot of those great English comedy songs were either produced or worked on by Beatles producer George Martin. I remember one occasion I was in George's AIR Studios in the canteen once and George joined us at our table. Everyone wanted to ask him questions about the Beatles, but I wanted to know about the comedy records he'd worked on when he was at Parlophone. Eric Sykes and Hattie Jacques. The Goons. The Peter Sellers version of 'A Hard Day's Night'. Those early 1960s comedy records were part of the nation's DNA when I was growing up, every bit as much as those records by the Dave Clark Five. Everybody knew them. When I used to visit Steve New from the Rich Kids' house, along with a lot of Frank Zappa, he often played this Harry H. Corbett (aka rag-and-bone man Harold Steptoe) record his dad had. All the percussion was played on old dustbin lids and whenever I hear Einstürzende Neubauten or some other cutting-edge German industrial band, I'm always reminded that Harry H. Corbett got there first.

same comical irreverence, and obviously a love of the English language in Kilburns songs like 'Rough Kids'.

'Rough Kids' was terrific, but its B-side might have been better still. 'Billy Bentley' was all about this young man's adventures in the big city. He comes to London and as he travels from borough to borough, he namechecks all these different places, from Clapham Common to Hyde Park Corner, and documents all these little snippets of London chatter. Dury writes these 'list songs' like nobody else: 'See the show, sir / Nice time, ducky / You'll be lucky / Billy Bentley, he's a caution.'

It's a pithy song and instantly conjures all these amazing images of the London I grew up in. There was no earth-shattering political commentary going on. He was just funny and unique, and those songs really tickle my fancy. He was years ahead of his time. Clearly, bands like Madness were paying attention to what he was doing.

The Pistols' rise to prominence almost ran parallel with Ian Dury and the Blockheads, so we'd see each other out and about occasionally. I didn't hang out with him that often, but I was friendly with him. Whenever we bumped into each other, he was always affable and full of interesting chat. He was a few years older and wiser than most of the other folks on the scene, so he was kind of like Uncle Ian to a lot of us. He and I once did a radio show together and while I was on air, he was sat across the studio from me and the guy who was hosting. While I was doing my interview, Ian just sat there twisting up a five-skin joint, before sparking it up and offering me and the presenter a toke. You couldn't smoke tobacco in the studio, let alone dope, so obviously the presenter was aghast. I'd packed up drinking by then, so I declined, too. Ian just shrugged and went ahead and caned the whole thing himself. By the time he had to come on air, he was totally blasted. What with being off his nut, and not able to walk that well at the best of times, he had to be carried downstairs after the show. He protested all the way, bless him.

8

FRAMED

When I first hooked up with Steve, Paul and Wally, we got to work rehearsing in Hammersmith. We had this amazing place on Lots Road, at the Riverside Studios. To look at it from the outside, it was just an old derelict 1930s building, but in its heyday, it had been a major television and film studio. A real hub of creativity. Classic British black and white movies like *The Happiest Days of Your Life* with Alastair Sim and Margaret Rutherford and *Father Brown* starring Alec Guinness were filmed there. Purportedly, it once had the best sound dubbing room in the whole of Europe, where orchestras would sit in their dickie-bows and dub the score in front of a giant screen. The BBC took the studios over in the 1950s and they made episodes of *Doctor Who*, *Dixon of Dock Green* and *Hancock's Half Hour* there for a time. That was long in the past, though. The place was pretty much a shell when we were there. While the place had fallen into disrepair, Wally's dad – who was an electrician by trade – had the job of sorting through whatever was left behind and deciding what, if anything, was worth keeping. We weren't supposed to be there, but Wally's dad had a second set of keys cut for the place, and we were given the run of the place.

As well as being a free rehearsal space, a place we could make a lot of noise and not bother anyone, over time it became an Aladdin's cave of stuff that Steve had stolen. Meanwhile, as Steve was nicking anything that wasn't nailed down, Paul was working an electrician's apprenticeship at Watneys Brewery during the day. Paul even set up a bar for us with a keg of beer that he'd nicked from work. So we drank beer, and while we drank beer, we played. It was still quite rudimentary stuff at this point. We played covers mainly; rock 'n' roll and old Small Faces tunes. We were trying a few songs we couldn't really play, but they ended up sounding nothing like the original, so that felt quite exciting. Amid all the cover versions, there were even a couple of originals. There was a song that I wrote called 'Where You Gonna Go' and an early version of the song 'Did You No Wrong' – although back then the song was called 'Scarface' and Wally's dad had written some lyrics for it: 'Scarface. Scars from ear to ear / Scarface. The girls don't even care.'

In among all the mess and loose wires, we had a clavinet that Steve had gotten hold of somewhere – don't ask – and I used to try my best to play 'Go Now', the old Moody Blues hit.[1] As a

---

[1] Malcolm once told me that Jamie Reid, the artist who created the Sex Pistols sleeves, was briefly a member of the Moody Blues, but Malcolm said lots of things.

singer, I think Steve imagined himself as a cross between Tom Jones and Steve Ellis, so we even had a crack at things like 'A Day Without Love', Ellis's old Love Affair tune. It wasn't exactly punk rock, but then punk hadn't happened yet, so nobody was doing that. Really, we were still learning how to play, knocking songs around. Nick Kent, the writer, one of the people who used to hang around the shop, would sometimes come down and jam with us. We were still trying to persuade Malcolm to step in as our manager, but he was keeping us at arm's length.

One midweek afternoon, when I was working at Let It Rock, the Sensational Alex Harvey Band walked off the King's Road and into the shop. They made for quite a sight. They were all dressed in heavy overcoats and Alex was wearing a pair of thick-framed NHS glasses. Chris Glen, the bass player, used to buy his dayglo socks from the shop, so the rest of the guys had followed him inside to see what all the fuss was about. The Sensational Alex Harvey Band were a group I used to follow, so it was a blast to see them at such close quarters. I'd seen them play in front of maybe fifteen people at the Greyhound and a dozen people at Kensington Town Hall before they started getting bigger, playing shows at the Marquee and further afield. While I was serving Chris, the door swung open and Malcolm burst in carrying a load of boxes from a delivery. Immediately he caught sight of the five overcoated men milling around in the shop. Malcolm looked aghast and motioned for me to follow him out to the back of the shop.

'Who's these blokes?' he said. He seemed a bit frantic. More so than usual.

'It's the Sensational Alex Harvey Band, Malcolm,' I told him. 'They're a band.'

He thought about this for a second. 'No, they're not,' he said. 'Get them out.'

'Malcolm. They're a band.'

'No, they're not.'

'Well, who do you think they are?'

Malcolm peered out onto the shop floor. 'They're tax collectors,' he decided.

'Malcolm. They're not tax collectors. They're the Sensational Alex Harvey Band. They were on *The Old Grey Whistle Test*,' I told him, but Malcolm remained unpersuaded.

Now, in fairness to Malcolm, looking at him, Alex Harvey in a dark overcoat could easily have passed for a tax collector, and given that everybody but everybody back then had long hair and wore flared trousers, the other guys, all a bit bigger and heavier-looking than Alex, could easily have been his henchmen. Ultimately, I didn't know what I could say that would convince Malcolm that he wasn't just being paranoid, so I went back out onto the shop floor, took Alex and the band to one side and quietly told them not to worry.

'My manager's just having a bit of a moment. Go over the road to the Roebuck and have a pint,' I told Alex. 'Come back in half an hour. He'll be gone and I'll serve you.'

By that point, the Sensational Alex Harvey Band had already been in the charts with 'Delilah', the murder ballad – a tune that had been a big hit for Tom Jones back in the day. I arranged to take Malcolm and a friend of mine from art college, a guy called

Nick Cash,[2] to their show at the Hammersmith Odeon. I knew it would be a great show, but mainly, I think I wanted to prove to Malcolm that they weren't tax collectors. The band came on and they played 'Framed', the old Leiber and Stoller tune, and this cover of a Coasters song they used to play. Malcolm, who was into all that '50s stuff, felt his ears prick up.

'Recognise them?' I turned to Malcolm. 'They're the guys you thought were tax collectors.'

Now, bear in mind that Malcolm had always been reluctant to manage us despite it never being far from our minds. Tonight, however, it was possible to see the little cogs creak into life and start turning in his brain.

'How much were these tickets?' he asked me. Back then, tickets were probably 75p, so I told him as much. Malcolm looked around at the crowd. 'How many does this place hold?'

'I dunno,' I said. 'Two and half, maybe three thousand?'

Malcolm did the maths in his head – 3,000 lots of 75p for a night's work.

'Tell you what,' he said. 'Let's have a little chat tomorrow about that band of yours.'

---

[2] Nowadays Nick Cash plays drums with the band the Members. It's worth noting that this particular Nick Cash was the *original* Nick Cash. I was sitting in the Ship pub on Wardour Street having a drink one day with Nick, when Keith Lucas from Kilburn and the High Roads (later of the punk band 999) poked his nose around the door, looking for somebody. I told him to come and have a drink with us and introduced him to Nick. 'Nick Cash? What a fantastic name,' he said. 'I'm going to nick that name.' From that day forward, Keith Lucas went by the name Nick Cash and suddenly there were two Nick Cashes.

9

ROADRUNNER

Strange as it may seem, I was still in sixth form studying for my A levels. Yet, somehow, I found myself living this second, far more exciting life, just a couple of bus journeys down the road from my family home. Technically speaking, the shop was at the wrong end of the King's Road, but while I was there, it started to become a real hub. The whole area was booming, becoming a real microcosm of people who did things a little differently. Every single day, the shop was bustling with interesting characters who drifted in from the King's Road and sometimes much further afield.

Chrissie Hynde was working there and pretty much ever-present. Chrissie had upped sticks from Ohio in 1973 and had done some writing work at the *NME* while working in the shop and plotting her next move. Siouxsie Sioux was in all the time with the Bromley Contingent, up in London from the suburbs on a cheap day return. William Broad, who used to get around town in an old Austin A35 GPO van, with the letters GPO crudely painted out, was another Bromley stray who found his way to the shop on a regular basis. Tommy Roberts, the wide-boy manager of Kilburn and the High Roads, would often pop in for a poke around and a chat with Malcolm. Roberts had owned the store before Malcolm, back when it was still the Paradise Garage. Roberts was an important figure and had helped set the tone in the early 1970s with his vintage-inspired fashion brand, Mr Freedom, over on Kensington's Church Street. He was a real larger-than-life, geezerish entrepreneur. Among Mr Freedom's many claims to fame, they had supplied Elton John with his winged boots during his 1970s heyday. Roberts turned the world of retail into a kind of theatre, and Malcolm and Vivienne had taken a lot of cues from his forward-thinking approach. After Mr Freedom folded, Roberts set up a boutique called City Lights Studio over in Covent Garden. If you have a copy of *Pin Ups* by David Bowie, flip it over. The suit David is wearing on the back cover is from City Lights Studio.

It wasn't just luminaries from the fashion and music scenes either. The ITN newsreader Reginald Bosanquet would stroll in from time to time to gawp at Jordan. Jordan started at the shop a little after I had, after it was remodelled and renamed SEX. She came in off the King's Road one day, in a pair of gold stilettos, a transparent net skirt, with her hair dyed white and piled high on top of her head in a striking bouffant style. Bosanquet was quite enamoured with her, and I think she was the main reason he came by so often. One afternoon, I sold a pair of shoes to Mick Ronson, from the Spiders from Mars and Mott the Hoople. He came in with his wife Suzi and his bandmate Ian Hunter. Mick had seen a pair of pink slip-on loafers in the window he wanted to try, and I gave him a fitting. It's not recorded in any glam rock tomes, but Mick had particularly tiny feet, and it took for ever to find a pair that fit. After trying on every pair in the shop, I started wrapping the shoes and looked back across the shop floor to see Mick clambering up the ladder and putting all the shoe boxes back on the high shelves.

'I thought you'd be annoyed having to put all these boxes back up there,' he explained.

'You're Mick Ronson. You don't have to do that,' I told him.

Ian Hunter, who was waiting for me to ring up his sale, just rolled his eyes. Anyway, Mick wore those same pink loafers in the Dylan movie *Renaldo and Clara*. It is a long, boring film, but I stayed in the cinema to watch the whole thing, just to catch a glimpse of the shoes. When Mick came on screen in his brief role as a security guard, as soon as I clocked the loafers, I couldn't contain my joy and made an announcement to the whole cinema.

'I sold him them shoes!' I cried out.

Almost as one, the entire audience of Dylan-heads at the Odeon Parkway in Camden shouted at me and told me to sit down and shut up.

Mick Ronson wasn't the only guitar hero who frequented Let It Rock. Chris Spedding, the legendary session player, used to stop in to buy his leather biker's gear with his girlfriend Nora Forster. Nora, of course, later married Lydon. Spedding held the joint distinction of helping with the Pistols' early demos *and* playing guitar for the Wombles. We all made a point of watching him when the Wombles appeared on *Top of the Pops*, I remember. Chris was the Womble with the flying-V guitar, wearing the leather biker's cap that he'd bought from Let It Rock. I also remember later, when he was flush with Wombles cash, seeing him pull up to the kerb outside the shop in a flash American motor and coming into peruse our latest leathers.

Some days we'd have David 'Piggy' Worth, the male model and stylist who was always appearing in *Vogue* spreads, showing his face. Piggy was always good for a laugh and a chat. And not forgetting Richard O'Brien and Little Nell (Campbell) from *The Rocky Horror Show*. This was in the days before *The Rocky Horror Show* became a movie phenomenon, but in our world, they were already a big deal. When I look back, I'm amazed at how I was never short of someone interesting to talk to or talk about. If you peered out the window at the right moment you'd catch Bryan Ferry sauntering past, deep in conversation with Antony Price, the fashion designer. It was a real melting pot of hip, happening people.

One regular, who was out of his head on Quaaludes half the time, was a slightly less celebrated customer of ours. He'd done a little time in Wormwood Scrubs for something or other, but when he got out, he told us he'd cleaned up his act and was now doing a job at Selfridges and to let him know if we ever needed anything while he was down there. When I asked which department he worked in, he muttered something vague about how they moved him around a lot and that it was hard to say exactly.

As it transpired, he wasn't on the Selfridges payroll at all. He was making a list and then shoplifting to order, presumably to fund his ludes habit.

Across the road, at the local pub we all frequented, the Roebuck, you'd usually catch sight of Angus Lennie, the actor who played the chef in *Crossroads* – and who famously appeared as the Mole alongside Steve McQueen in *The Great Escape*. Lennie was a regular fixture, enjoying a lunchtime livener, while his boyfriend pulled pints behind the bar. That pub was a weird fusion of all different types of people. There were all the regular people that Malcolm referred to as the fashion victims and drug victims from around the area, and there were all us types from the shop, but it was always brimming with these rough-around-the-edges Chelsea characters, too. Tough-looking blokes who could easily have been heavies from *Callan* or *Minder*, propping up the bar or whispering in dark corners. They usually described themselves as diamond dealers, but their pug noses and cauliflower ears told another story. Really, they were just straight-up gangsters.

All the ingredients were there for something exciting. Music and fashion were all in the stew together. I'd help the punters with their suits and brothel creepers and put records on the radiogram to soundtrack the day. I remember playing a Brinsley Schwarz record I'd picked up from the Virgin store in Notting Hill one time. Malcolm was unimpressed. After hearing a couple of bars, clearly disgusted with what he was listening to, he marched over to the radiogram and took the record off.

'Not in my shop,' he sneered, giving me the side eye.

After that, I tried my luck with something else. I bought an LP from Rock On records at the unfashionable end of the Portobello Road. The album was by Art Blakey and the Jazz Messengers, and I brought it along to the shop one Saturday. It was the soundtrack album to the movie *Les Liaisons Dangereuses*. I can still remember taking it out of its sleeve, dropping the needle and watching as Malcolm's ears pricked up. *Les Liaisons Dangereuses* had been a big beatnik movie, so he was surprised that the Saturday boy knew something so hip. He let that one play, to his credit. Aside from the records we'd bring in, we used to have a copy of *Fun House* by the Stooges, as well as the New York Dolls LP, both of which were in heavy rotation around that time. The radiogram stayed in situ, but after a while, the shop got its own jukebox, too. I was there the day it was delivered. Malcolm filled it with the most eclectic selection of old 45s you could imagine. I was already listening to John Peel and had been through the 1960s pirate radio phase and worked through the pile of old 78s my uncle Colin had given me, so Malcolm's madcap selections were yet another layer to my musical education. It was a real mishmash of wacky stuff, some of which I hadn't heard before and some tunes that verged on the ridiculous: 'You Need Hands' by Max Bygraves – which Malcolm later covered in *The Great Rock 'n' Roll Swindle* movie; 'Ya Ya' by Lee Dorsey; 'Saturday Night at the Duckpond' by the Cougars, which was a kind of up-tempo Shadows guitar instrumental take on *Swan Lake*; 'Rocking Goose' by Johnny and the Hurricanes; 'Don't Gimme No Lip Child' and 'Little Things' by Dave Berry; 'What Do You Want' by Adam Faith; and tunes by Johnny Tillotson, Arthur

Alexander, Tommy Steele; the Small Faces; and the Stones' 'Have You Seen Your Mother, Baby, Standing in the Shadow?' Screaming Lord Sutch, he of the Monster Raving Loony Party, had the honour of having two discs on the jukebox during my time there: 'Monster in Black Tights' and 'I'm a Hog for You'.

There was a guy in leathers, two pairs of trousers, who came in a lot. He was the *NME* star writer Nick Kent. Initially, he had his eye on Chrissie Hynde, and he would float between Malcolm's shop and Granny Takes a Trip, just a little further down the King's Road. The Granny Takes a Trip people were all friendly with Malcolm, but their clothes couldn't have been more different. Granny Takes a Trip sold more dandy-style fashions, the type of stuff you would see the Stones and the Faces wearing. I understand they also had a sideline in selling a little weed from under the counter.

One day, Nick came in and handed us a tape of this American band he was hip to and that his friend had produced. Nick Kent being Nick Kent, and having all those connections at the *NME*, none of us were surprised when we found out his friend was John Cale from the Velvet Underground. In any case, the band on the tape was Jonathan Richman and the Modern Lovers. There were only half a dozen songs on the tape, so there was just half an album at this point, but it was probably a long time before the album came out that we got to hear it. The song, 'Roadrunner', grabbed me right away. Beyond the fact he was singing about driving around Boston, I didn't really know what it was about, but Richman made it all seem so exotic. It wasn't until years later, driving outside Boston myself and seeing my first Stop 'n' Shop, that I realised it wasn't that exotic at all. None of that detracts from the record, though. It remains one of my favourites to this day: 'Roadrunner, roadrunner / Going faster miles an hour.'

We liked the song so much that Steve, Paul, Wally and I absorbed it into our Lots Road rehearsals almost immediately, and it's never really gone away. The Pistols played it as an encore when we re-formed in 2008, for the Isle of Wight Festival. I think I might have been daydreaming when we played it that night because Paul was waiting for a cue I'd missed for the climax. I remember Steve was looking over at me, and instead of winding down when it should have, the song ended up going on and on for ages. John, who hadn't wanted to do the song on the basis that it went on too long, was just standing there across the stage giving me the stink-eye.

I can't write about Let It Rock, and subsequently SEX, without a few words about Vivienne Westwood. From the outset, I could see she was an incredibly driven, capable person. I was really taken with her from the first time we met. She wasn't scrawny exactly, more like thin and edgy, a bit wiry. She was always decked out in a black leather something or other, with this wayward blonde hair. Whenever she spoke, she was completely direct, and she had a very particular northern accent that I'd never come across in west London. While I was still in sixth form and I first applied for art college, I approached Vivienne for her advice. You needed two referees in those days, so I got one from the family GP and I asked Vivienne if she thought Malcolm would give me the other if I asked. Malcolm was around less and less. He was travelling a lot between London and the States, building a web of contacts for the shop. With the benefit of hindsight, I think Vivienne was maybe a little put out that I hadn't asked her, but that probably went over my head at the time.

'What do you need a reference for?' she asked.

'I'm thinking about going to art school,' I told her, and she looked me up and down.

'That's interesting,' she said. 'But I don't think you want to ask Malcolm. He's been thrown out of every art school in London.'

As I understand it, Malcolm made a habit of getting into colleges, claiming a full grant for the academic year, and then applying to another college and getting another grant from them. Still, when Vivienne eventually told Malcolm I was applying for Saint Martins, Malcolm's perception of me shifted. Before, I was just the Saturday boy, but suddenly that made me more interesting to him and, in turn, he started to seem more interesting to me, too.

Once it was established that I might be, let's say, not uninteresting, Malcolm and I hung out from time to time. We had some fun times, and occasionally got into some scrapes. A bunch of us would go to gigs together or take in late-night movies. One night we went to see Sha Na Na, who were a kind of pastiche 1950s-style doo wop band dressed in gold lamé and leather jackets and with pompadour and ducktail hairdos. Nostalgia always seems to go in twenty-year cycles, so the 1950s revival was huge around that time. Sha Na Na's leader was a greaser guy called Jon 'Bowzer' Bauman, who was kind of like the Fonz from the TV show *Happy Days*, but years before *Happy Days* hit our screens. Bowzer spent the night greasing his hair back with a comb and striking James Dean kind of poses, before calling for someone from the audience to come up on stage with the group. We were right up in the gods, so to get to the stage meant going down a couple of flights of stairs and walking through the stalls, so it looked like more trouble than it was worth, but a couple of minutes later, Vivienne Westwood was up there bopping around in her leather. Bowzer mistook her for a fella, which pissed her off no end, so when the number was over, she refused to get off the stage. We were all laughing but Malcolm had his head in his hands in embarrassment.

I remember one afternoon Malcolm and I were browsing the shelves in a dusty second-hand bookshop. While Malcolm bustled around me, I pulled a book down from the shelf and began to scan the pages. The book was about the 1960s student protests and that era's political movement. Among other events, it included details of the protests at the London School of Economics buildings in 1968 when, over the course of three days, 600 students occupied the buildings. While I was leafing through the pages, Malcolm tapped me on the shoulder.

'I'm in that book,' he beamed. He didn't tell me where in the book, but as I scanned through the pages, I read that while the protesting LSE students were deliberating, taking votes on whether to break a door down to get into a room filled with their student records, there was a description of this red-headed, bearded anarchist. Apparently, this guy had become bored of waiting for the vote. He appeared out of nowhere and just broke the door down with a sledgehammer. Now, given my experience of the man, I couldn't imagine Malcolm doing anything like that, but the bearded ginger anarchist was the only person in the book who could possibly have been him. I mean, he always seemed more interested in making money than anarchy, but those lines would blur soon enough.

10

CAN'T STAND MY BABY

Essentially, the foundation course at Saint Martins was a year or so of me trying my hand at a bit of everything. The idea being that during the first year, you'll ultimately land on the subject that you select to be your discipline when it came to a degree course. It was a lot of fun, and such a far cry from the maths and physics I'd studied at A level. I learned the rudiments of everything. I took life classes, painting, screen-printing, a little bit of sculpture, photography, and learned how to use a darkroom. The college also held extra-curricular classes where we studied movies and discussed their meaning with the hippy film studies tutor. Having spent so long in science and maths classes, it was a real gear change. We'd have to dissect the hidden subtext of George A. Romero's *Night of the Living Dead* and the Soviet silent film *Battleship Potemkin*. I remember we had Ivor Cutler come in once and he gave a talk to the students. I'd heard Cutler on

John Peel a few times. His talk was most memorable for him constantly referring to the fact that he was wearing odd socks. I guess he was being eccentric, but having worn odd socks myself from time to time, I wasn't sure it made for the most illuminating subject matter for a lecture.

I loved being exposed to art and to new ways of expressing myself. I was already into Lautrec – I'd chosen a book on his work as the arts and crafts prize when I left school – but I soon discovered and became more interested in twentieth-century painters and visual artists. A little later, I started to get hip to the Pop Artists, but from the outset, I was quickly turned on by the Dadaists. I really loved collage as an artform and a means of communicating ideas, and I found myself drawn to John Heartfield. Heartfield was a German collagist, born Helmut Herzfeld, but he was so vehemently against the Nazis that he anglicised his name and relocated to England following the Second World War. He created these incredible photomontages with a striking anti-fascist message. Obviously, that hadn't endeared him to the regime in Germany between the wars.

I also loved the French artist and sculptor Marcel Duchamp and his 'ready-mades'. The notion of taking a physical object like a urinal, signing it, and then placing it in an art gallery seemed such a revolutionary thing to do. Because the artist decrees that a thing is art, it becomes art. Learning about things like that gave me a good grasp of artistic theory and I think that was my main takeaway from art college. It's not just about becoming competent in your field; it's about having a greater understanding of what you are creating. Being able to explain why you placed a certain mark or brushstroke in a particular place, and why those decisions are important. If used correctly, it's a great discipline to have. On the other hand, it can lead you down the path of talking total bollocks, so it's crucial that you remain vigilant on that front. On a positive note, it can help you identify bullshit in others.

I remember when Bernard Rhodes used to hang around with the Pistols. Bernard was this guy who was around the shop all the time. He knew Malcolm from way back and he was the one who knew how to screen-print T-shirts. When the band started making a bit of progress, Bernard was constantly trying to get us to justify our existence. What was it that made us different from the other bands out there? Why did we want to express ourselves this way, rather than that? I thought what we were doing was a reaction to all those bands like Barclay James Harvest and concept albums about hobgoblins or whatever. Bernie thought we were the opposite: action, rather than reaction, and maybe he was right. Considering Malcolm's artistic bent, he always thought that kind of discussion was a load of nonsense, but, in a small way, some of the theory I'd learned in college helped me to understand what I wanted from the band and what I felt we should be expressing. Interestingly, Bernard, who at that time just seemed to be dabbling in a bit of this and that, would go on to apply much of the same philosophy with the Clash.

It was during my foundation year at Saint Martins that I found myself right at the heart of London's art school scene. And it really was a scene. Everything felt like it was interconnected – the shop, the band, and art school. Saint Martins, Central

School of Art and Hornsey Art School were all really happening back then. It was around this time I discovered that the Royal College of Art held a disco every Friday night and so I started going along. I got to be good friends with the social secretary, this guy called Edwin Pouncey. Among the many strings he has to his bow, Edwin was later known as the Savage Pencil, the cartoonist and illustrator du jour at the *NME*. He used to put on a good disco, so I invited Steve and Paul along one week. There was a band playing that night, and while I was idly chatting to Edwin, suddenly there was a kerfuffle going on over by the stage, which escalated quickly into a major furore. Apparently, this was because Steve and Paul had been caught trying to nick the band's cymbals. Of course it was. I looked at Edwin and he was having a meltdown.

'What did you bring these horrible louts around here for?' he yelled.

Eventually Edwin would go on to embrace punk. It was a little later, but he was one of the people behind the Royal College of Art Summer Ball they put on in 1976, the 'Night of Treason' gig that the Clash played. That was kind of the culmination of the art school punk scene before everything blew up and punk started to go overground. It was also probably around that time that I bumped into Mick Jones and Viv Albertine from the Slits for the first time. They'd all met at Hammersmith School of Art, out in Lime Grove, and like me they were out at gigs every night. I was the only one in the Pistols with that art school background, but all the bands that were emerging at the time had at least one member who attended art college.

For the record, my favourite of the 'art school songs' was by the Rezillos. There was a time shortly after the Pistols, I was travelling up to Glasgow to meet this guy, Midge Ure, and I happened to bump into Mike Thorne, who was EMI's junior A&R man at the time and had been instrumental in signing the first Pistols deal. He asked if I wanted to check out this band, the Rezillos. They were playing a show at this strange Scottish country club. They were great. They had a terrific song, 'Can't Stand My Baby', which takes me right back to my life as an art school kid: 'Don't love my baby for her curvy hips / I love my baby 'cos she does good sculptures, yeah!'

It was written by Jo Callis, the guitarist in the band, and it had an incredible riff. Jo later co-wrote 'Don't You Want Me' by the Human League.

Scroll forward a few decades and, as of 2022, I'm now an honorary fellow of the arts at University of the Arts London/ Saint Martins, an honour conferred on me at the Royal Festival Hall, by Grayson Perry, no less. As an old alumnus, I was recently asked to take part in a talk, alongside designer Sebastian Conran, one of the guys who booked the Pistols for the Central School of Art show, and Esme Young, the English fashion designer and now a BBC television presenter. Esme was one of the Swanky Modes girls who designed a lot of the fashion associated with the punk scene in the 1970s. After the event, I posted a picture on social media, and I haven't had a reaction like it. My followers, in Japan in particular, were very excited to see me pictured with Esme from *The Great British Sewing Bee*. After I gave my speech, I bumped into Phil Oakey from the

Human League, who I probably hadn't seen since the Human League were supporting Iggy Pop in the UK and were following us around the country in their beaten-up transit van. I imagine everyone experiences these little coincidences, but it never fails to amaze me how much in life is interconnected. You tug on a thread here, and you see the result further down the line.

11

DID YOU NO WRONG

I think Malcolm seeing the Sensational Alex Harvey Band with me was the precise moment he started to take the band seriously. Maybe not us, but he definitely started to take *the idea* of us and our potential seriously. I suppose the thought of maybe 3,000 people, each paying 75p to see us, was probably a great motivator, and he started to take a keener interest. After we had our band meeting the next day, Malcolm started throwing some potential band names into the mix. There were a few floating around that we tried on for size but didn't like. Names like Kid Gladlove and the Damned, and Crème de la Crème, if you can imagine that, but they all seemed a bit naff. They still do. Then, finally, we landed on QT Jones and His Sex Pistols, and that was the name that stuck. I believe the QT came from Paul's local postcode, which was 8QT. Malcolm had recently changed the name of Let It Rock to SEX, and shifted focus from brothel creepers to the more subversive fashions associated with punk. The idea was that we would be the Pistols from the SEX shop. Wally and I decided we didn't want to be 'and the' anything. There was a lot of that about at the time, stuff like Disco Tex and the Sex-O-Lettes and Dr Hook and the Medicine Show, and we were thinking maybe it wasn't so cool for us to be 'and the' something. After Wally and I lobbied for a change, we dropped the QT Jones entirely and became just 'the Sex Pistols'.

Malcolm was showing up at a few more rehearsals and chipping in with suggestions. Sometimes he'd bring along one of his associates to see what they thought. One evening, he arrived with Herbie Flowers in tow. Herbie is one of the greats. His CV reads like a roll-call of 1970s rock and pop aristocracy. He'd played bass for Bowie, T-Rex, Elton John, Lou Reed, and he's featured on literally dozens of legendary records. Malcolm had known Herbie for some time, and he brought him along to Lots Road to watch the Pistols rehearsing and see if we were up to snuff. Steve was singing and Wally Nightingale was on guitar, so it's a fair guess that we probably weren't at that point. Herbie wasn't impressed by what he saw at all. We were pretty shambolic, admittedly. Having said that, he apparently told Malcolm he thought the bass player was good at least.

'Who was that?' I asked Malcolm as Flowers departed. 'That wasn't Herbie Flowers, was it?'

Malcolm looked me up and down. 'How do you know who Herbie Flowers is?'

I think, on some level, Malcolm always underestimated me, so I always loved to surprise him. Whenever I mentioned a book or used a word or phrase that he presumed I didn't or shouldn't know, he'd always recoil in surprise: 'How do you know that?' It was like when I played the Art Blakey album in the shop that time. There was always this underlying subtext of, how could Glen – the Saturday Boy – possibly know about this? From Malcolm's perspective, I guess I was just some straight kid in a Take 6 corduroy suit that he had working in the shop and who didn't know the ropes. As I saw it, those little moments when I surprised him were like stepping stones towards gaining his approval.

With the band's name settled, the next issue, at least as far as Malcolm was concerned, was the band personnel. First things first, he told us, we had to sack Wally Nightingale. It was a difficult moment for us because everyone liked Wally. Bernard Rhodes, who was hanging around with us back then, liked Wally. Steve and Paul liked Wally. I thought he was a decent guitarist and, ultimately, Wally was a good guy. Maybe he needed to work on his look a bit, but sack him from the band? That seemed harsh. Steve Jones will always be the heart of the Sex Pistols, but really, it was as much Wally's band as it was anyone else's. But Malcolm said he had to go, so that was that. I suppose we must have prevaricated a while, because no one wanted to pull the trigger. As I said, we liked Wally, and Wally was the reason we had the rehearsal space. Eventually, when Malcolm returned from one of his trips to the States to find Wally still in the band, he was livid that we still hadn't given him his marching orders. I remember pushing back a bit out of loyalty to Wally, but by then the die was cast. The next time the subject came up for discussion, Paul told me it was time to let Wally go.

'I dunno why you're defending him, Glen,' he said. 'He's always trying to get rid of you.'

After hearing that, I agreed that it was the end of the road for Wally. So, as Malcolm had decreed, we invited him to leave the band. Of course, sacking Wally was made a little more complicated by the fact that our rehearsal space had all been laid on a platter for us by Wally's dad. So, when Wally left, that arrangement went tits up. However, it was pretty much all over at Lots Road anyway. Around the time of Wally's departure, we had a run-in with the law. Steve got into trouble, but surprisingly it had nothing to do with his light fingers. Although, thinking about it, he may have been using his fingers for something.

During the last days at Lots Road, we'd all started to notice that Steve had a habit of disappearing every day during our sessions, and always at the same time. We found out later that he'd discovered that one of the studio's windows overlooked a little cul-de-sac, which had a reputation locally as a lovers' lane. It turned out that Steve had found a vantage point from one of the windows and was peeping on a couple of regulars getting hot and heavy, and they reported him to the police. When the coppers arrived at the studio, they were looking around at the bar Paul had installed and all the stolen equipment. We were asked to leave. That was the final nail in the coffin of the Riverside rehearsals and the end of Wally in the band.

I didn't see Wally Nightingale again for a long time. I think he took his sacking quite badly. Wally was Paul and Steve's mate when all was said and done. They'd all gone to school together in Shepherd's Bush and I think he felt quite betrayed. In fact, when we reconnected a few years later, Wally told me that he was going to take us to court.

'The band was all my idea,' he said. 'If it wasn't for me, Steve would still be nicking fur coats and purses. It was *my* idea for Steve to nick guitars so we could form a band.'

I told him that probably wasn't going to stand up in court and, ultimately, he agreed. He was, in his way, the mastermind, though. Like Noël Coward in *The Italian Job*. Holed up in Wormwood Scrubs prison, pulling all the strings. Initially, at least. Still, it must have been hard on him. After he departed, he had another band that didn't get off the ground and some substance abuse problems followed. He overdosed shortly before the Filthy Lucre reunion tour in 1996. The song 'Scarface', later known as 'Did You No Wrong', had been Wally's initial riff and his dad – his dad who got the second key to the Riverside Studios for us – had written the lyrics. In later years, there was a legal dispute over the songwriting credits. It seems only right that people should get their due, so I went to bat for Wally, and he won the case. I heard, and I don't know if this is true, that the royalty cheque for his part of the songwriting arrived the day after Wally died, so it was more than a little bittersweet.

It wasn't such a small step, getting rid of Wally and Steve taking over guitar duties, but after Wally got the elbow, Steve started to apply himself more and his guitar playing improved a lot. Partly it was application, but also some credit goes to Nick Kent, who took Steve under his wing and gave him some pointers. Also, Steve had met Chrissie Hynde through Malcolm's shop, and as we know, Chrissie could play the guitar a bit.

Personally speaking, I had liked Wally and hadn't really wanted to get rid of him. He was a decent player – he had that Ronnie Wood style that I'd always liked since the Faces days – but then Steve's playing started to improve, and we just moved on. Now we just needed a rehearsal space. And a singer.

12

EIGHTEEN

After Wally Nightingale was despatched and finding ourselves banished from Lots Road, we located a new rehearsal room above the Rose and Crown pub in Wandsworth, which Malcolm stumped up the cash for. It wasn't a long-term solution, however. The pub's landlord had partitioned off a rehearsal space upstairs but hadn't bothered to soundproof the room. He'd just put basic hardboard up, so when we plugged in, all the regulars in the pub downstairs started to complain about the racket we were making. They started banging on the door and telling us to pipe down, but we told them we'd paid our money to rehearse there and weren't going anywhere. That was the last time we tried that place.

Still, you could feel there was a renewed focus within the group. There was just one niggle. It was evident that Steve was never going to cut it as a singer, so we started looking for somebody to act as frontman. The brief was short: we wanted someone with a bit of charisma, and we wanted them to have short hair. It was early 1974, so it was relatively easy to identify someone with the right look, because 99 per cent of people still had long hair and wore flared trousers, so 99 per cent of people had un-wittingly ruled themselves out from the get-go. The 'No Hippies' rule helped to whittle down the populace somewhat and helped us sort some of the wheat from the chaff. Everyone involved with the shop knew we were looking for a new singer. Malcolm and Vivienne and a few others started to put out feelers on our behalf for someone kind of interesting. If someone strayed into the shop or if they noticed a guy in the street who they thought had the right look, they would buttonhole them and see if they were interested, and then report back to us. I even did it myself a few times if I saw someone who I thought might fit the bill. It was Bernard Rhodes who told us to keep our eyes open for this guy called John. I think Bernard must have collared him one time when he came into the shop and told him we were looking. He was just some guy who'd come into the shop looking for a pair of sneakers. I don't think I'd even seen him at that stage. When Bernie came down to see us a while later, he was a bit puzzled.

'I thought I told you to look out for this guy called John?' he said. I told him we had. 'Not that John,' he said. 'The other John.'

He was talking about John Beverley, better known as Sid Vicious. Beverley was one of a gang of marauding Johns. They'd all been to the same college, the place you went when you'd buggered up all your O levels. In no particular order, they were: John Beverley, John Wardle, John Gray and John Lydon. Because they were all called John, they came up with nicknames to differentiate one from the other: John Gray went by his surname, Grey; John Wardle was Jah Wobble; and John Beverley became Sid, who had taken the name from his pet hamster. John Lydon, who was the leader of the pack, and probably the alpha of the gang, remained plain old John, but only for a while longer. They were a whole different crowd of people. They had nothing to do with us west London lot. Lydon hailed from north London. Our reaction was something along the lines of: *Finsbury Park? Where the fuck is that?* They weren't anything like us. We were more working class, like the hoi polloi, and they were kind of druggy types. They struck me as a bit weird, but in a contrived way.

Apparently, Sid's name came into contention as a possible singer when Bernard caught sight of him strolling along the King's Road one day. Some old dear had given him some stick for something or other, and in response, Sid stopped in his tracks, undid his trousers, and waved his willy at her. Apparently, Sid's willy-waving antics had piqued even Malcolm's interest. 'You've got to have something going for you to be able to do that in broad daylight,' he noted, when discussing Sid as a possible singer. Later, it turned out that Sid was quite a good singer in his own right. You can't deny that he would have looked the part, but he certainly didn't have the same gift of the gab that the other John had.

Anyway, there was a miscommunication somewhere along the line. It wasn't *that* John that joined, it was the leader of the

Finsbury Park gang, John Lydon. I think Malcolm promised him a free pair of brothel creepers and arranged for us to meet and for us to try to suss him out in the Roebuck after work one Saturday. Lydon arrived with his mate John Gray in tow, acting as his entourage. Lydon was wearing a Pink Floyd T-shirt, on which he'd scrawled the words 'I hate' in Magic Marker, so the legend now read 'I hate Pink Floyd'.[1] Despite how it's been portrayed in the recent Danny Boyle TV show, it was me, Paul Cook, Steve Jones and Malcolm who attended the meet. After we'd done the introductions, John asked me the name of the band and I told him it was the Sex Pistols.

'That is dreadful. It's so bad,' he said. 'I love it.'

We all got acquainted, although it was a bit frosty between Steve and John, and after a drink John was invited back to the shop, where he gave an audition. I say audition, but in truth, he just larked around in front of the jukebox over a couple of records. Someone cued up 'Eighteen' by Alice Cooper, and Malcolm handed him an old showerhead as a prop microphone and told him to behave as if he was on stage and we all stood back by the jukebox and watched him perform. It was an awkward, edgy display all told. But it was also funny, and we were

---

[1] A few years down the line, I was playing with my band at a literary festival and David Gilmour was in the audience dancing around and singing along to 'Pretty Vacant' with his missus. After we left the stage, and we got to hanging out afterwards, I overheard him explaining to a friend of mine the significance of the I Hate Pink Floyd T-shirt. The Pink Floyd exhibition at the V&A displayed a replica of the T-shirt a few years back, so I'm pretty sure he saw the funny side of it.

all chuckling while he scuttled around the shop like he was Richard III or Quasimodo. It was a weird performance, and you couldn't put your finger on it exactly, but you could tell he had something. Us being all lined up in judgement was an embarrassing scenario for him, but John made the best of a bad situation and obviously he got the gig.

'Cor blimey, mate,' Steve piped up in the aftermath. 'Your teeth are rotten.'

And that was that. Malcolm dubbed him Johnny Rotten, and he was duly installed as our new singer. I think we were just going to see how it went, but it almost fell apart at the first hurdle. We got off on the wrong foot with John right out of the gate.

We arranged a time to meet for a rehearsal a week later at a place Malcolm had lined up. The rehearsal space was at this hippy commune in Rotherhithe called the Crunchy Frog. We'd rehearsed there a couple of times after the plug got pulled on Lots Road and the room above the pub fell through. The week we arranged to meet John, Paul and Steve didn't turn up – which was a particular speciality of Paul and Steve's back then. Meanwhile, I was busted en route for bunking the fare on the Circle Line and didn't make it either. It wasn't the most auspicious start to our collaboration. The next day, we got an angry call from John, who had schlepped all the way to Rotherhithe, only to find none of us had bothered to turn up.

Understandably, he was none too pleased. I don't blame him. As I remember it, he had to be coaxed out of his sulk by Malcolm before he'd agree to try again. Then, not long after we'd all left John in the lurch, I spotted an advert in the *Melody Maker* for a place in Denmark Street, right in the heart of London's Tin Pan Alley. I showed the ad to Malcolm, and he told me to call up the guy and offer him £1,000 for the place, sight unseen. Bearing in mind the times, a grand was a lot of money. I told Malcolm I thought he was mad, but he insisted I do it anyway. So I made the call and the guy said we could talk business.

The guy who answered the phone was a chap called Bill Collins. Bill had been an old jazz band leader from way back and, unlike Malcolm, had some connections in the music world. He'd even played in a jazz band with Paul's dad, James McCartney, and he told me he had roadied for the Beatles on a couple of occasions. Also, Bill was the father of Lewis Collins, who was in a few beat bands in the 1960s, including the Mojos. They cut a few singles, but aside from a couple of minor hits, they never really made it. Bill managed the Mojos and later steered the career of Badfinger, the old Apple Records band. Lewis, Bill's son, would later find fame as Bodie, the guy in the silver Capri in the ITV show *The Professionals*.[2]

I don't recall whether Bill ever got his £1,000 from Malcolm, but we took over the lease of the place on Denmark Street and for a while, he kind of took us under his wing. I moved

---

[2] If ever you went around to Bill Collins' house, which was out Finchley way, sometimes you'd bump into his son Lewis. I saw him once, pulling away in an ambulance he'd converted into a dormobile. He'd long since abandoned his pop career and was leaving to do repertory theatre for the first time. He was travelling around the country performing in little provincial theatres and sleeping every night in this camper van. Not exactly a Ford Capri, but I guess it got him wherever he was going.

out of my mum and dad's house out in Sudbury Hill, towards Greenford – where we'd moved to from Kensal Green a few months earlier. I could have killed them when they announced the move. Living in Kensal Green meant you could always get back home if you stayed out too late or missed the last train. Getting back to Greenford was twice as far and twice as hard, so I jumped at the chance of having my own place in the centre of everything. Seventeen years old and living right in the heart of Soho! After surveying the place, Steve and I moved into Denmark Street almost immediately.

13

WITHOUT YOU

We were being carried forward by our own momentum at this point. We thought we were the bee's knees, and now I think about it, even at that embryonic stage, we probably were. Looking back, I'm always surprised at how easily everything was falling into place for us. It reminds me of that movie *The Blues Brothers*. Jake and Elwood getting out of jail and travelling all over Chicago, getting the band back together. I didn't think we were on a mission from God, but I did feel that we were on a mission to do . . . *something*.

Bill's earlier charges, Badfinger, had held the lease on the place on Denmark Street before us. They were a good band, with a knack for making classy pop music, but had gone tits up after struggling to score a big hit. They wrote the song 'Without You', and Bill had recommended an orchestral arrangement, but they dismissed the idea out of hand. Not long after, 'Without

You' ended up as a worldwide hit for Harry Nilsson, with pretty much the arrangement Bill had suggested, but by then, Badfinger were no more.

It was a pre-Victorian building that at one time had been a sweat shop, with seamstresses and machinists packed into the place like sardines in a can. Our rehearsal room was about 10 feet square and situated on one floor. Just upstairs, there was a tiny room with a sink and pretty much nothing else, where Steve and I shared digs. That became our hangout, our bedroom and our office. We stayed for probably the best part of a year, living on top of each other and right next door to the old Tin Pan Alley Club. The Swinging Sixties were long dead, but even then, the Tin Pan Alley Club was like a scene out of a movie. They had all types in there, a proper rogues gallery. All the Denmark Street music spivs, rent boys and gangsters used to congregate there, as well as the junkies, who used to shoot up and leave their used needles on the ground outside in our backyard.

Still, in purely practical terms, it proved to be a great place for us. When you're in a band, it's a constant pain having to book rehearsal rooms, lug all the gear, set up your equipment, chat about what you're going to do, mess around with the leads because something isn't working, only to discover that nobody has any decent ideas and then, at the end of the rehearsal, you have to take everything down and start the whole cycle again when you book the next room. Having our own place at last meant we didn't have to do any of that. We just kept all our gear there, all set up and ready to go whenever we fancied. And because you have nothing better to do at that age, you meet up, bursting with ideas and full of enthusiasm. If the worst comes to the worst, you just meet up again the day after that and you're still ready to go. It was a great place to make noise. Paul would attack his drums at full tilt and Steve was always of the opinion that if you had an amp that went up to ten, it was a waste of money and effort not to use the full ten available to you. And because Paul and Steve were basically at ten the whole time, I couldn't hear the bass, so I had no option but to turn up to ten myself. We were like any band starting out in that sense, except everyone else at that time was wearing great coats and flares. We all had short hair and were decked out in drainpipe trousers. John, who had never sung before, only had a little 50-watt PA system in the corner and probably couldn't hear himself at all. I imagine that was a contributing factor in terms of his vocal style. I mean, God knows what the neighbours thought. I have tinnitus today, and I think I can trace that directly back to standing in front of Paul's drumkit in that little room on Denmark Street.

London wasn't gentrified back then, so we shared the place with a few mice who scurried around the place while we played. John tried to convince us that the mice were rats, and so Malcolm bought me and Steve a cat, which I named Tom, after my grandad. Malcolm hung on to the place for ages, and still had the lease after I eventually left the Pistols a few years later. As you might imagine, the place wasn't all that much to look at, but we were kids basically and we were living right in the heart of the West End. It was an exciting time. I was at art college, and I had my own place. It was such a novelty, living there, sometimes I used to just make up excuses to pop out and explore. Say, if I needed a 2B pencil or a sheet of cartridge paper, I would head out on an errand, deliberately taking the long way around to see what I might see. I'd walk all the way down Old Compton Street and stroll past the French House or the York Minster pubs in Soho and maybe see if I could catch a glimpse of Jeffrey Barnard writing his next column. On the way back, usually he'd have moved on and would be sitting in the open window of the Coach and Horses drinking a pint after he'd finished his copy and submitted it. Sometimes you'd see Keith Waterhouse or Denis Norden or some other luminary, all these faces and people I'd read about. Because the pubs used to close in the afternoons at 3 p.m., everyone moved on to the drinking clubs like the Colony Rooms on Dean Street, where you'd see Francis Bacon heading in for a lunchtime livener. Just popping out for a pencil, I'd get to see all these fantastic slices of London and history happening around me. Fascinating people from the 1940s and 1950s, closing out their era, just as we were setting out on our own path.

Beyond my life in the band, my fellow students and I quickly settled into our lives outside of what we thought of as straight society. It was a real mixture of people from differing social backgrounds. There were kids like me, from working-class stock, rubbing shoulders with the debutante crowd of students and everything in between. There were so many debs in our midst, the café next to Saint Martins where we used to hang out sold Sobranie cocktail cigarettes over the counter, so the posh girls didn't have to slum it when they fancied a smoke with their cappuccino. Obviously, from the point of view of this red-blooded teenager, it didn't go unnoticed that, as well as being a lot more sophisticated, a lot of the girls were also quite attractive.

Over time, we began to imagine ourselves as bohemians. Outside of lectures, we'd smoke cigarettes and drink coffee in these places we thought were exotic cafés, because we'd heard somewhere that it was once a beatnik hangout. Usually they were just greasy spoons that served egg and chips all day long, but we enjoyed the air of mystery, even if it was all in our imagination. We'd sip our espressos, wondering if that bloke at the other table was Lucien Freud or some other notable society figure, but Lucien Freud had enough acclaim that he was probably having his lunch at the Ritz, or some flash gentleman's club by this time. Still, in my eyes, there was a real mystique about the place, even though the seedy side of Soho was still on display. Wherever you were, you were only ever a hop, skip and a jump away from that other Soho. Wander down a side street and there would still be girls lined up offering a nice time to the passers-by. In upstairs windows, there would always be signs for 'Large chest for sale' on your way to the peep shows and the Raymond Revuebar.

That part of town was still run by Maltese gangsters, and they were an everyday sight, collecting protection money from the shops and cafés. There was a barber shop near mine and Steve's place on Denmark Street where I regularly went to get my hair cut. One time I was in, the barber was giving me a trim and finishing off the hair on the back of my neck with a cutthroat razor. While he was making small talk and starting to tidy up, in the mirror I noticed the reflection of someone standing in the doorway of the shop. He was a little stocky guy, wearing an expensive-looking sharkskin suit. As he crossed the threshold, and the little bell over the door chimed, he opened his jacket to reveal a gun in a shoulder holster. The barber's face drained of all its colour.

'But . . . I paid you last week,' the barber told him.

Without missing a beat, and paying me no mind whatsoever, the guy in the sharkskin suit told him, 'You paid me last week. You pay me this week. You pay me *every* fucking week.'

'Come back later. I've got a customer,' the barber implored him.

'Oh, I *will* come back later.' The guy grinned and left.

The barber seemed as if he was pretty shaken, which seemed an understandable reaction. When he picked up the cutthroat razor to finish tidying up the stray hairs on the back of my neck and I noticed his hands were still shaking, I dusted myself off and told him, 'You can leave that, mate.' I wanted my hair cut, not my neck sliced to ribbons.

A lot of my history is tied to that square mile of London, so I still have an affinity with the place. Even now, I keep finding surprising connections with the area. A few years later, after I'd left the Pistols, I was renting a flat and the rent collector was a guy called Big Mac. Big Mac had an office above Hank's Guitars on Denmark Street, just a few doors down from where I'd lived with Steve. Mac worked for Harry Hyams, the property magnate who owned Centrepoint. Later still, when my nan passed away and I was going through her affairs, I learned that she had been born on Denmark Street, just a stone's throw from mine and Steve's place and our rehearsal room.

Soho was a different world in those times. Six days a week, it was completely buzzing, but in contrast, on Sunday mornings it was like waking up in a different part of the city. I would pop out to this little grocery store on Old Compton Street and get a pint of milk and a tin of cat food and there was never a soul around. Soho was so quiet; it was like a village.

More than any of the others, I became quite friendly with Bill Collins over time, and we often chatted about the history of the area and the local characters. Bill was a friendly guy, and he knew everyone's backstories. During our time there, there used to be a curry house, and I was fascinated by this big tubby bloke who was always sat in the window seat scoffing curries.

'Have you ever seen that ad in the back of the *Melody Maker*: "Your lyrics set to music"?' asked Bill. 'Well, that's him. That's Morgan Jones. He used to be the pianist in a swing band, and he has this one tune, and whatever lyrics people send him, he sets them to that one tune. As soon as he gets paid, he's straight down the curry house to stuff his face,' Bill told me.

Because it was next door to mine and Steve's place, we spent a lot of time at number 9 Denmark Street, La Gioconda Café, which held a storied place in British pop music history. Nowadays it's an upmarket steak house, but when we were there and for years beforehand, it was the go-to place for a coffee and a confab in Tin Pan Alley if you were in showbiz or trying to break your way in. It wasn't just Sex Pistols who sought refuge and a cuppa there. From the 1950s onwards, everybody who was in, or trying to make it in music, used to hang out at La Gioconda. Because Dick James Music was based on Denmark Street, Elton John and Bernie Taupin were in there all the time. While he was still climbing the staircase to stardom, you'd often find David Bowie nursing a cup of tea for a couple of hours, hoping someone would spot him. In fact, for a time, Bowie lived in a converted ambulance that he parked on Denmark Street, presumably so he'd have easier access to the street's star makers. The Small Faces signed their contract with music tycoon (and noted shark) Don Arden in La Gioconda. Kenney Jones of the Small Faces once told me they were in there one day and Bowie came over to tell them what a big fan he was. Apparently, the Faces had a show that night in Tottenham somewhere and David asked if he could tag along and maybe get up and play with them. Steve Marriott told him he could come, but only if he helped carry the equipment, and David duly agreed. Bowie was out of his mod-about-town and Tony Newley periods by this point and had entered his short-lived solo, acoustic troubadour phase. The music he was playing was what Kenney referred to as 'Ban the Bomb' music, kind of acoustic protest music in the style of Donovan or Dylan. They played the gig and Bowie was down at the front the whole show, and between every song he'd ask if he could get up and play and the guys told him, 'After the next one.' Every song, it was, 'Yeah, David. In a minute, mate. After the next one.' Finally, as they were about to play their last song, David asked if he could get up and they told him yes. After the next one. He duly got up, at which point the Small Faces exited, stage left, and Bowie took the stage as the crowd started filing out. Don't let it be said that Bowie never suffered for his art.

14

SUBMISSION

Briefly, before we'd taken up residence on Denmark Street, we found a place to rehearse in Camden at the Roundhouse. They had a little rehearsal studio in the basement that was owned by Gerry Bron, the founder of Bronze Records. Malcolm had booked us a couple of days there, and although there's no blue plaque up on the wall outside commemorating the occasion, completely by accident, it was the site of the Sex Pistols' first ever radio broadcast. They were putting out a live classical concert for the BBC World Service from the main auditorium. A few minutes after they began transmitting, someone from the BBC came down and said the microphones were picking up the sound from our rehearsal and asked if we wouldn't mind turning the volume down. Being as we were Sex Pistols, and snotty kids, we told them that we did mind actually, and we carried on playing. My heartfelt apologies if you were in Botswana that day, expecting to hear Grieg's *Piano Concerto* and got an earful of us playing 'Roadrunner' in the background.

On the second day of rehearsals at the Roundhouse, Paul and Steve pulled another one of their disappearing acts and sloped off somewhere. Me and John waited around for a while, but when it became clear they weren't going to show, we cut our losses and reconvened to the pub across the road. Over a pint, John asked me if I'd seen Malcolm lately.

'As a matter of fact, I have,' I said. 'He's suggested a song title for us to work on.'

'Oh yeah, what's that, then?'

'Submission,' I said, and John rolled his eyes.

'What, all bondage and domination and that sort of stuff? I'm not having that.'

Malcolm was still trying to tie the Sex Pistols to the shop in some way and assumed we'd be amenable to writing a few songs to his specifications. Around the time John became a Pistol, Let It Rock had gone the way of the dodo and was superseded by Malcolm's infamous SEX boutique. In fact, I'd helped create the four-foot-high pink foam rubber letters that went up on the façade. Inside the store, the changes were just as stark. It was out with the chintz wallpaper and grandma's house aesthetic and in with the chicken wire and sprayed graffiti. Rubber curtains were hung from the walls and a blood red carpet was fitted. For the most part, the drape suits and 1950s stylings were out and replaced with something far more subversive. The SEX boutique sold fetish and bondage wear supplied by specialist underground fashion labels like London Leatherman, alongside

Malcolm and Vivienne's own designs. Considering the times, they really were confronting our uptight little nation's social and sexual taboos and enjoying a bit of notoriety among the faint of heart. Famously, the shop was selling T-shirts of the Cambridge Rapist's hooded face, Jim French's 1969 illustration of half-naked cowboys (the bottom half being naked, naturally), and the trompe-l'oeil breasts that Steve was pictured in from time to time and wore on the Bill Grundy show. Among the designs were clear plastic-pocketed jeans, zippered tops, and Anarchy shirts. Seeing as nowadays, many of those items are museum pieces, fetching astronomical prices, I kind of wish I'd hung on to a few items from my time in the shop.

John was already wary of Malcolm and neither of us fancied the idea of a song about bondage and whatnot, so while we were in the pub, we changed the brief. Instead of writing a song about S&M, we wrote a song about a submarine mission, just to see if we could get a rise out of Malcolm. It was a lot of fun. We traded lines back and forth over a pint or two until the song was written.

John would say, 'I'm on a submarine mission for you, baby.'

Then I'd say, 'I feel the way you were going.'

John: 'I picked you up on my TV screen.'

Me: 'I feel your undercurrent flowing.'

I read that John said it was the closest thing the world got to a love song by the Sex Pistols, but it was just an exercise in mischief really. A gold-plated opportunity for us to have a bit of fun at Malcolm's expense. When we had the words, I went home and worked out the chords, which wasn't particularly hard, as it's basically 'Hello, I Love You' by the Doors. It was the only song that I sat down and wrote with John in that old-school, Tin Pan Alley-ish, two-guys-working-together-in-a-room kind of fashion. It was a cool moment, even if the song is quite a throw-away number. If I'm honest, as a fan of the three-minute pop song myself, it's at least a minute too long. It always felt even longer when we played it live, but it helped pad the set out. It's not like we're blessed with the biggest back catalogue, so we need all the help we can get on that front. I don't know if it's worth noting, but we played the song at our first ever show and we played it when we last played together.

'Submission' ended up on the demos that were later released as the *Spunk* bootleg album, which has gone on to have a kind of legendary status among punk aficionados. The *Spunk* demos were recorded at our place on Denmark Street by the two hip-pies who became our sound engineers: Dave Goodman and his sidekick, Kim Thraves. Dave had been in a few bands, dating back to the 1960s, and was into the whole alternative hippy life-style. Kim, on the other hand, was a cool, good-looking, long-hair type, with a bit of a groovy *Catweazle* vibe going on. Kim used to drive around in an old Mark II Daimler Jag and always had an eye for the ladies. We met them when we played our first gig at the Nashville in April 1976. Between them, they had a PA company and a van, which was all we were looking for at first, but they worked out for us and wound up working the sound for all our gigs. They were there when we made our first forays out of the capital and up to the grey north. In May we'd tried a few demos with our friend Chris Spedding at the recording desk, including 'Problems', 'Pretty Vacant', and a few takes of 'No Feelings', but we knew we could do better.

Afterwards, Dave let us know he had a Revox four-track tape recorder and suggested we do some recording at our rehearsal place, so in July, we regrouped with Dave on Denmark Street. I don't know if it was because we were playing on home turf, but the songs immediately started to sound better than they had on the Spedding recordings. Dave said it might be worth taking the backing tracks to a recording studio to do all the vocals and overdubs and the final mix, which is what ended up happening. And those were the demos that had the record labels sniffing around us, and eventually got us the deal with EMI.

Presumably this was all coming out of Malcolm's pockets, but he didn't say. It wouldn't surprise me to discover that he hadn't paid anyone, but I wasn't hip to Malcolm's financial machinations. I don't think any of us were. If you asked about anything like that, he'd just give you a load of flannel about seeing you all right. We just knew we were in an actual recording studio, and it felt like we were getting somewhere.

15

SOS

I finished my foundation course at Saint Martins in May 1975 and applied, and was accepted, for a degree in fine art painting. The band was going great guns at this point and there was a growing sense that we might be embarking on something significant, but we still didn't quite know what. I was hanging out with John a bit more and we were regularly bouncing ideas around for songs. And the dynamic in the group was changing.

The Johnny Rotten persona didn't arrive fully formed, but kind of evolved over time. Sure, John brought a different energy. He had a sort of Jonathan Swift-ian, sideways way of looking at the world, and that really appealed to me. By the same token, I think maybe as a second-generation Irish kid, he carried a chip on his shoulder that the rest of us didn't really appreciate. I remember one set of lyrics he pulled out early on, an odd rant about the Archangel Gabriel. My upbringing had been strictly

C of E, so I was immediately struck by the differences in our experience of the world. But it wasn't a million miles away from the pivotal line 'I am an anti-Christ' in 'Anarchy in the UK'. From my perspective, it felt like he had a totally unique take on the world. I read later that he hadn't even considered his Catholic upbringing as having an effect on his lyrics and his outlook in general until he'd read something I said in an interview, but it was always clear to me. Every one of us, whatever our backgrounds, carries something of our childhoods with us into later life, whether we realise it or not. It's there and, in our case, it led to some culturally seismic ideas. It doesn't take a psychologist to tell you that John was a prickly character back then and how that was in stark contrast to my own personality, not to mention Steve and Paul's.

I suppose all of us were tiptoeing around each other, finding a way to work together. We got to hang out a lot at the rehearsal space on Denmark Street. We were still feeling each other out, but over time, John and I started to form a tentative songwriting partnership. Steve had a few things cooking, tune wise, and John had a plastic carrier bag filled with the lyrics he'd been furiously scribbling since he passed the audition at Malcolm's, so right from the offset, there was a lot for us to draw upon. We started knocking out some songs and throwing a few ideas around, one of them being the song 'Scarface' that we'd had since the Wally Nightingale times. We persevered with the tune, but John came in with some lyrics about one of his mates' suicide attempt.

I remember thinking, *Jesus, we're not going to go there, are we?* You could feel the shift in gear. Even for us, it felt very dark, so we didn't do that. Eventually the song morphed into 'Did You No Wrong'. Then there were other covers we were working up, as well as one of Steve's tunes, 'Seventeen'. John later adapted the lyrics, and that became 'Lazy Sod', although the words were still kind of related to Steve.

Culturally, we were right at the fag-end of the glam rock era, but also getting into art rock territory; Bowie and Lou Reed's *Transformer*, which we were all into to varying degrees, but John was especially hip to all that, as well as bands like Captain Beefheart and his Magic Band and CAN. One of the best gigs I ever saw was CAN at the Hammersmith Palais, but John loved them deeply. If you had your ears open, it was an exciting time. A great amalgamation of sounds and ideas. We were all listening to the New York Dolls and Iggy and the Stooges[1] on a loop. We were seventeen and eighteen years old and we had our feet in the waters of fashion, rock and art, this demi-monde of happening people.

Obviously, the tensions in the band have been written about a thousand times over, but at the start, relations really were more amicable. Of course, we would all take the piss out of each other, in what I thought was a good-natured way, but some of us were better practised in the art than others. I was the youngest member of the band, and maybe not so streetwise as the other three guys. I certainly wasn't as cocksure as Steve Jones, but,

---

[1] I know John saw the Stooges play at the 1972 show at King's Cross Cinema, the one that's pictured on the cover of *Raw Power*. Mick Rock, who took those photographs, was a frequent visitor to Malcolm's shop.

then, who is? John was a different kettle of fish and spoke a lot more directly. He would tell you how horrible he thought you were, and you'd laugh it off and he'd fix you with that Lydon look of his.

'No, I mean it,' he'd tell you.

The next minute, it'd all be quite good-natured again. John and I would nip to La Gioconda Café next door and split a plate of jam roly-poly and custard between us for lunch, because John's dole had run out or we'd spent all our money on beer. We'd rehearse and argue and discuss whether the second chorus or whatever should come in after the bridge or the second verse. It was usual band stuff, a lot of the time. But Lydon wasn't cut from the same cloth as Steve, Paul and me, that much was clear. I hadn't met anybody like him before. Once the honeymoon period was over, I think John started looking for an opportunity for a kind of hostile corporate takeover, with his ally Sid waiting in the wings. I would be usurped, if you like, and then it would be a straight two vs two fight. Politically, what I think was happening, personal politics I mean, was that John, being the last man on board, tended to have a mindset that it was three against one and that it was an unfair balance. It wasn't really like that. If anything, it was a triumvirate; you had the double act of Steve and Paul, a kind of union block vote, and then there was me and there was John. I don't think John ever really appreciated that.

Ultimately, and as we progressed over the following year, there was always a bit of needle between John and me. I think that was kind of the reason he wanted to get his mate Sid in, to redress the balance. The assumption being that with Sid in the band, he would have someone on his side, but as history has already noted, it didn't really work out like that. Also, on some level, I think John held the art school thing against me. I've seen John's art. He created the artwork on some of the PiL records. He's a talented painter, with a genuinely interesting and subversive take on the world. But maybe because I went to art school and he didn't apply, I think there might have been some resentment simmering away somewhere. Maybe he would have liked to have gone down that path himself? I don't know. At the time, whenever it came up, he made out that he saw it as a kind of bourgeois pursuit of mine, but really it wasn't. Not that it should matter, but I wasn't middle-class. I'm a working-class guy who just managed to make it work somehow. That was one of the best things about art college. Admittedly, there were a lot of students whose rich parents had sent them there as some kind of finishing school, but, at the same time, there were a lot of working-class kids too and it was an uphill struggle for us to make it. I don't just mean academically, either. I was always a year up on where I should have been at grammar school, and because of that, I didn't receive a student grant in my foundation year because I was too young to qualify.

Whatever John's opinion, I got to Saint Martins because I grafted hard for it. I bunked the fares every day and I paid my way by working in Malcolm's shop. Ever since I was a kid, I've always supported myself. In some shape or form, I've been working since I was eleven or twelve years old. It's 2023 and I'm still working all the time. I worked in a lino warehouse. I worked stacking shelves and delivering groceries. I had the gig at Whiteleys. Even while I was at Saint Martins, I had to take a summer job in the accounts department at Rolls-Royce. Good money for the time, too. £40 a week, and that allowed me to pay for my Fender Bassman cabinet to go with the head that Steve Jones had acquired by less honest methods, obviously (he stole it from *The Rocky Horror Show*), but then he was never renowned for his work ethic. Lazy sod.

Over that summer, I carried on working for Malcolm and Vivienne in my capacity as Saturday Boy and store detective. Malcolm wasn't always around, though, still travelling backwards and forwards between London and New York. Initially he was trying to make connections with like-minded souls in the rag trade, so he could source original Teddy Boy fashions for the shop. After a few trips, however, he expanded his brief, and started making contact with other hip and happening people over there. After a time, he started to make connections with people in the New York music scene. When he flew back to London, he would come back to the shop buzzing with ideas, talking about Richard Hell and Tom Verlaine from Television, and telling us how they reminded him of the French new romantic poets. He'd show us these photos of the New York punk scene and would come back with pockets full of flyers and setlists for these shows he'd seen. He was so full of excitement, even though none of these people had even made a record at this point. Through Malcolm, I heard about Television and the Heartbreakers, and they seemed so far away and exotic, and here was Malcolm meeting all of them and making these connections. None of the bands' line-ups had settled yet, but it was clear that something interesting was going on over the Atlantic and we were aware of that – via Malcolm – before everyone else on this side of the pond. I think it was a month or two later when he decided to get involved with the New York Dolls. He'd hooked up with Sylvain Sylvain from the Dolls at, of all places, a US clothing convention. While he was still in the Dolls, Sylvain used to have a clothing company called Truth and Soul as well as a blue jeans emporium. When Sylvain and I became friends, he told me his claim to fame was having sold a pair of dungarees to Janis Joplin. Sylvain had invited Malcolm out one night and that had started the ball rolling – at least as far as he was concerned.

Malcolm was staying in New York a lot around that time, going to CBGB's and reporting back to us on the King's Road. His networking was starting to pay dividends, too. After he'd run into Sylvain Sylvain, the band must have taken a shine to him, because they started inviting him along to their shows when he was in town. Aware of how persuasive he could be, I knew it was only a matter of time before he got to work on them. Before too long, he'd twisted their arms and Malcolm stepped in as their manager. He only managed the Dolls for a short while, until they broke up, but there's probably a whole book in that story. I remember once he sent us a picture of the Dolls dressed in red patent leather, in front of a hammer-and-sickle backdrop that he'd organised. When Vivienne saw the photo, I remember she was indignant that she could see David Johansen's ugly grey socks in the frame. She wasn't shocked by the Soviet imagery or how provocative it was. She just thought they'd ruined the aesthetics of the image by showing the grey socks. Apparently,

Malcolm thought the picture would cause a bit of a furore and he proceeded to book the band on a tour of all the redneck US states, all so they could court a bit of controversy. I don't know if Malcolm was really the great provocateur everyone thinks he was, but I'm sure *he* thought he was. Looking back, that whole New York Dolls escapade of his feels a bit like a dry run for the Anarchy in the UK tour.

Among the flyers and photos Malcolm brought back from his trips to New York was a setlist for a Television show. It all seemed very cryptic and cool. Consequently, these little flyers pinned to the pinboard at work caught my imagination. I saw the phrase 'Blank Generation' splashed across the top, and that phrase stayed with me. In a roundabout way, it got me thinking about how there was nothing going on in London. The world was an exciting place inside my art college bubble, but outside of it, there was a real air of despondency and desperation with the constant strikes, the IRA, three-day weeks and power cuts. There was a sense of emptiness that had crept into people's lives, and I felt that maybe we were the blank generation. Many years later, when I met Richard Hell, he told me he hadn't meant it that way at all. He'd meant it to be optimistic. He saw the blank generation as a fresh page in a book, the future unwritten and filled with possibility. I was feeling like our generation had nothing available to us, so I wrote a song about the exact opposite. 'We're so pretty, oh so pretty / We're vacant.'

In a quiet moment, I started work on the song and it wasn't too long before I had the set of chord changes and the rest of the lyric, but I was short of a riff to give the song its momentum.

To my mind, there are three kinds of songs: first you have the songs that have a great set of chord changes and a beautiful melody, like the Kinks' 'Waterloo Sunset'. Second there are songs that have a memorable riff, songs like 'Whole Lotta Love'. And thirdly, you have the songs that are a combination of the two: songs like 'Satisfaction', which has a killer riff, but also some clever chord changes happening. With 'Pretty Vacant', I knew the riff needed to be melodic and memorable, but it just wouldn't come to me.

Then one day I popped into my old art school local above Mooney's on Cambridge Circus. I was sitting by myself enjoying a quiet pint and someone put a record on the jukebox downstairs and my ears suddenly pricked up. It was muffled, but suddenly the missing piece of the jigsaw fell in to place. Being a bass player, I'm always tuned in to the bass parts in other people's records and there was a really neat change in the bass part, and I thought, *I'm having that*. It wasn't the exact riff, but it alluded to it, and provided the jumping-off point for me. The song was 'SOS' by the Swedish pop band ABBA. That little bass part inspired the riff I needed. I finished off my pint and walked back up the road to Denmark Street and picked up Steve's guitar. Within a minute, I was banging out the riff and everything fell into place. When everyone came together later for a rehearsal, I gave the lyrics to John, showed Steve and Paul the changes and the song was born. Because I could never hear what John was singing when we played live, I didn't notice until the record came out that John, unbeknown to me, had changed a couple of lines in the second verse. 'I don't believe illusions 'cause too much is real / So stop your cheap comment, 'cause we know what we feel.'

I can't even remember what lines I wrote initially, but to be fair, John's were good.

Regarding the ABBA influence, I looked at it as kind of like sampling, but before sampling became a thing.[2] In some ways, it was kind of inspired by Duchamp's ready-mades, taking something that already existed and repurposing it for my own little piece of art. Over the years, I've taken some stick for liking ABBA, but as pop writers, I think they're fantastic. 'Pretty Vacant': it's part Matlock, part Duchamp, part ABBA.

When I showed 'Vacant' to John, he seemed impressed. I remember he liked the fact that he could sing the line as 'We're so pretty, we're vay-cunt'. It hadn't occurred to me, but the idea that he could basically sing the word 'cunt' onstage or, better still, if the song ever got on the radio, obviously appealed to his sense of humour.

---

[2] Just for the sake of clarity, when I take inspiration, I consider it to be an homage. However, when someone does it to me, it's a nick, so be warned. Incidentally, I mentioned the ABBA inspiration in an interview a few years ago. I don't know how he found my address, but every Christmas for the next ten years, until he passed in 2015, Rutger Gunnarsson, the bass player with ABBA, used to send me a card offering his fond regards for the festive season.

16

WHATCHA GONNA DO ABOUT IT?

Despite the widely reported tales of Malcolm's managerial nous, it was yours truly that set up the Pistols' first shows. I did the legwork during the summer of 1975. After months of us badgering Malcolm to pull his finger out on that front, there was a tangible sense of frustration that we weren't getting out there. It was clear to see we'd gotten better over the course of the summer, and we wanted to test ourselves in front of an actual audience. We kept on at Malcolm to get us a gig, telling him we were ready, but he felt we weren't there yet. He was playing for time, I think, because he didn't know how to do it or how the business worked. His address book was okay if you wanted to get the number for the IRA or Yoko Ono, but if you needed to get in touch with the art school student unions around Greater London, you would be shit out of luck. I don't want to big myself up, but when it became clear that nothing was going to happen if we relied on Malcolm's time-table or address book, I took the bull by the horns and went out and got some gigs myself. I don't like to let the grass grow. You can procrastinate and put things off for ever, but to my mind, there's nothing better for focusing the mind than having a deadline. I figured if we had a show in the diary, it would be something for us to work towards.

Punk historians note that the first Pistols show took place at Saint Martins College of Art on 6 November 1975. Technically this is true. We did play, after a fashion, but in reality the show was a bit of a debacle. Personally, I consider the second gig at Central School of Art to be the first real Pistols gig, but we'll come to that.

I'd successfully completed my foundation at Saint Martins and been accepted on the fine art painting degree course, starting in September 1975. I wanted to keep my options open, so I did scout around a few other art colleges to check out their degrees. I took a tour of Alexandra Palace, which was part of Hornsey Art School back then, and popped my head around one door and saw a pre-Adam Ant Stuart Goddard standing at his easel, taking a life-drawing class. Some of the courses looked promising, but ultimately, I decided to accept the offer and to stay at Saint Martins. Up until that summer, it was my intention to continue my studies and see where that led me. I don't think I realised at the time quite what a big deal that was, if I'm honest. My enthusiasm for the band was reaching its high watermark and, because it seemed so obvious how we were improving as a unit, I think my focus was slowly shifting from art to music. Towards the end of the summer, we were really starting to take the Pistols seriously. It felt as if we were really onto something. There was an urgent, feral electricity at rehearsals. We were all of us getting better and, obviously, having John on board brought something different to the party. Something that nobody had seen before. All the ingredients were in the pot. We were ready.

The show intended as our first, in Holborn, at the Central School of Art, was booked with Sebastian Conran and Alexander McDowell. I'm great friends with Al to this day. He lives and works in California as a university professor and runs an eminent design company. He's what they call a narrative designer, in today's parlance, and he's the man to go to if you want to learn about the future of storytelling. To put it bluntly, if Al doesn't know it, it probably isn't worth knowing. He's a proper visionary renaissance man. Besides being a respected professor, he's also one of the chief designers behind a clutch of Hollywood movies – *The Watchmen*, *Charlie and the Chocolate Factory*, *The Terminal*, *Fear and Loathing in Las Vegas*, to name just a few. Also, that's his design on the cover of the Rich Kids album, *Ghosts of Princes in Towers*. When we signed for EMI, we helped set him up with the design studio he had in Berwick Street, Rocking Russian. The guy who used to be the tea boy at Rocking Russian was Neville Brody, who designed the font for *The Face* magazine and went on to become one of the most celebrated graphic designers of his generation. A couple of years later, along with Dylan Jones the editor, he started *I-D Magazine* working at my kitchen table. He now lives in Silver Lake, a very hip part of Los Angeles. Just recently, I was in California playing some shows with Blondie, so I arranged to meet Al for lunch one day. Before I set off, I asked someone how to get to Silver Lake and he told me, 'Sure. First thing you need to do is go to art college.' It's that kind of place. A real hub for artists and cool people. Still, any false modesty aside, Al's real claim to fame is that he was the first person, along with Sebastian, to book the Sex Pistols.

I don't think I caught him on his best day when I rocked up at his office in the summer of 1975, though. I walked into the student union office and found the two of them arguing the toss over who was the social secretary and who was the assistant social secretary. I stood in their office for a full minute while they squabbled among themselves, each of them telling the other that they were the assistant. Eventually, they realised I was there.

'I don't know who's the social secretary and who's the assistant, but I've got a band and we'd be interested in playing a show for you,' I told them.

Sebastian looked me up and down. 'And what's the name of this band?' he said.

'The Sex Pistols.'

'Fantastic,' Al said. 'With a name like that, you *must* play for us.'

Al remembers the exchange slightly differently. He swears blind that I told him we'd play the show for free, but I suppose we'll just have to agree to disagree on that one. They put the Sex Pistols in the diary to play for them on 7 November. I'd booked our first show. Then, flush from my success with Al and Sebastian, I walked across to Saint Martins to set up a second Pistols show with the student union on the top floor. I spoke to some hairy bloke who was a couple of years older than me, and I said I had a band and asked if we could play. He told me he had this other band lined up for 6 November, but because the support band had pulled out, there was an opening for us to fill in. We were given the slot supporting Bazooka Joe. I'd heard of Bazooka Joe. They were one of two or three bands that were on the art school circuit with a kind of rockabilly thing going on. Brent Ford and the Nylons were another and as far as I remember, I believe they were the band that had to pull out of the show and created the opening for us.

With a second show booked, I took myself down the hall to the bursar's office and explained that I wouldn't be accepting the degree place they'd offered me. This was despite Vivienne Westwood telling me I was daft. She advised me not to tell them, so I'd still qualify for a student grant – as Malcolm would have done. She said I could spend the money on a guitar, but she couldn't dissuade me. I'd decided I was going to be a musician, not an artist, and that was that. Later I realised I needn't have been so headstrong. I was too honest for my own good, I think, or maybe too stupid. Practically everyone on the scene – Mick Jones, Keith Levine and all those guys – had signed up for their respective courses, pocketed the grant, and then disappeared off to Denmark Street to find the nearest guitar shop. I wish I'd thought that through better, but my mind was already made up and I departed the course before it even started. Whatever the case, my conversation with the bursar was a short one.

'I'm not coming back. You can give my place to somebody else,' I said.

The bursar barely looked up from whatever paperwork he was doing. It was a disappointing reaction, but I pressed on regardless.

'I'm joining a rock 'n' roll band,' I told him, like he'd never heard anyone say that before.

I didn't imagine he'd fall to his knees and beg me to reconsider, but I'd assumed that he'd at least try to persuade me to stay and tell me I was desperately needed on the course, but sadly no. The bursar merely shrugged. He located my file and moved it from one pile to another and, just like that, my scholastic life came to an end. A place on the fine art painting degree at Saint Martins was, as it is now, highly sought after, and there were a lot of people clamouring to get a place, so you can understand why my declaration wasn't greeted with any open weeping and wailing in the bursar's office. Still, on a positive note, my departure from the course meant I had good reason to take the band seriously. I'd burnt my bridges, so I had no other option. None of us really had anything else going on, so we were all equally motivated to succeed. As summer turned to autumn, we rehearsed constantly until, eventually, November and the night of our first show arrived.

Bazooka Joe had a few 1950s stylings and were causing a minor stir on the pub rock circuit. There were still a lot of hippy casualties floating around the scene at the time, but Bazooka Joe's lead singer was this guy, Danny Kleinman, who was quite a handsome rockabilly bloke, so he really stood out from the crowd. I seem to recall their drummer was studying in the year above me at Saint Martins. I couldn't help but remember him.

He was a haemophiliac, so every time he got a little nick in his finger when he was cutting a piece of cartridge paper, he'd start bleeding profusely and need to be rushed to hospital. More than once, I looked out the window and saw an ambulance parked outside on the Charing Cross Road waiting to whisk him off to casualty. More famously, Bazooka Joe also featured Stuart Goddard on bass. Stuart left Bazooka Joe shortly after the Saint Martins show and transformed himself into the pantomime prince of punk pop, Adam Ant.

And, as for Danny Kleinman, he did all right for himself, too. Years later, in 2006, I took myself off to the cinema to see *Casino Royale*, the latest Bond movie. I'd read the book as a kid, so I was interested to see what they'd done with it. I was immediately taken with the opening title sequence, which had this amazing, spiralling collage of graphics depicting elements from the casino. I was so taken with the look of it, I stayed until the end of the credits to see who the designer was, and it was Danny Kleinman. A while after that, a mutual friend was at a dinner party with Kleinman and texted me, and Danny and I had a chat over text. We both realised we hadn't seen each other since that night when the Pistols supported Bazooka Joe.

There was a little friction as we arrived at the Saint Martins student union bar that night. I thought it was agreed that we'd be using Bazooka Joe's backline as well as the PA, but when we went to soundcheck, they told us point blank that we couldn't use their gear. We didn't have a road crew, obviously, but fortunately our equipment was only around the corner at our place on Denmark Street. It was rush hour and it was pissing with rain, so once we'd dragged all the gear from Denmark Street and lugged it up six flights of stairs and set up, there wasn't a lot of time for first-night nerves or whatever adrenaline rush you normally get before a show, and it was by no means glamorous. When you start out on the road to becoming a musician, you have all these daydreams of playing Wembley Stadium, but they couldn't have been further removed from the reality. Fast-forward forty-odd years to last night, I played a show at the Chelsea Arts Club. The place was rammed, just a great night, but at 1 a.m. after the show, it was still me humping my bass amp up the stairs. *Plus ça change*, I suppose.

Before the show, there was a tiny miracle that took place. He was never famed for his largesse, but on this occasion, Malcolm put his hand in his pocket and bought each of us a drink. They were student union prices, but even so. He even gave me a quarter bottle of vodka he'd smuggled in, so my playing was a bit ragged. I was eighteen years old, brimming with adrenaline, but with hindsight I probably should have paced myself and made the vodka last a little longer. The night was something of a blur. There was no stage to speak of, and the PA was just set up in one corner of the common room, across from the bar. Truth be told, it was all something of an anti-climax. We only played five songs, two originals and three covers, including 'Whatcha Gonna Do About It?' by the Small Faces, with lyrics amended by John: 'I want you to know that I hate you, baby / And here we are, we're the Sex Pistols . . . Whatcha gonna do about it?'

It wasn't a huge crowd. There were maybe thirty or forty people there altogether, and presumably most of them were wondering what the hell was happening. With the passing of time, things have gotten a little hazy, but my abiding memory is that we were just incredibly loud. Loud and shambolic. It wasn't the best PA, and we were all playing on ten when we probably should have been on two. Until someone pulled the plug on us. We knocked out five songs and then it was over. Following the fifth number, a fight broke out because they'd unplugged us. It was probably a right old mess. I later found out from Danny Kleinman that they didn't pull the plug on us because we were too loud or because someone didn't like the performance, but because John was kicking the PA – possibly because he'd never heard the sound of his own voice through a PA before and didn't like the results. But he was kicking the PA and it wasn't even paid for. Bazooka Joe had got it on HP and there were still a ton of instalments left to pay on it.

As with everything with the Pistols, there are varying accounts of what unfolded, but an altercation occurred over who pulled the plug. I wasn't involved in that. And not because I wasn't up for a fight. I wasn't averse to having a punch-up if a punch-up was required. I just didn't get involved in the fracas because I'd invited Sebastian Conran and Alexander McDowell to give them an idea of what they'd booked for the following night. When the fight kicked off, I walked through the melee and tried my best to reassure them that we weren't usually like this, and that we'd bring our A-game when we played for them. It turned out that I needn't have worried. They both found all the chaos around us highly amusing.

Once we'd nursed our hangovers and wounds from the Saint Martins debacle, we regrouped the following night for the Central School of Art in Holborn. Earmarked to support us that night was a band called Roogalator. They were another group making a name for themselves on the pub rock circuit. They were quite an interesting band and had been around for a fair while at this point. They would go on to support Dr Feelgood at the Hammersmith Odeon in early 1976. I don't recall if they ever sorted out who was whose underling, but whoever ended up as social secretary and assistant social secretary, Al and Sebastian's whole operation was a good deal slicker than Saint Martins' had been. For a start, there was a proper stage and lighting rig, so that's the show I consider to be our first proper gig. Also, instead of us seeing the plug pulled and an ensuing fracas, the night ran smoothly. We played our entire set from start to finish. All eleven songs. No one unplugged the PA, no fights broke out, so all in all, that felt like progress. The setlist was almost a 50/50 split between originals and covers: 'Did You No Wrong', 'Seventeen', 'Submission', 'Pretty Vacant', and covers of the Stooges' 'No Fun', the Moody Blues' 'Go Now', 'Don't Gimme No Lip Child' by Dave Berry – which had been on the jukebox at Malcolm's shop – 'I'm Not Your Stepping Stone' by the Monkees (or Paul Revere and the Raiders, depending on which side you like your bread buttered), plus a couple of Small Faces tunes. I recall that the gig went down well. I'd invited Bill Collins along to see us and he came to me afterwards and complimented us on the show and 'Pretty Vacant' in particular. He was impressed when I told him that was one of my tunes. He turned to Malcolm and told him he thought we had something. As I've mentioned before, Bill knew a thing or two about the music business, so I'm sure Malcolm took note when he heard that. We'd all had a couple of drinks by then, and I'd probably had another quarter bottle of vodka, so I was feeling quite pleased with myself. When we were humping the gear out after the show, John sidled up to me.

'Glen,' he said. 'I don't understand you. Most people when they get drunk get really horrible and miserable. But you . . . you seem to get happier.'

'Yeah, so what?' I shrugged, and John looked at me as if I'd just stepped out of a UFO.

'What is wrong with you?' he shook his head gravely and walked away.

Like a lot of things John said, it's hard to know how much to take at face value, but it struck me as quite a telling moment and illustrates the contrast in our personalities. It wasn't as bad as it was going to be, but there was an obvious misalignment in our dynamic even then. Much further down the line, Malcolm would manipulate that misalignment, which was kind of our undoing ultimately.

After the Holborn show, we suddenly found ourselves on the art school circuit, getting shows right across the board. Again, I booked some of the shows. At the time, we knew we didn't want to play the pub circuit, because we didn't want to be lumped in with the pub rock scene. I loved a lot of what pub rock had to offer, but we wanted to stand apart from all that. I had a few contacts through my circle of art school pals and that was a big leg-up for us. John may have decried the whole art school thing, but because those people were generally more open-minded, and willing to give us a try, we started to get a foothold. I got talking to the people I knew at the Royal College of Art, and Malcolm, possibly feeling there was some potential, following Bill Collins's enthusiastic endorsement, booked Chelsea School of Art, and Ravensbourne College in Chislehurst. After the first two shows, I think he saw how good we could be.

He upped his game a tad, even if some of his best efforts involved him trawling through the gig listings in *Time Out* magazine. He found a couple of random nights. One was at Frognal, which was a teacher training college just up the Finchley Road, and another at the Queen Elizabeth College in Kensington. He didn't book the shows, however. That would have been too conventional, I guess. He merely spotted these places had events and had us turn up on the relevant night with all our equipment. I don't know if it was intended as a kind of guerrilla tactic, or if it was just common-or-garden incompetence on Malcolm's part, but in fairness, it did work. Once we arrived and explained that our manager had told us we were playing, rather than deal with the headache of a gaggle of scruffy kids, because we weren't asking to be paid for our services, they just tended to let us play. It was probably less hassle.

In the run-up to Christmas, we had the Ravensbourne show. My girlfriend at the time was attending Ravensbourne, and Chislehurst being not too far meant that the Bromley Contingent were all in attendance. It felt like a home fixture, in that respect. Steve Severin and Siouxsie and Billy Idol, who all used to hang around in the shop with us, were in the crowd. There was a sense that the little bubble we occupied was growing a little. Obviously, we'd only played half a dozen shows, but already there was this small band of people who were starting to dig us and there were just the slightest hints that things might start to snowball. From the vantage of 1975, the following year was showing a lot of promise even then.

Promise, but also peril, as it turned out.

17

ANARCHY IN THE UK

'Anarchy in the UK' arrived in the second batch of Pistols songs after John joined the band. I felt like I was coming up with a lot of ideas, and my confidence was growing in terms of writing songs. Steve wasn't throwing in so many ideas, so I challenged him to come up with something for a change. Conversations like that were standard fare for us. We didn't stand on ceremony with each other. Everything was in service to the band, so I don't think any of us took it personally if someone said something was a load of shit. Because there were no new ideas, we took a break for a couple of days and when we came back, Steve played a few things he'd been working on. They didn't exactly set the world on fire. It was probably written all over my face, because immediately he got a bit defensive.

'What've you got, then?' he said.

I had the kernel of an idea in the back of my mind, for the opening bars of a tune that had been nagging at me for a while. For some reason, I was thinking of something that worked like a TV theme. It sounds a bit daft, but I was thinking something like the *da-da-da-da* overture to *Tonight at the London Palladium*, which I used to watch with my mum. I didn't have much, but I was thinking something grand, a descending chord sequence that would announce the arrival of the song. I started to play, and Steve picked up on it and I started giving him cues for the verse and the chorus. I was making it up as I went along really, but after that, it fell into place quite quickly. Steve came up with the key change and added the 'Let's Spend the Night Together' Rolling Stones riff and suddenly we were at the races.

John never once asked us to work out music for the lyrics he was carrying in his bag. Who knows what we might have come up with if he had, but it was always the other way around. I would come in with some chord changes or a tune, and if he heard something that fit, he would dip into the bag and have a fish around for the words that worked with the music. It always struck me as the wrong way around, but that's how it came together with 'Anarchy in the UK'. We already had the basic spine of the song up and running by the time he showed an interest.

'At last,' he said. 'I've got something to go with this.' He already had the lyrics to 'Anarchy in the UK' scribbled out, almost word for word.

The process was very quick, and I thought it sounded okay. I mean, personally speaking, I've always thought that having to resort to a key change is the last refuge of the scoundrel in song-writing terms, but it all gelled somehow. As with everything, we messed around with it until we got it right. We fine-tuned the order a bit, arguing about moving the second chorus to after the bridge, and shifting the verses around, but that's just something you do when you're in a band. Lyrically, it's all John's handiwork, and you can see evidence of where we'd been hanging out with Malcolm and Jamie Reid, Malcolm's associate and future Pistols sleeve designer. Malcolm and Jamie shared a similar student agitprop background, and both had played a part in the late 1960s sit-ins at Croydon Art College, so it's fair to say they liked to shake things up a bit. The Guildford Four and the Birmingham Six were still fresh in the nation's memory, so to be writing lyrics about the UDA (Ulster Defence Association) and IRA (Irish Republican Army) probably seemed incendiary to some people. But from John's perspective, as a second-generation Irish kid, that stuff was at the front of his mind. It couldn't really be further removed from the way I write songs. I always think of my songs as me having a word in someone's ear. Even with some of the more political songs I've recently written, I try to keep that conversational dynamic. John's words here are delivered as snippets of information, like news sound-bites, but they're delivered direct from the front lines. To John's credit, it's filled with great lines and, looking back, a lot of what he was saying feels prescient. The line 'Your future dream is a shopping scheme' still hits hard, I think. There didn't used to be shopping malls anywhere, but they're all over the country now. It's like religion was the opium of the masses, but if that doesn't work out, maybe shopping for trinkets will keep the population in their trance-like state. It's filled with moments like that, a kind of angry cynicism and mischievous wordplay, switching the word 'enemy' for '*NME*'. I don't know if it felt like an earth-shattering moment at the time, but looking back, maybe I can see it now. Certainly, for a bunch of scruffy kids, it was a big statement of a song.

I don't think too much about the impact of 'Anarchy in the UK'. I do remember that when Captain Sensible first heard it, he said he thought it sounded like Bad Company, the band Paul Rodgers started when he left Free. I think that's down to the fact that Damned's idea of punk was that everything they played started at 200 mph and just got faster and faster. Person-ally speaking, I wanted us to stand apart from that kind of stuff. 'Anarchy' still had that kind of grandeur that I'd originally envis-aged when I was thinking about the *Tonight at the London Palladium* overture. I don't mind a bit of grandeur, but I do draw the line at grandiose. There's an important distinction. I mean, Bowie's 'Heroes' is grand, but you could never say it was grandiose. When 'Anarchy' was released as a single later in the year, journalist Caroline Coon, who'd cut her teeth in the underground press in the 1960s, called me up at my little flat in Chiswick and asked me how I'd describe the intro. I told her it was a punk overture, and she used the phrase in her article. I do like to think that because of that grand framing, the song delivers more punch. The lyrics scan and there's room for the music to breathe. Consequently, it's a more powerful song. We didn't want to play everything at breakneck speed; we wanted something with a bit more stately aplomb to it than that. In fact, when we recorded 'Anarchy', we had a real battle on our hands not to go down the road at full pelt. I'm glad we weren't persuaded to speed the song up. The descending chord sequence was like the Sex Pistols overture in miniature that I'd imagined in my head. The song swells. It felt like we were summoning the troops.

18

BOREDOM

In the clubs of Great Britain, the summer of 1976 was turning into a wild ride. The country was baking in one of the longest heatwaves on record and a new sound was exploding in the capital and, more tentatively, out in the provinces. We were finding our feet, playing more shows in London, but also, we were making tiny strides outside our own backyards. By the time we played the 100 Club in May, it was clear that word was getting out. There was a slow trickle of five, ten, fifteen more people than there were at the last show every time we plugged in. By the time the summer arrived, instead of playing to dozens of people, we were playing to a hundred or more. Very slowly, we started to see more like-minded people and, for the first time, it began to resemble a scene. It looks rough and grainy in the footage that you see nowadays, but it felt enlightened and forward-thinking at the time. Before it became better known as the Roxy, the venue was a gay disco called Shagarama where cool people would get down to early Roxy Music and Lou Reed's *Transformer*. We didn't discriminate. They were just these other people we knew from around town. I just considered them to be fellow outsiders and we welcomed them into our fold.

Outside the capital, we still had our work cut out for us. The provinces weren't quite ready for the Sex Pistols *just* yet. Before the Bill Grundy incident, our progress was more 'slow and steady' than explosive, while a faint pulse was slowly building. You might be playing in the face of adversity, or downright indifference sometimes, but the adversity helped to steel us, make us tighter as a unit and, ultimately, more confident.

It was outside London where things sometimes got weird. We weren't playing big-city venues, but somehow we found our way to towns like Scarborough long before the famous shows in Manchester or Birmingham or Sheffield. These were strictly one-night affairs, with us piling into the back of the van after the gigs and driving overnight back to London for the next show. It wasn't until later in the year when Malcolm brought a booking agent on board that you could describe what we were doing as 'touring'. In truth, they were more like reconnaissance missions. During one of our first ventures up north, we played a Conservative Club. That seems weird in and of itself, but add in the fact that we were asked to stop playing after a couple of numbers because the old dears couldn't hear the bingo numbers being called in the lounge and you'll have an idea just how strange things sometimes got. Another night, we played in Northallerton at a kind of chicken-in-the-basket discotheque-cum-cabaret.

The comedian and compère, a Bernard Manning-type in a crushed velvet dinner jacket, introduced us on stage.

'Ladies and gentlemen. Please put your chicken down and welcome to the stage, all the way from London . . . Sex *Pistol*!'

Another night at Middlesbrough Town Hall, we played supporting Doctors of Madness. They wouldn't let us use their set-up, so we had to play through a tiny H&H 50-watt amp. We must have sounded dreadful. To get them back, when they took to the stage after our set, Steve ransacked their dressing room, rifled through their pockets and spat in their stack-heeled boots. They got off lightly, all things considered. I bumped into Kid Strange, the Doctors of Madness lead singer, a few years later and he was much more forgiving than I would have been. He said they probably deserved it.

Over time, we started to see the same familiar faces turn out whenever we played – in the capital at least. There was the Bromley Contingent and that lot in London, but they weren't there when we played Liverpool. They weren't there when we played Manchester. It wasn't like a movie where there's a queue of twenty people waiting outside to get in, then the next week it's eighty people and then the week after that there's a line around the block and your name is up in lights. It may have been starting to buzz around London, but when you've schlepped all the way to Redcar for a gig, it was like a blank slate, and you had to start all over again. Some places were more hip than others. I remember meeting Steve Strange, later of Visage, at a gig in Newport. He was wearing, very stylishly I might add, a black plastic bin liner. We stayed in touch, and when I had my own flat after we signed a record deal, I put him up for a while when he first escaped from the Welsh valleys and came to live in the capital.[1] Eventually there was a whole coterie of forward-looking kids from Newport and Pontypridd and all these little towns in the valleys jumping on trains to Paddington and decamping to the King's Road and beyond. Then, after a while, people start writing about you and your face is in the paper a bit, and you can feel a . . . shift. Believe it or not, one of our first mentions in the press came in the society magazine *Tatler*, after we played at one of Andrew Logan's events. As more bands started popping up around us, it started to feel more like we were at the vanguard of a movement, rather than just another band on the circuit. We even helped Joe Strummer see the light.

We played a show at the Nashville supporting Joe Strummer's band, the 101ers. I knew Joe already, and we used to hang out a little bit. I'd met him at one of his gigs with Mick Jones, when I was still at art college. The day before the Nashville show, I took Steve Jones along to check out the competition when the 101ers played the Acklam Hall, which was a kind of community centre under the flyover by Portobello Road. Steve and I went into the dressing room before the band went on stage and crept up behind Joe. We were larking about, putting Joe off while he tried to tune his guitar. Nobody had those electronic tuners back then, so Joe was using one of those pitch pipes. You found the

---

[1] I remember I came home one evening and found Steve in the hallway of my flat, standing in front of the mirror trying on all the clothes I had accumulated from my time at Let It Rock.

note you wanted, blew into the pipe, and tuned your guitar by ear. That was the theory anyway. It wasn't happening for Joe because every time he blew into the pipe, me and Steve made a loud ooh sound, so he couldn't find the tuning. Joe wasn't happy. He dropped the pipe and guitar and made his feelings known.

'Sex Pistols, eh?' he snarled. 'We'll see tomorrow night.'

There's always rivalry between bands. You always want to blow the competition off the stage. That's part of being in a band. You want to be better than your peers. I don't remember much about the night, but I know we wanted to make a splash. We played a couple of shows with the 101ers. One night, the curtain went up and Steve, who'd been caught short, was taking a piss at the back of the stage. On the second occasion, a ruck broke out down the front. It wasn't a big crowd, but over the years I've learned that there are two things that never help if you're trying to play a show. First, if a girl takes her top off, no one's going to be looking at you. It's the same thing if a fight breaks out, so we were trying to calm things down. This was meant to be our spotlight moment. When you see the photos, however, it looked as if we were part of the chaos, and it was splashed all over the *Melody Maker* the next week. I don't think the 101ers even got a mention, but Joe Strummer saw what we were like, and the impact we had, and it was as if he'd seen the future. He split up the 101ers shortly after and started the Clash with Mick Jones. Bernard Rhodes later fell out with Malcolm, went on to be the Clash's manager and helped Mick put the line-up together. Having seen how Malcolm handled our career, he promised that he wasn't going to play the same games and would keep the band together. They didn't last for ever, but four or five albums down the line, with Bernard at the helm, the Clash broke the States.

Malcolm, to be fair, had started doing a better job. The London shows were coming thick and fast, and the music press started to catch on as we headed into the summer. We had Dave Goodman and Kim Thraves working the sound for us and driving the van by then, and they had a wealth of contacts that they shared with Malcolm. The first time we played Liverpool, we had a booking at the legendary Eric's Club, on Victoria Street. Eric's Club went on to be one of the key punk and post-punk venues in the north-west of England, but there were only a handful of people who turned out to see us that night. It seemed a long way to travel, only to have a couple of dozen people bother to check us out. After the show, I went downstairs where there was a local band called the Yachts playing, a kind of power pop trio, and that's where I met Clive Langer and Jayne Casey from Big in Japan for the first time. It was cool to discover there was something new happening outside of London as well.

In July, we played Manchester. It was a big show for us. It was our second gig there in the space of a month. Famously, word hadn't really got out before our first show at the Lesser Free Trade Hall, and it wasn't exactly packed to the rafters. Having said that, some of the future luminaries who attended went on to form some of the bands who would follow in our wake: Joy Division, Buzzcocks, the Smiths and the Fall. For the second show, a month later, we were supported by Slaughter and the Dogs and, playing their first proper gig, rather than just as paying punters, Buzzcocks. The place was rammed. We opened with 'Anarchy', the first time we ever played it to an audience, and it got an amazing reaction. I watched Buzzcocks from the side of the stage and they were great. They had even less money behind them than we did, and they obviously didn't have access to a master thief like Steve Jones to nick gear on their behalf. I remember Pete Shelley was thrashing around on this trashed old Woolworths 'Winfield Special' guitar. The top half of the guitar body looked like it had been sawn off. I asked Pete afterwards why he'd cut the top off his guitar.

'Oh,' he said. 'It just kind of fell off.'

They finished their set with 'Boredom' and that interminable, two-note guitar solo, before Howard Devoto ended the show by just pulling out Pete's plug. I don't know if it was because he'd had enough or if it was a kind of pre-arranged artistic statement, but I recognised them as kindred spirits. I liked them a lot. I thought Howard Devoto had a kind of arty quality to him. Pete Shelley sadly died in 2018, but I still see Steve Diggle around from time to time. He's still touring and recording with the band. I was at a press conference recently and Steve was there, so we caught up a bit. When the Pistols bandwagon started rolling, we always said we wanted there to be loads of bands like us. The same, but different. They were and I've always rated them.

Back in the capital, we stayed true to our plan to not play the pub rock circuit, so along with the art school shows, we played random venues like the Screen on the Green in Islington and the El Paradise strip club in Soho. That one was an eye-opener. We walked in on the night and the place was disgusting. Without going into too much detail, it was like walking into a crime scene.

We went across the road to a hardware store and bought a mop and a bucket and cleaned up before we played.

We went north of the border for the first time in October, travelling by rail to Dundee and staying in a little hotel on the banks of the River Tay. I remember we made it down in time for breakfast and just in time to see the 1950s crooner and entertainer Frankie Vaughan come in with a bevy of beauties on each arm. It was like something out of a film, a proper star getting his coffee and toast, while the four of us loaded our plates with kippers and smoked haddock. Malcolm wasn't best pleased when he was presented with the bill. We were never allowed to order room service again.

19

SHAKE SOME ACTION

The summer heatwave had turned into a drought when we took our first steps as a band onto foreign soul, with two shows at the Chalet Du Lac in Paris in September. The owners of the club had put out feelers to find the most fashionable English rock band of the time and ours was the name that came up. Malcolm may still have been learning the ropes of band management, but these were connected, high-fashion people in Paris, something he understood better than most people, so it's probably not a surprise that we got the gig. I've heard that Malcolm struck a deal for the Pistols to play two shows for a cool £1,000, with hotels and flights thrown in. As with all things related to Malcolm and money, it's difficult to verify. You can be sure we didn't see much of it. Still, it was an exciting experience and an important moment in punk's emergence into the wider world.

It was the first time I'd travelled by air since I was a kid, when I took a trip to Spain with my aunt and uncle. Back then, the seats faced the back of the plane. When I boarded the flight with the Pistols, I expressed my surprise that the seats now faced forward. Everyone looked at me like I was an idiot and obviously it was grist for the mill for Rotten in particular. Personally, I suspect he'd never been on a plane in his life, but even so, being John, he took the piss mercilessly. I seem to remember he spent half the flight joking that we were all going to die in a crash.

I love Paris. I'd been the year before, with the money I'd saved working at the lino factory during the summer, so I knew my way around the subway system, and I knew a few cool places to hang out. That trip to Paris the year before formed a key, informal part of my education and my growing into an outward-looking person and, yes, a European. I realise that sounds like a funny thing to say, but it used to be something we Brits aspired to. Having said that, my first trip to Paris wasn't all baguettes and détente. One afternoon I was sitting outside a café having a chat and drinking a coffee with a mate and I overheard one of the locals refer to me as *le rosbif*. I guess back then in those less enlightened times, we were all calling the French 'frogs', so no harm, no foul. It turned out the guy calling me *le rosbif* did us a favour in the end. A minor altercation with my Gallic interlocutor resulted in us missing our train – one that was held up at gunpoint before all the passengers were robbed blind. It was a lucky escape. I was happy to take the culinary insult instead.

I almost moved to Paris a few years ago, but the pandemic came along and my plans had to change. Even so, I consider myself to be a Europhile, and could happily settle in Paris. I go there regularly. I play shows, I visit galleries, I call up old friends. It is a remarkable place and it's almost on our doorstep. Recently, at a Paris memorial for Vivienne Westwood, Paul Cook and I reconnected with the fashion designer Jean-Charles de Castelbajac. He was a friend of Malcolm's in the fashion trade and one of the people who helped set up the Pistols shows at the Chalet du Lac. I don't think Paul had seen him since, but I'd caught up with him a couple of times over the years and, while it was a sad occasion, it was so good to see him again. He showed us the sights when we were over with the Pistols and was the person who taught me how to drink tequila properly, with a dash of salt and a lemon slice. He also gave Steve Jones a ride on his motorbike up to Rue Saint-Denis to get his leg over with a Parisian lady of the night.

Club Chalet Du Lac was previously a discotheque but had recently been repurposed as a live music venue. Essentially it was a restaurant with a dancefloor set on the banks of a small lake, kind of reminiscent of a pavilion in Regent's Park in London. Our appearance was set to mark the grand reopening after it had been given a spruce-up by the owners. The first show on 3 September was absolutely heaving. Estimates say that there were 2,000 people that night, with hundreds left outside. The crowd was mostly made up of the original discotheque goers, who were highly sceptical of the UK punk scene, but there were a few French proto-punk types who knew what was happening on the other side of the Channel. The cooler kids who were on our coattails in Paris were into the Flamin' Groovies. Everywhere we went we heard their tune, 'Shake Some Action'. We did meet the band briefly – just long enough for Steve Jones to 'acquire' the Groovies' Phase 45 pedal that he used on the recording of 'Anarchy in the UK'. Alongside the kids who would go on to be the first French punks, there was a demi-monde of the hippest French boys and girls and Johnny Hallyday fans in their black leather biker gear. There were a few more familiar faces from back home, too. Siouxsie and Steve Severin had made the trip, and Billy Idol had come across on the Dover-to-Calais ferry in his little yellow GPO van. We didn't see it, but a few locals apparently weren't too impressed when they saw one of the Bromley Contingent was sporting a swastika. I gather there was a little scrap, followed by a group of disgruntled Parisians trying to topple Billy's GPO van over onto its side. We opened our set on the stroke of midnight with 'Anarchy in the UK' and closed with 'Did You No Wrong', with all the usual stops in between. The discotheque people had never seen the likes of us.

The Pistols' second show on 5 September was in the afternoon at 4 p.m. We had to play a much shorter set as we needed to make our flight back to London. Only 200 people turned up. When I asked where all the people were, one of the people at the club told me in pidgin English that it was full on Friday because the drinks were free.

After the Chalet Du Lac, it felt as if the ball was rolling. We played a run of gigs outside London: Whitby, Leeds, Chester, Blackburn, then the show at Chelmsford nick, and then it was the punk festival at the 100 Club. It was a key moment for punk, even if my memories are a bit on the hazy side. Siouxsie famously assembled a band featuring Steve Severin, with future Ant Marco Pirroni on guitar and Sid on drums. They were added to the bill after one of our support bands pulled out last minute. I would love to tell you what a historic, monumental event it was, but in my memory, it was just another show. I do recall I'd decided to wear a rubber jacket with a pair of rubber drainpipe trousers. I thought I was looking sharp, but because they were rubber, they literally acted like drainpipes, and I ended the night carrying my underwear around in a plastic bag.

20

EMI

Mike Thorne was the junior A&R man at EMI, and he was instrumental in us getting our deal. He was the guy who persuaded Nick Mobbs, the head of EMI, that we were worth a punt. EMI were the biggest label in the country, if not the world, so it's arguable they didn't need us. They had Pink Floyd on their roster and had released all the Beatles records, so without Mike in our corner, it's doubtful they would have signed us. Mike had been down to see us play at the 100 Club a few times, so any connection we had with EMI was entirely down to him.

They weren't the only label looking to sign us. For an unsigned band, we were generating a lot of heat in the music papers, so all the labels in London were circling at some point. CBS, who would later sign the Clash, were chasing us. Chris Parry, the Polydor A&R man, was desperate to land us a deal and they did a lot of the early running. They even went so far as to pay for us to go into the studio and record a few demos. Parry missed out on us and later failed to secure a deal with the Clash, after they turned him down. The day after we signed on the dotted line with EMI, Chris came along to see us at a recording studio in Holborn – the sessions Polydor were funding – to see how we were getting on. Malcolm hadn't bothered to tell him, so it was left to me to give him the bad news. Chris had been working tirelessly to get a deal over the line, and he was understandably choked. Don't feel too badly for him, though. Parry went on to the sign the Jam in 1977, and later the Cure. He did okay.

Everything up until then had been done on a handshake, so we had to sign a management deal with Malcolm, which was drafted by Malcolm's shady lawyer. Of the four of us, I was the only one to read it. Malcolm was on a 25 per cent cut, which seemed steep to me. Most music managers are on between 15 and 20 per cent, so I queried that, but I guess it fell on deaf ears.

'You've read it. I haven't,' John told me as he signed. 'If there's anything wrong with it, it's your fault, Glen.'

Given that we'd been playing non-stop throughout 1976, the record companies chasing our signature, the demos for Polydor, the management deal and signing with Malcolm all took place in the space of a week. We signed to EMI records on 6 October for £40,000, which was a very tidy deal at the time, even if Malcolm was going to cream 25 per cent off the top. Malcolm put us on £25 a week, plus a few quid so

I could rent a little flat in Chiswick, which I shared with my friend Mark.[1]

Once we signed for EMI, if you'll forgive the understatement here, we found ourselves at the centre of a maelstrom. That whole period felt kind of bonkers at the time. Looking at it through the rear-view mirror, though, it was almost a procession of these little historic moments. We played our legendary shows in Paris, we recorded and released 'Anarchy', there was the Bill Grundy fiasco, the Anarchy tour, and our becoming Britain's public enemy number one, all of which occurred in the space of a few short weeks. No doubt it was exciting, but it was hard to keep tabs on everything that was going on around us.

EMI wanted an instant return on their investment, so we were despatched to the studio almost before the ink was dry on the contract. 'Anarchy in the UK' was earmarked as the first single. Nowadays, I subscribe to the Nick Lowe adage about recording: go into the studio, bash out the tune and then tart it up, but back then, I didn't really understand what a producer was supposed to do, if I'm honest, and we were still wet behind the ears.

At first, we went into Lansdowne Studios in Notting Hill with Dave Goodman, our sound guy. That session was a swing and a miss, but it seemed only fair to give him a shot. Dave had recorded the demos that helped secure the record deal with EMI in the first place, and we had a good rapport with him. If there was an issue, it was that Dave was a bit beholden to

---

[1] Mark Helfont later worked with the Clash and can be seen on the cover of their 'Rock the Casbah' single, dressed as a Hasidic Jew: different times.

Malcolm, who decided he wanted to be in the studio with us. Malcolm was there with Dave the whole time, like a devil on his shoulder, telling him it wasn't exciting enough and to make it faster. We played it over and over and I think in the end, we got fed up with Malcolm constantly giving notes on how it should sound. If anything, Malcolm's suggestions knocked the stuffing out of the song. Eventually, we put our collective foot down and effectively went on strike. It wasn't Dave's fault by any stretch, but it clearly wasn't working out. We needed somebody with a bit more cachet, who wasn't going to be told what to do.

I think Paul suggested a couple of potential replacements for Dave, one being Bill Nelson, who was the singer in Be-Bop Deluxe, and the other was Chris Thomas, who'd recorded all those early Roxy Music records and had mixed *Dark Side of the Moon*. Chris Thomas knew about us through our mate Chris Spedding. Also, he'd been to one of our shows to check us out, so he had the added benefit of at least being curious, if not interested. Those kinds of things made a difference, so we decided to go with Chris.

After the disappointment of the Dave Goodman attempt, John didn't come along initially, but the remaining three of us regrouped at Wessex Studios with Chris. Because we'd told him we didn't want Malcolm in there interfering, we laid down the track in five takes. Without Malcolm acting as a third wheel, Chris just got on with it. He instinctively knew when it sounded right. I think the version that's on the record is two takes that have been spliced together: the first half is from the third take, and the second half is the fifth. Once we had it, we started calling around trying to locate John to get him to come down and lay down his vocal. It took a while, but we eventually caught up with him.

'Where are you?' we asked.

'You can't have done it,' he said, surprised by our progress. We assured him we had. 'But you can't play,' was all he said.

153

21

GOD SAVE THE QUEEN

When we started the abortive sessions for 'Anarchy in the UK' at Lansdowne Studios with Dave Goodman, I found a piano in the studio. I was bored with all the bickering with Malcolm, so I sat down, lifted the lid, and started tinkering around with the keys. After a few minutes, I had a riff and started playing it over and over. It was only part-formed, but while I was noodling around, it started to become a bit of an earworm. I was driving everyone mad with it. The way I've always worked is, if you get a little idea, leave it to gestate a while and see how it sits with you. If you find you can't remember it later, don't sweat it. It was probably never meant to be. However, if you find you can't get the melody out of your head, that's different. The moment it becomes an earworm, you're going to need to do something about it. So the riff stayed in my head a while, stored away for later use. We took it to the rehearsal room and messed around with it.

Steve thought it sounded like 'Love Me Do' by the Beatles. The riff had shades of that Eddie Cochran 'C'mon Everybody' rhythm, but I was also thinking about 'Fire Brigade' by the 1960s band the Move. I was a big fan of Roy Wood's songwriting growing up. Eddie Cochran had died when I was a kid, so I didn't get the chance to apologise to him for using that guitar motif, but I did get to confess to the Move homage when I bumped into Roy Wood in a Maida Vale pub a few years ago. We got chatting, and inevitably one of us mentioned 'God Save the Queen'.

'People think that's an Eddie Cochran nick,' I said. 'But actually, it's quite a bit like your "Fire Brigade" single.'

Roy fixed me with a good-natured glare.

'I had noticed,' he said.

In what was now a familiar sequence of events, once we played around with the song a while, John had a rummage in his carrier bag of lyrics and found something to fit the bill. I think we'd all got used to John by now, so I don't remember any of us thinking it was shocking, but they are impactful words: 'God save the Queen / The fascist regime.'

It's powerful stuff. And to this day, it still rings kind of true. Anything that embarrasses the royal family, or exposes their hypocrisy and brings them to account, can only be a good thing. I still have people ask me if I care about the royals, hoping to generate a soundbite from a Sex Pistol and maybe make someone's grandma faint with horror. Well, I care about them about as much as they care about me. In some ways, I see the royals as a kind of sop, thrown out there to the population to keep us distracted and in our place. I think it's created a false patriotism. You criticise the Queen – or the King, if you want to keep current – and there's an army of newspaper columnists waiting in the wings to say that you hate your country. It's sophistry, to some extent. The truth is, you didn't say anything about the country, but they reframed the argument while no one was looking. I guess it's ironic now that John subscribes to all that Trumpian *Make America Great Again* bollocks, which is just fascism under a red cap.

The song was finessed a bit. We ironed out a few wrinkles along the way but essentially the song they recorded is the same one we laid out after the Lansdowne Studios session. There are some demos around somewhere that we recorded with Mike Thorne of EMI, and there was a whole middle eight section that we removed at Mike's suggestion. In its original form, the song was too long, but I remember now, during the middle eight, I was playing the bass line from Isaac Hayes' 'Shaft'. I don't think that version has ever seen the light of day, sadly. The song was still going under the title 'No Future' at that point in time. It wasn't until later and all the upcoming Silver Jubilee hullabaloo, when someone thought there might be some capital in changing the title. The words were still the same, the only thing that was changed was the title.

The first time we played it was at the Winter Gardens in Cleethorpes in December.

I know we played it on my final shows with the band at the Paradiso Melkweg club in Amsterdam in early 1977, which was a bit of an eye-opener for me. In the foyer of the venue, they had a trestle table laid out and were openly selling bags of marijuana. It wasn't something you saw in Neasden. I know while we were there, we recorded a TV appearance, which I haven't seen since. I think the TV company must have recorded over the tape, but I wish I could see it. We were booked onto the same show as Golden Earring, the Dutch rock band, and the Three Degrees. At the soundcheck, they had a dwarf juggling plates in front of us. We said we weren't having that, but when we took to the stage for the live recording, the dwarf was still there, still juggling crockery.

This year, to mark the release of my new album, I played a launch show at the 100 Club in London. The gig was kind of mischievously scheduled to coincide with the coronation of King Charles III. I like to have a little pop at the establishment from time to time, but I was presented with a small problem. The thing is, I can't play a show and not play 'God Save the Queen'. I like to play the new songs and mix things up a bit, throw the occasional curveball, but the fact remains there are certain old chestnuts that people expect you to pull out when they pay for a ticket to see you, and I understand that. I mean, if ever I'd gone to see Bowie and he hadn't played 'Heroes', I would have gone home disappointed. The trouble was, it seemed kind of weird singing 'God Save the Queen' when the old girl wasn't around any more, so we decided to do something, but only for the people who were there in that moment. As a one-off, my band and I played an alternate version of the song: 'God Save the King'. Because of a lot of complicated rights issues, there's no way I could or would ever release it. It was intended as a 'one-night-only' spot of irreverence to mark the occasion. Naturally, I soon realised that if I simply switched the words from Queen to King, there'd be a butterfly effect on the rest of the words, and I'd need to change half the lyrics because nothing rhymed any more.

I didn't have a bag of lyrics lying around, so I worked with what I had: 'God save the King / And his ill-gotten bling.'

That morning, there were a few TV cameras congregating outside Chez Matlock, and the story ran in the papers, so it was kind of cool to prick the pomposity of the occasion, even if it was only in a very small way. A few of John's fans came out of the woodwork on social media to tell me it was a sacrilege, that it was John's song and not mine to change, but really, it's our song. It was just a one-off, so if you were at the 100 Club on the day Charlie got his new titfer, you heard it. If you weren't, you missed a never-to-be-repeated show.

22

WINDY

On 1 December 1976, Freddie Mercury got a toothache, and the world would never be the same again. According to Eric Hall, the legendary 1970s record plugger, the only reason that the Pistols were on the Thames TV *Today* show at all was as a last-minute replacement for Queen, our label-mates at EMI Records. Queen were forced to cancel after Freddie Mercury had to attend an emergency dentist's appointment. So, depending on your point of view, you can either blame Freddie Mercury or you can thank him for what happened next.

It was a bit last minute and we were all feeling exuberant. Exuberance that was only exacerbated by all the beer we drank in the green room at the TV studios and the fact we had a small entourage of our mates standing behind us. I was only twenty, and I think I was a bit bemused by the whole interview. Bill Grundy had been presenting the *Today* show for a few years and he had a kind of bored, detached style, giving the impression that the show was a bit beneath a man of his talents. I subsequently learned from an old friend who knew him that Grundy used to be a big wheel in journalistic circles. He had a regular column in *Punch* magazine, and he used to write for *The Guardian* back in the days when it was still the *Manchester Guardian*. It used to be the case that if Elizabeth Taylor and Richard Burton were coming into town and only doing one interview, they'd want to do it with Bill Grundy. I would feel worse for the guy, but whatever happened next, he brought it all on himself.

We were acting up – we were still kids really – but not out of control. He was a bit superior with us, killing the last couple of minutes of the show so he could get down the pub. There was a bit of back and forth. When he expressed disbelief that we'd been signed for £40,000, I told him we'd spent all the money down the boozer. I stood my ground with Grundy. I didn't swear, but I think I was righteously non-deferential to the bloke, who clearly had the idea that we'd be easy meat. I've heard whispers that there was some power play going on behind the scenes between him and the producer, but whatever the reason, Grundy arrived in the studio in a foul mood. He'd probably enjoyed a proper old-school journalist's liquid lunch and was clearly unprepared for the two and a half minutes that was going to torpedo his career.

Really, he was the architect of his own downfall. He made it perfectly clear he didn't want to be there, and he tried to take it out on us. He probably thought we were another of those 'here today, gone tomorrow' bands, but either way, he had underestimated us. The mood shifted when Bill Grundy tried to make John look bad, but John gave him no quarter. John accidentally said 'shit', but Steve had already let out a 'fuck', which kind of went unnoticed. When Grundy asked John what he'd said, John repeated the word back, but louder and more clearly, and Grundy kind of sarcastically scolded him as if he was a naughty school kid. You would think he'd have learned from that mistake, but no. Possibly to run the clock down, Grundy tried to chat up Siouxsie, who was standing behind us, and Steve called him a dirty old man. The weird thing is, Grundy still thought he had the measure of all of us, but he was dead in the water the minute he turned to Steve and said the immortal line, 'Well keep going, chief, keep going. Go on, you've got another five seconds. Say something outrageous.'

'You dirty fucker,' Steve told him. You've seen the clips a thousand times, I'm sure.

What you didn't see was Malcolm behind the cameras, pleading with us to stop. *Promote the tour! Promote the single!* At the same time, the producers were up in the gantry, doing their own pleading with Grundy via his earpiece. They were begging Grundy to stop poking the bear, but by then it was too late. Grundy was probably thinking, *What the hell, it's just a regional TV show. What could possibly go wrong?* In two minutes flat, everything came crashing down around him. A couple of fucks and a shit later, and our first live TV interview went from regional to national news in a heartbeat.

When the scene had played out and 'Windy', the jaunty, end title music, started incongruously playing over our goofing around, Grundy walked off set. He was obviously wondering, *What have I done?* while Malcolm was coming in the other direction, equally berating us, 'What have you done?' Around us, it all went off. Panicked researchers were scurrying around with their clipboards and headsets and the cameramen's jaws were on the studio floor. I wanted to go and have another drink in the green room, but Malcolm collared me, dragged me outside and threw me into the limo EMI had laid on for us. As we pulled away from the kerb, a black maria rolled up and half a dozen coppers with truncheons at the ready spilled out of the back and entered the studios. I remember we gave them a sarcastic wave as we drove off. Malcolm was mortified, but he needn't have been. It was the moment that ended Grundy's career and kick-started ours.

As soon as the show finished, the switchboard was overloaded with complaints from the public and everything changed from that moment on. We'd spent the previous six months chasing the weekly music press, the *NME*, *Melody Maker*, *Sounds* and the *Record Mirror*. Slowly but surely, we were climbing the greasy pole of the music papers and had progressed from the occasional mention to live reviews, before finally we started getting cover features. It was working well on that front, ticking over nicely. Then, suddenly, we were the scourge of all the red-top newspapers. Malcolm had a kind of Damascene conversion and made out that it had all been part of his masterplan, but the truth of the matter was Malcolm had been bricking it. He was devastated after the show and was screaming at us, telling us we'd blown it for him. It wasn't until the next day that he changed his tune. Instead of having to hustle to get us in the newspapers, now they were beating a path to our door, and he wanted more and more of that. In a way, it was a kind of easy route to finding fame, and I can see why he'd find it so seductive, but it was almost as if the year of hard graft we'd all put in to reach that point suddenly didn't mean as much to him. Why work hard when you can just have a gimmick? He made hay while the sun was shining with that approach for a while, but it didn't take long for it to become a kind of cartoonish parody. The controversy got shifted to centre-stage, and from Malcolm's perspective, I think the music became less and less important than the freak show.

Having avoided the police and their truncheons, the limo took us back to Denmark Street, and I think maybe we went out for a drink afterwards because I remember bumping into the Heartbreakers in town and being asked how it went.

'Oh, you'll see,' I told them.

I ended up back in my local in Chiswick and drank a skinful. When I woke up the next day I had a thick head, but otherwise it was just a regular day. Then I got a call from Sophie Richmond, Malcolm's assistant.

'You've got to get to EMI now,' she said.

I got dressed and jumped on the bus, smiling at this girl I used to see round and about and who used to smile back at me. She didn't smile at me that morning. Outside of the dirty looks John used to give out on a regular basis, she gave me the most pointedly filthy look I think I'd ever seen. I was scratching my head, wondering what had happened to my morning smile, when all the pieces began to fall into place. I arrived at EMI HQ on Manchester Square, but I was late for the meeting and had to run a gauntlet of press to get in the place. I could see Steve, Paul and John hanging out of one of the windows, jeering me as I made my way past the gentlemen of the press. Twenty-four hours earlier, we couldn't get arrested. Today, a procession of Fleet Street's finest were lining up to tear us a new one.

23

PROBLEMS

There's a lot of talk these days about cancel culture. As if the notion of trying to cancel somebody just turned up on social media in the past ten years. I'm here to tell you it's been around for a lot longer than that. I know this because in 1976, I was cancelled by great swathes of the United Kingdom.

The Anarchy tour morphed into something else after the Grundy appearance and the subsequent press brouhaha. Around the country, dozens of local councils started getting jittery and wondering if we were going to be bringing Sodom and Gomorrah down on their little towns. When you see the list of shows that were cancelled by local authorities across the nation, it seems a ridiculous over-reaction. The tour started two days after Grundy, and the itinerary was as follows; Norwich University (cancelled); Derby (cancelled); Newcastle (cancelled); Leeds (played!); Bournemouth (cancelled); Manchester (played!);

Lancaster (cancelled); Liverpool (cancelled); Bristol (cancelled); Cardiff (cancelled); Caerphilly (played!); Glasgow (cancelled); Dundee (cancelled); Sheffield (cancelled); Southend (cancelled); Guildford (cancelled); Manchester (played!); Birmingham (cancelled); Cleethorpes (played!); two shows in Plymouth[1] (played!); Torquay (cancelled); and the final shows in Paignton and London, both of which were cancelled. It wasn't as if the shows were pulled before we headed out on the road either. We didn't spend three weeks with our feet up. No. We headed out on the road in an old-school *Magical Mystery Tour* coach, with our support bands, the Heartbreakers, and the Clash, with no idea whether the shows were cancelled until we arrived. Plus we had to go to every single venue, or we'd have lost half the deposit money we'd shelled out to secure the shows. If we hadn't shown up, we wouldn't have been paid at all. You have to wonder what it was exactly they were so scared of.

I think over the course of that tour, the band was becoming more factional than ever. Steve and Paul were keeping their distance and John was being John, so I found myself hanging out with the Clash and the Heartbreakers most of the time. I shared hotel digs most nights with Mick Jones because we got on so well, but I suppose in a way, that only marginalised me from the rest of the Pistols even more, but also, I was more vocal in questioning what was going on. I even briefly mulled the idea of leaving the Pistols and joining one of the support bands. Every band has

[1] Of the two Plymouth shows, incidentally, no one even turned up for the second show because no one knew we were playing.

166

its fall guy, I guess. I was the Pistols fall guy, but Billy Rath was the Heartbreakers'. Johnny Thunders was trying to push Billy out and egging me on to join the band in his place. Personally, I liked the Heartbreakers, and I liked Billy, so I didn't want to go down that road. And I doubt I'd be here now if I had.

Although I didn't realise it at the time, the seeds of my next move were already being sown before I left the Pistols and Malcolm penned *that* telegram to the *NME*. When we played the shows in the Netherlands, I was getting the impression that Steve and Paul were starting to freeze me out. I knew how they worked, because I'd seen how it had been with Wally Nightingale when he was on the way out. In the meantime, John had Sid in his earhole, pestering him constantly to join the band. He was telling him that he was better than Glen: 'I look better, I wear a leather jacket better, look – I've got a dog chain around my neck.'

For my money, all those cosmetic punk stylings were becoming a cliché even then, but because Malcolm was thinking in terms of us as something out of a comic strip, I think eventually the idea of Sid coming into the fold started to chime with him. Malcolm wanted someone a bit more lairy, to live up to that cartoon characterisation of the group he'd been formulating. Obviously, in that respect, Sid fit the bill, and ultimately it was to the band's detriment. Possibly it was forgotten that I'd come up with a lot of the tunes. It's not as if there's a bunch of great songs that were written after I departed. When I left, I wasn't watching that closely, but from the outside, it just seemed like a slow-motion car crash. With hindsight, it turned out to be a short-sighted gambit on Malcolm's part, but perhaps he didn't really know what we had together. Obviously I would say that, but I think a lot of people have come around to my way of thinking as the years have gone by.

It was a horrible time for me, but it wasn't just me who could see the writing on the wall, and I won't forget the friends who stood by me. Just after Christmas, one friend in particular, Mike Thorne from EMI, called me and invited me out for a curry. I gave my standard response.

'Who's paying?' I asked.

Mike assured me that EMI would pick up the tab, so, seeing as I wouldn't need to put my hand in my pocket, I decided to go along. Besides, I always got along well with Mike. He'd always been very supportive of me. Plus it turned out to be a decent curry, to be fair. We chatted for a while and then, over the plates of poppadoms and naan, Mike laid his cards on the table. As a friend and representative of EMI, he told me he could see maybe it wasn't working for me with the Pistols. They knew there was a problem between John and I, and that the situation was worsening by the day. By this time, I already had a sense the jig was up with the band, but Mike reassured me that whatever happened, EMI remained in my corner. Obviously, they hoped we could solve our own problems, but if we didn't, they'd be more than interested in helping to plot my next move. The feeling at EMI was that I was the main tunesmith of the Pistols and if I ever wanted to get out, they'd find a home for whatever project I had going forward. It was reassuring to know someone was pulling for me.

Mike Thorne is a lovely guy and to this day a good mate. After cutting his teeth in A&R, he went on to have an illustrious production career – he worked with Roger Daltrey, John Cale and Blur – and is probably best known for producing Soft Cell's 'Tainted Love'. For me, however, he'll always be the guy from EMI who turned up with a parachute, just as the plane was about to go down. It was a comfort to know EMI had my back, but it wasn't just them. Just a couple of weeks later, EMI dumped the Pistols and Malcolm signed the deal with A&M records outside the gates of Buckingham Palace. When word of my departure reached Derek Green, the head of A&M, he dropped the band like a stone.

24

NEVER MIND THE BOLLOCKS

28 February 1977

Telegram to Derek Johnson, NME, *King's Reach Tower.*

*YES DEREK GLEN MATLOCK WAS THROWN OUT OF
THE SEX PISTOLS SO I'M TOLD BECAUSE HE WENT
ON TOO LONG ABOUT PAUL MCCARTNEY [STOP] EMI
WAS ENOUGH [STOP] THE BEATLES WAS TOO MUCH
[STOP] . . . LOVE AND PEACE MALCOLM MCLAREN*

I remember seeing an interview with Jerry Nolan from the New
York Dolls. He said that when I was in the Pistols, there was
a delicate balance between all the members. Once Sid arrived,
he was so outrageous, and craved so much attention, the balance we'd had before was completely turned on its head. John
might have wanted his friend Sid to join the group, and to act

as my usurper, but as the saying goes, be careful what you wish for. Instead of having the ally that he'd wanted for so long, Sid became a liability and John ended up more pissed off with the situation than ever. I wasn't in the band, though, so it wasn't my problem any more. I wasn't there on the outside with my face pressed up against the glass, wondering what was happening. If I heard one of my songs on the radio, I wasn't overwhelmed with feelings of what might have been. If I'm honest, I just thought the bass could have sounded better. I don't know that I had any sense of schadenfreude when they inevitably went belly up, because by then, I felt I had other things going on.

After the Pistols, I didn't have a set idea as to what I wanted to do, but I knew whatever form a new project was going to take, it wasn't going to be an out-and-out punk band. If I'm honest, I never saw the Sex Pistols as a punk band either, but I guess that's a matter of perspective. Possibly history has already made its decision on that front. Already, in early 1977, with the Pistols growing in notoriety, I could see there was a lot of bandwagon-jumping as the punk movement gathered pace in the main-stream. A lot of old pub rockers were sticking safety pins through their noses and crossing out their ages on their passports. I knew that whatever my next move was going to be, I wanted to swim against the tide a little.

Pick up the music papers and you could see bands were form-ing all over the country in the Pistols' wake and doing things, I think, that we'd already done to some extent. Not everybody, of course, but that was the general impression. In some respects, it was a lot like the British Invasion bands the decade before, following on the coattails of the Stones and the Beatles. A lot of bands who were in their slipstream were either copyists or weren't as earth-shattering. In any case, I didn't want to get tarred with the brush of being a copy of something I'd helped instigate in the first place.

From the outset, I had a small clutch of songs or ideas for songs that probably didn't fit the Pistols template. I wanted to do something a bit outside the box and to write about things from a different perspective. Maybe that was a kind of fiscal stupidity on my part, but my head was in a different place. I knew it would have been very easy for me to come back with a kind of second division Pistols thing, but I'd done the Pistols already. With this new band, I just wanted to do something a bit more musical. Rather than simply trying to be the latest anarchist in town, I felt like I wanted us to stand apart. I mean, being an anarchist has its merits, but I genuinely do like pop music that has some edge. A little more bollocks, if you like.

As for personnel, I didn't have any great masterplan in place. A good deal of how things got started with the Rich Kids had more to do with serendipity than any overarching plans and schemes I might have been working on. Take Steve New, for example. Credit where it's due, Steve New was an incredible guitarist. He could play everything – a whole spectrum of music from elaborate Charlie Christian, Barney Kessel jazz guitar kind of stuff, right through to three-chord punk. He looked good, he played great, and he was a lovely guy. He was a few years younger than me, but we got along like a house on fire right from the outset. I think because I was an only child, over time, he kind of became the younger brother I never had. I mean that in the sense that I used to love him, but there were times I felt like I wanted to strangle him. Of course, whenever I told him I thought of him as a kid brother, he was always quick to tell me that he had a younger brother himself, so he wasn't in the market for an older brother.

The first time I encountered Steve New was back in the Pistols days. We'd placed an ad in the paper looking for a second guitarist. Personally, I didn't see the need for a second guitarist, and nor did Steve, but Paul Cook was pushing for one. Steve and I felt like we were ready to start playing some shows, but Paul started muttering that Steve wasn't up to the task. That wasn't the real reason, though. Paul was getting close to completing his electrician's apprenticeship at Watneys Brewery in Mortlake at the time, and he was stalling so he could get his qualification. The second guitarist ruse was just a smokescreen.[1] That was my take anyway. Whether that was Paul's plan or not, we had to go through the rigmarole of advertising for a second guitarist in the music papers. The ad ran in the *Melody Maker* on 13 September 1975.

WHIZZ KID GUITARIST
Not older than 20
Not worse looking than Johnny Thunders
Auditioning: Tin Pan Alley

---

[1] When Paul eventually passed his apprenticeship, he was taken out by the lads at the brewery as a send-off. We played a show that night – I think it was at Chelmsford Prison. Paul was pissed as a fart. If you have the bootleg, you can hear him falling off his drum stool in the middle of the set. To his credit, he did manage to keep the beat going. What a pro.

After the ad ran, we had a ton of people turning up on our doorstep and chancing an arm. Practically no one fit the bill. I remember one fella who strolled in off Denmark Street, looking like a member of Queen, with a big Freddie Mercury scarf trailing behind him and an attitude to match. He didn't even have a chance to get his guitar out of its case. As he entered, Malcolm looked him up and down.

'The ad said good looking,' he told him, and sent him on his way. The poor guy looked crestfallen.

We saw a few players, but Steve New was the only one who made the grade. He was a Harrow Road boy, so from my neck of the woods, and I felt an affinity with him right from the off. I think he was only fifteen or sixteen at the time, and he arrived at his audition with his girlfriend, Rose. Rose was also his secondary school art teacher. She wasn't that much older than Steve, to be fair, but that didn't stop us from thinking he was a dirty sod. Still, dirty sod or not, when he plugged in, we could all see he was a great guitarist, and after he tried out, he was sort of in the Sex Pistols briefly, if only for a week or so. He played a few things for us, and he was incredible. We didn't exactly have a dress code, but when we pointed out that his hair was too long, Steve refused point blank to have it cut. It was left to me to give him the ultimatum: no haircut, no gig. He decided he didn't want to get his hair cut that badly, but by that time, Paul had suddenly cooled on the idea of hiring a second guitar player, so Steve New was out anyway. But he had left an impression.

In the aftermath of the Pistols, for the first time in a couple of years, I took myself down to the King's Road. To me it had all stopped being real. I was twenty years old, and I simply couldn't see the wood for the trees. Really, I should have been keeping my head down when the news broke about my leaving the band. There was obviously a story circulating, which McClaren's press release ultimately elevated from myth to fact. Everybody's heard it. For those not paying attention at the back, the story was that I'd been sacked from the band for liking the Beatles. It bores me to have to say it again, but it was total bollocks. Malcolm had been trying to pit me and John against one another, trying to manufacture some kind of friction almost from the start. John had really begun to change since he started getting his face in the newspapers, while Malcolm started to believe his own press that he was this Svengali figure and that everything we'd achieved was down to him. After a while, he seemed to start thinking of us as a kind of punk rock version of the Archies, like we were all cartoon characters and ultimately expendable. Worst of all, he stopped being honest. By the end of the Anarchy tour, Malcolm was playing to the gallery.

From his perspective, the circus around the band was more important than the band. He liked to tell us we were banned from playing, but I had promoters approach me and they were desperate for us to play for them. It was just Malcolm building this pointless mystique around us. It was frustrating. The reason I'd got into a band in the first place was to get out and play, but we were hamstrung by Malcolm. The final straw came when I heard that they'd rehearsed without me a couple of times, with Sid trying out on bass. I think I'd just had enough of the bullshit at that point. There was a meeting, and I told them I was off.

'Can't you just pretend you like John?' was Paul's response.

'Like you two?' I said. 'Never saying boo to him?'

My walking out was the upshot. It was my decision. Malcolm had engineered it this way, which is a shame. The infamous telegram to the *NME* was just Malcolm trying to capitalise on my exit and maybe save face in the press. The reason it still kind of rankles with me is the dishonesty of it all. It was a cuntish thing to do. When I left, I went back to Denmark Street to pick up my stuff. We'd shaken hands – everyone except John. I realise it wasn't the best situation, but I thought we'd parted amicably. A week later, Malcolm sent the telegram. Steve will tell you it was just a bit of fun, but it was a bit of fun at my expense, and it's been an albatross around my neck for years. I think that when I was in the band originally, we were more like bands I grew up with, rather than the circus the Pistols were about to become. Originally, I'd seen us as being like the Who in their early days, not sounding like them exactly, but a band by the kids, for the kids. When I fell out with them and they bought in Sid, the band became Malcolm McLaren's puppets, and I didn't like that in the slightest.

Malcolm was a one-off kind of guy and it's a pleasure to have known him, really it is. He was funny, stylish, and had a wild imagination. His place on the King's Road was like a magnet, drawing in all these oddballs and people who wanted to do something different with their lives. He was a lot of fun to be around, but he also had this other side to him. He used people and he spat them out. Still, this Beatles story was spreading like wildfire. To this day, people still ask me about it. It's like that old saying: a lie gets halfway around the world before the truth has a chance to get its pants on. The lie was halfway around the world that I was pushed when, the truth is, I'd walked. It still gets reported as a fact, even today. It's the embodiment of the newspaperman adage: when the legend becomes fact, print the legend.

In strictly pragmatic terms, I wasn't exactly in a rush to leave the band. It didn't make a lot of sense for me economically. We were yet to strike a deal regarding my departure and so I was still receiving a £25 per week wage from EMI, plus the few quid I got for the flat. So really, when I had fallen out with the Pistols, until we sorted out my severance deal, I had to maintain a low profile because I was worried about keeping a roof over my head.

I had all that swimming around upstairs and this vague idea for a new band, and I found myself drifting into the Roebuck, the pub where we all used to hang out. It was the same day that *Sounds* magazine had come out and they ran the story that I was going to form a new band. I hadn't been in the place for maybe a year and a half, and it felt kind of weird being back at the scene of the crime, so to speak. I got myself a drink at the bar and I'd barely got my top lip wet when Steve New came running into the pub. He said he'd been looking for me and this was the only place he could think to find me.

'What are you gonna do?' he said.

'I'm gonna put a band together,' I told him. 'Me and you, right?'

'Don't worry,' he said. 'I'll cut my hair this time.'

And that was it. Simple as that, I had my guitarist.

A couple of days after the chance meeting with Steve New, I went to a gig at the Nashville in Kensington to see Rockpile – Dave Edmunds' band – and I was approached by a tall lad with this mountain of strawberry blonde hair piled on top of his head. He introduced himself to me as Rusty Egan and started telling me what a great drummer he was and that I should give him a shot. He was talking nine to the dozen, telling me how he'd just tried out for the Clash, but they wouldn't commit to hiring him.

I gave him a once-over. 'Alright, mate. You're in.' He carried on pitching, telling me how good he was, and I cut him off. 'Shut up. You're in,' I told him, knowing full well that if he wasn't any good, I didn't have to keep him. I was glad I met him, though. Knowing Rusty came in quite handy later that night. I was waiting around for the band to play, when this pretty American girl made her way through the crowd and buttonholed me.

'Hey, are you a Sex Pistol?' she asked.

I hadn't signed the exit agreement at this point, so I told her, 'Well, technically I am. Why are you asking?'

'Come outside and I'll fight you.' She fixed me with a look. She didn't look like she was joking.

As Rockpile took to the stage, their manager, Jake Riviera, marched into view. There was always a bit of needle between Jake and Malcolm, but I didn't have any beef with him. Jake thought Malcolm was an airy-fairy poseur and he didn't mind who knew it, while Malcolm made no bones about the fact that he thought that Jake and his pub rock bands were dragging music backwards towards the Stone Age. Despite the grudge between them, I assumed we were on friendly terms. Jake said hi and asked what was going on.

'You won't believe it, Jake,' I told him. 'But this lovely young lady here just asked me outside for a fight.'

Jake looked at her. 'Is this true?' he said, and the girl shook her head.

'I don't know what he's talking about,' she said.

'She really did,' I told him, and the atmosphere changed suddenly.

Riviera had a face like thunder. 'Are you calling my girl a liar?'

And with that, he started swinging these great haymakers at me. As far as I was concerned, any feud with Malcolm was between them, but I guess I was still in Camp McLaren to the outside world, whether I liked it or not. I mean, the very next day I was going to sign on the dotted line that I wasn't a Sex Pistol any more, so it seemed like a ridiculous waste of testosterone, frankly. That's what I was thinking anyway, when Rusty emerged from the crowd, took stock of what was occurring, and punched Jake Riviera spark out. In the street afterwards, I asked him how he'd managed to bail me out like that. It was a comprehensive knockout.

'I used to be southern England borstal boxing champion,' he explained.

If he wasn't in before, he'd certainly made the grade now. He wasn't exactly a bruiser, but he knew how to handle himself. So just on that front, Rusty being handy with his fists was certainly an added attribute. Later, when I finally brought Steve New and Rusty together, it transpired that they already knew each other. Steve had taken over Rusty's job as a runner for WEA Records when he left, so they already had a rapport. Like so many things in my life, strange little connections along the way have become a recurring theme.

25

RICH KIDS

In no time at all, we were putting songs together, writing, rehearsing and laying down some demos here and there. I had a couple of songs, like 'Rich Kids', which I'd put forward to the other guys when I was still a Pistol, but my voice wasn't exactly getting heard then. With the songs I was working on with Steve and Rusty, initially I was singing, but eventually we decided that perhaps we should cast a wider net to find a singer. I sometimes wonder if maybe I should have put myself out front as singer, but at the time I was mindful that I only had a limited range. Back then, my vocal range floated between E, G and A, with maybe a bit of C thrown in there for good measure. I knew how to write songs and play, but I think I didn't really have any understanding of how keys worked, so I decided I'd stick to what I knew. I would look around for a singer.

I was trying out a variety of different vocalists, as well as a few additional guitarists. I did have a conversation with Paul Weller. I'd always rated him and, importantly, I got on with him. We're still friendly – in fact he lives in the same neighbourhood as me. Nothing really came of it with Paul, though, as the Jam were starting to take off at that point. They weren't massive yet, but they were making a name for themselves, playing shows at the Marquee and across town, and it was probably around the time they signed with Chris Parry at Polydor. Funnily enough, the conversation with Paul got turned around and I found myself talking about possibly joining their line-up as a second guitarist. I was going to join them on stage at the Roxy one night, and Rick Buckler and Bruce Foxton came over before the show.

'We hear you might be joining us?'

'Maybe,' I said. 'Let's have a play and see how it goes.'

'You gonna wear a suit?' Bruce asked.

At the time, the Jam wore these black suits. As a look, I suppose it set them apart from the other bands around, but those suits were these horrible cheap-looking things. I'd spent enough hours working in Malcolm's shop to know what good fashion was, and those suits certainly weren't it.

'What, from Carnaby Cavern?' I laughed. 'You must be fucking joking,' I said, and that was the end of that.

My real focus was on starting my own thing. Getting a vocalist on board and seeing if we could get something happening. The lack of a singer was an immediate and frustrating problem. Practically all the singers I met had the same issue: everyone but *everyone* just wanted to be Johnny Rotten. Firstly, John is kind of inimitable, bless him. Secondly, no offence to John, but another Johnny Rotten was the last thing we needed. I wanted to distance myself from that sound and attitude right from the get-go, have someone who could carry a tune and create something with a bit more melody.

We auditioned a load of guys, but the procession of sub-par singers became a grind. There was a fella who came down one time to this little rehearsal place we had lined up, but I couldn't really hear him sing because the PA wasn't great. I hired another place with a bit more space, to give him another try. The rehearsal room was underneath the Photographers' Gallery around by Little Newport Street in Chinatown. I think the place used to be a beat club in the '60s, and there were a couple of old dears down there who used to complain about the noise. The second try with the singer wasn't any better, to be honest. He was a nice chap, but he just wasn't what we needed. I was disappointed, so I called time on the rehearsal there and then.

Having found Steve and Rusty so quickly and having that feeling that things were falling into place so naturally, the length of time it was taking to land a singer felt agonising. The music scene in 1977 was moving so quickly, the slow pace of progress felt like a let-down in that respect, and I didn't want us to be left behind. As I walked out of the session, one of the women stopped me to give me a piece of her mind.

'You lot will never make it,' she told me. 'You boys are too bloody loud. We've had them all in here, you know – the Kinks, the Stones, the Who – and they were never as loud as this.'

We had some potential management people scheduled to come down and give us the once-over that day. I'd already had the assurance from Mike Thorne that EMI were interested, so that took some of the pressure off, but I was still feeling a bit distracted by the fact we hadn't nailed down the lead singer spot. I decided to take myself off to Leicester Square and drifted into a record shop, still pondering the singer problem. Flicking idly through the racks, I found an album by the band Slik. They were a Scottish pop band from a couple of years back. Slik hadn't quite been and gone by this point, but they were on their last knockings, so to speak. They'd started out as a kind of glam rock band, but probably they were best remembered for their bubblegum pop hit 'Forever and Ever', which got to number one in 1976. Obviously, a lot can happen in the space of a year, but bubblegum pop and glam were both pretty much dead in the water by early 1977, so it struck me that the singer might be in the market for a new band. I didn't want to wind up the punk crowd, but I suppose in the back of my mind, I knew that having a famous pop singer in the group would ruffle a few feathers.

I had a tenuous connection with the singer in Slik. He was a guy called Midge Ure. The story was that Midge had met Malcolm and Bernard Rhodes outside a music shop in Glasgow a few years back. Bernard and Malcolm had gone off on a mad trip around the country to buy old clothes for Let It Rock, and while they were on their magical history tour, they tried to offload some other stuff. They had some hot gear that Steve had purloined on one of his nocturnal escapades and wanted to shift, as far away from London as possible. While they were in Glasgow, they went into a music shop hoping to sell a stolen amplifier. This was back in the days when practically everyone had long hair, but I remembered Malcolm telling me about this cool chap in Glasgow, Midge, who had his hair styled in a quiff. Midge had overheard the conversation between Malcolm and the shop owner and after the guy wouldn't strike a deal, Midge bought the amp from Malcolm himself. Intrigued, Malcolm took his number, and I called him when Steve, Paul and I were looking for a singer, but he was just getting this other band off the ground, so it was a no-go. How different things might have been. I wondered what he was doing now.

It wasn't long before Midge was down in London, trying out for us over the course of a weekend. Immediately, he seemed a great fit. Things clicked quite quickly, but it was still a while before we had him fully on board. Midge was technically still a member of Slik at this point and getting him wasn't going to be straightforward. He had this big-time manager called Frank Silver who would need to be won over before any progress could be made. Silver wasn't impressed with how disorganised we seemed, and even though Slik weren't having hits any more, it was clear he would need a bit of persuading. Geographically speaking, it was slightly painful. Midge was based in Glasgow and, once the Pistols exit agreement was signed, I'd moved out of my flat in Chiswick and into a squat. We used the downstairs as a makeshift rehearsal space. Essentially, we had no organisation around us, we had no money, and although we had potential managers circling, there was nothing definite in place. But we were ambitious, had a few good songs, and there was a relaxed camaraderie. Also, I knew Midge was intrigued by the slight perversity of an ex-Pistol getting together with a former member of Slik, so I had a good feeling that he would eventually sign up for duty.

It wasn't easy, however. Some days it seemed as if he was going to join the band, and some days it seemed like he wasn't. It became a bit of a test. I had to go backwards and forwards to Glasgow to meet with Midge and his manager a few times.

On one occasion, I went up on the sleeper train to Glasgow with my friend Al McDowell, who had started managing us. The whole journey was like a comedy of errors. Somebody had given us a little something to help keep us awake, which in retrospect was a daft thing to do on a sleeper train, but we were delighted that you could summon the guard to your cabin through the course of the night and he was allowed to sell little miniatures of various spirits. It wasn't our finest hour. At some point during the journey, the train pulled over into a siding and the guard seemed to have disappeared. By this time, we'd finished all our miniatures and were both feeling pretty wired, but we carried on pressing the bell intermittently, hoping to get the guard to come and bring us a few more drinks to take the edge off. After a while, it was clear no one was coming. The train had come to a halt and all the passengers were tucked up in their bunks. There was no announcement, so we were completely clueless as to what was happening. I started to feel increasingly edgy. In that heightened state, I could feel panic setting in. I needed to get to Glasgow to see Midge. My career was depending on it! I peeked through the window to see if I could make out any visible landmarks. I could just about see the Top of the World club, which had a giant model of a rocket fixed to the front of the place, so I could see that we were in Stafford. A long way from London, but further still from Glasgow. We gave it one last try with the guard and pressed the button for service again, but there was still no sign of life. Out of sheer desperation, Al and I decided to take matters into our own hands. We climbed out of our respective bunks and ventured out of the cabin and into the carriage, dressed only in our underpants and socks, and began searching for the guard. At the end of the carriage, we opened a sliding door and found his empty little cubicle. With no sign of life, we crept in and started to help ourselves to bottles of vodka and scotch. It wasn't as if we weren't intending to pay – we thought we'd grab a few and let him know we'd taken them when he finally showed up. However, the next thing we knew, the train lurched to a start and the sliding door slammed shut behind us. Shut and locked, as it turned out. We rooted around the tiny space in search of a key, but to no avail. We simply had to wait for the guard to come back from his rounds, or wherever he'd gone. He wouldn't be long, would he? Eventually the train moved out of the siding and pressed onward, but for some reason the guard never returned to his office. The door stayed locked the whole way and we were just stuck there, unable to sit down, all the way from the Midlands until we arrived in Glasgow. All that we could do was stand bolt upright, bracing ourselves against the train's movement, drinking miniature after miniature. By the time the train pulled into Glasgow Central station at around 7 a.m., we were a complete mess, and we were met by the Glaswegian transport police and a barrage of snapping police dogs. I'd love to say we were arrested, because obviously that would be a more rock 'n' roll outcome, but sadly we weren't. We were taken to one side, they quickly established that we weren't ne'er-do-wells, just common-or-garden nitwits, and they let us off with a warning.

Emerging from the station, we made our way to the nearest hotel to grab a couple of hours' kip and to freshen up before our meeting with Midge and Frank Silver at 11. As we arrived, Frank asked if it was okay if someone sat in on the meeting. It was some new guy that Silver had signed to his management stable, this long-haired hippy-looking fella with a wispy beard, but he seemed friendly enough. I gave the guy a nod to say hello and said that was fine, and then we got down to discussing a few matters with Frank and Midge.

While we were chatting things over, doing our best to persuade Midge to come back down south and join the band permanently, I suddenly realised my legs were itching. I gave my shins a casual scratch and hoped no one had noticed. A minute later, I had to scratch again. I looked over at Al and noticed he was scratching his legs, too. As the meeting wore on, the sensation started getting worse. After five minutes or so, I couldn't concentrate on what was being discussed, because I was feverishly scratching away at my legs. Before too long, it became unbearable. I rolled my trousers up from my ankles to investigate and realised my legs were riddled with fleas. The hippy bearded guy who was sitting in on the meeting looked down at me furiously scratching my legs.

'What's going on there?' he said. He had a broad Glasgow accent.

'We had a bit of a run-in on the train,' I explained. 'We decided to freshen up at that hotel over the road.'

The bearded guy started to smile. 'Which hotel?'

'I dunno,' I said. 'The big one over on the corner.'

'Oh right.' He started laughing. 'You dinnae wanna go there. That's the dossers' hotel.' He was howling with laughter now. 'It's a flophouse, basically. Place is riddled with fleas.'

He proceeded to make total mincemeat of us, joking with Midge and Frank at our expense. It turned out we were getting a private roasting from Billy Connolly, the Scottish comic who had signed up with Frank. We were laughing so hard we didn't care that Midge and Frank clearly thought we were idiots.

26

GHOSTS OF PRINCES IN TOWERS

While Midge considered his options, I thought we should test the waters with a few live gigs. Because he had some downtime from the Clash, I asked Mick Jones to play with us and he joined us for maybe half a dozen shows. We didn't have an itinerary. We were just blagging gigs and turning up and playing to whoever was gathered there. We played one night at the Vortex, which was the club on Wardour Street. After the Roxy was forced to close its doors, for a few short months in 1977, the Vortex became London's premier punk venue. We took to the stage that night, decidedly out of step with the safety-pin and torn-shirt clientele. Steve New still hadn't got his hair cut, I was growing mine out, and Mick was going through a Keith Richards phase in terms of his styling, so we didn't exactly look like the embodiment of punk rock when we played that show. A fanzine review described us as taking to the stage looking like the 'ghosts of princes in towers'. *That's a good title for a song*, I thought.

I'd come from a family where the only reading matter was the *Daily Mirror*, but I was always trying to broaden my literary horizons. The more interesting things you expose yourself to, the wider your influences, so subconsciously, and possibly consciously too, I was absorbing a lot of different themes into my songwriting around that time. I was reading all the existentialists and I'd fallen in love with the films and writings of Jean Cocteau. I devoured *Les Enfants Terribles* and was struck by a line of prose describing the characters as poor, but rich in ideas, and that became the inspiration for the band name, the Rich Kids. We may not have been wealthy in monetary terms, but we were rich in ideas and thought. After I read Cocteau's *Thomas the Impostor* and *Les Enfants Terribles*, I began toying with an idea that was inspired by those novels. We were always on the lookout for something different or interesting to do, beyond the usual high jinks of being a band about town. There was always a late-night movie to take in. The Acklam Hall used to run midnight showings of Jean Vigo's *Zéro de Conduite* and *L'Atalante* and all these French realist movies. I remember one night going with Mick Jones to see Cocteau's *La Belle et la Bête*. It's a great film and there's a moment when La Belle is being harangued by her brothers and she says, 'You two are just wastrels.'

In the darkness, Mick turned to me and said, 'That's us, that is.'

Sometimes as a songwriter, you have a lot of disparate ideas fighting for your attention, but you can't always bring them together because you need something to hang it on. 'The ghosts of princes in towers' line in the fanzine became that unifying element. The late 1970s was a violent, frustrated time. There was a lot of pent-up aggression in the air around London and across the rest of the country. Meathead Teddy Boys were fighting the upstart punks and the punks were scrapping with the mods and it seemed that wherever you went, people just wanted to stave one another's heads in simply because they were wearing the wrong uniform. I tied all that together in the lyric. Steve New came up with the riff and a neat middle-eight major scale kind of thing and I assembled all the pieces into a finished song: 'You know there are those who make it / And those who never may.'

It was only a temporary arrangement between Mick Jones and us, but I enjoyed playing with him. In August '77, we played a show supporting the Tom Robinson Band at the Brecknock pub in Camden. Tom and the band were celebrating signing their record deal with EMI, so there was quite a party atmosphere. I have a cassette of the show somewhere that someone recorded from the audience. You can hear us playing our hearts out in the background, while in the foreground, people are ordering their pints at the bar. I like that. It reminds me of the Velvet Underground *Live at Max's Kansas City* album and the folks in the crowd loudly ordering Pernod while the Velvets bash out a version of 'Waiting for My Man'.

That night, we decided to mix things up a bit, so we closed our set with a cover version. Covers are an important ingredient to add into the mix when you're finding your feet as a band. Anyway, during the song's opening bars, you can hear Roger Armstrong from Rock On Records, in his thick Irish accent, comment loudly, 'Oh, they're doing "I Think We're Alone Now" by the Rubinoos!', and that always makes me smile. Obviously, this was a long time before Tiffany recorded her hit version, but a while back, I was playing in LA with Camp Freddy at the Whiskey a Go Go. Camp Freddy were this kind of celebrity super group, and they persuaded me to perform 'Pretty Vacant' with Tiffany on lead vocals. She's no Johnny Rotten, but she gives it a go.

Over the summer of '77, I travelled to Scotland a couple more times and Midge started to come down from Glasgow on these little reconnaissance trips. I'd call from time to time, to check on his progress, and his mother would answer the phone. When I said I wanted to speak to Midge, she'd call up the stairs to her 'Wee Jimmy' and tell him it was a call from London. It took a while to get him to join. I think he was testing the water, but he was edging ever closer to joining the band. On my last trip to Scotland, he seemed a little lost. He and some of the other former members of Slik, who had sensed that the wind had changed, decided to go in a more punk direction, and they'd put together a new band called PVC2. They were getting set to release an EP. One of the songs on the EP, 'Put You in the Picture', would wind up on the Rich Kids album. Really, I think I broke that band up, but ultimately it was Midge's decision to leave PVC2 and finally throw his chips in with our little lot.

Despite all the comings and goings north of the border, I was still around and about the scene in London, charming my way into shows when I could. One night, after we'd got together for a rehearsal, I took Midge and the guys down to see a band at the Hope and Anchor in Islington and, as I usually did, I was trying to blag our way in. I was explaining who we were to this big fella called John, who was working the door. We tried every trick in the book to get in, but Big John wasn't having any of it. I insisted that we were a band, but he was equally insistent that we should pay to get in. Just then, this smaller guy – also called John – appeared behind him and started muttering about the support band not showing up for the gig.

'We'll play,' I said, ever the opportunist.

'What's your band called?' Little John asked.

We still didn't have a name at that point, but given he was in a jam, he said we could play. He still made us pay to come in, but he agreed to give us our money back if he liked the cut of our jib. So we played that night supporting the Police, who were just starting out. The Police were a four-piece at the time, with Henry Padovani on guitar. Henry became a friend of mine, but I don't think he was that night. None of them were. Obviously, we hadn't planned on playing, so we had to use the band's instruments. Steve New hadn't held back particularly and shredded all the strings on the guitar he'd borrowed. Still, even if the Police were irritated, Big John and Little John were satisfied at least. Not only did they give us our money back, but they also slipped us an extra fiver for all our trouble and paid for our night out.

Later that same night, we went on to a party at Shad Thames, near Tower Bridge. I'd heard that Andrew Logan, the renowned sculptor, was hosting his annual Alternative Miss World pageant. I'd played at the previous pageant with the Pistols in 1976 and it had been a riot. The Alternative Miss

World had started life in the early '70s when Logan decided to start a kind of unconventional version of the Miss World style of beauty competitions. Logan's left-field take on those naff pageants was like a celebration of unconventional people of all ages and genders: transvestites, drag queens and people dressed as teapots. The venue that night was this Victorian-era cargo warehouse on the banks of the river. Nowadays that's quite an upmarket area, filled with well-to-do apartments, but in 1977 the place had seen better days. The warehouse was basically one giant squat. Still, I'd heard there were some bands playing, so we went along to check it out and maybe see if we could sneak onto the bill ourselves. One of the squatters was Anne Bean, the artist. She spent the night walking around in an outfit that was made from raw bacon and cuts of meat, wrapped in cling film. Midge, who was quite a straight guy from Glasgow, had never seen anything like it.

'What the fuck is going on here?'

I didn't let on, but despite my art school leanings and my time on the fringes with the Pistols, I hadn't quite seen anything like that either. As we had done earlier, we blagged our way onto the stage and ran through maybe four or five songs before getting back to the party. I caught sight of a few familiar faces when we played. I noticed Sid was there, along with his girlfriend Nancy Spungen. While they were outside having a cigarette, someone on one of the floors above us took a piss out of one of the windows, thinking they were peeing in the river. I'm not one to hold a grudge, so I did my best not to chuckle when the phantom pisser missed the river entirely and soaked Sid instead.

In late 1977, with Midge finally in the fold, we signed our deal with EMI Records. EMI offered us a load of money to sign for them. We'd spoken with all the labels in London by this point and EMI's was the best offer. Partly it was a case of better the devil you know, but I was still on friendly terms with the people there and had a good rapport with Mike and Nick Mobbs. Despite all the shit talk from Malcolm in the aftermath, the people on the shop floor at EMI hadn't wanted rid of the Sex Pistols. That edict came from much higher up in the organisation. As a company, EMI was an electronics and technology giant. They were a global concern with a hundred divisions and fingers in pies all over the world. The company was such a big deal, the MD used to have dinner with the Queen from time to time. The reasons behind the Sex Pistols' sacking from EMI were far more complex than whatever press releases Malcolm sent to the *NME*. EMI invented the CT scanner, which they hoped to roll out to hospitals all over the world. They had all these delegations of US evangelical conservatives coming over to the UK, offering funding for the new technology, and, meanwhile, we were on the front of all the papers and on TV singing 'I am an antichrist'. Something had to give. The record side of their business, despite having Floyd and the Beatles and all these million-selling artists, was not a primary concern for them, so that's why the band was shown the exit. The people in the record company themselves didn't have any issues with us.

Although we made the decision to sign with EMI, we kept the other labels dangling for a bit because they were all so eager. For a while, it was like having a Rolodex of people who wanted to take you out for lunch or dinner. Let me tell you, whoever said there's no such thing as a free lunch was way off the mark. If I was hungry of an evening, and the cupboard was bare, I'd put in a call to someone at Virgin or Polydor and see if they fancied taking us out for a bite. It seemed rude not to take advantage of their largesse.

27

HUNG ON YOU

With the Rich Kids line-up settled finally, we demoed furiously, played a few shows around the country, and recorded our one and only session for the John Peel show. The shows were getting good reviews. Our first single, the eponymous 'Rich Kids', hit the top thirty and we were on *Top of the Pops* and blaring out of radios across the land. I'd even find my phone ringing with calls from the *NME* for my take on this or that. I always reacted the same, 'Why are you asking me?' It wasn't false modesty. I didn't feel that my opinion mattered that much, but briefly I found myself flavour of the month and there was an expectation that the Rich Kids were going to achieve great things. I guess some of that was down to who I was and where I'd come from, but it was kind of surreal, all the same. It was a different set-up to the Pistols, but I was starting to feel that sense of momentum building again. After all the shit with the way my time with the Pistols ended, it was a good feeling.

The songs we were working up were sounding good. We all felt a shared excitement. 'Hung on You' came about not long after I'd left the Pistols. I took the title from a shop I had read about in the Nik Cohn book *Today There Are No Gentlemen*, which is about the changes in the Englishman's wardrobe in the years since the war. If you get the chance to read it, it's a fascinating book. I was learning all about these people like Cecil Gee, who had one of London's first clothing boutiques selling American-style zoot suits and those black and white Gatsby-looking correspondent shoes.[1] In the book Cohn also wrote about Hung on You, which was a 1960s London fashion boutique set up by the designer Michael Rainey, which was famous for its garish, psychedelic flowery shirts and kipper ties. I didn't particularly fancy the idea of a kipper tie, but I thought 'Hung on You' would make a terrific song title. The Pistols telegram and all the related bullshit was still at the forefront of my mind, so the song became about that. In particular, it was about John: 'I don't care for your exhortations / No, I ain't hung, for your information / On you, oh no.'

At the same time that punk was on the rise, reggae music was also growing in popularity. There was always a synergy between punk and reggae. At the start of the punk boom in 1976, there were hardly any punk records released, so Don Letts, the

---

[1] The correspondent shoe, or spectator shoe, was a style of low-heeled Oxford brogue constructed from two contrasting colours and had a kind of disreputable reputation. It earned the name correspondent shoe because it was viewed as the kind of footwear a co-respondent to a divorce petition might wear. You needed a fair bit of front to put a pair on and they were a favoured style of shoe among gangsters and spivs.

DJ at the Roxy, used to play old Blue Beat and Ska 45s between bands, so all the fledgling punks were switched on to reggae. There were a lot of great bands and records coming out. I found the Burning Sounds record store on the Harrow Road. It was a great shop specialising in reggae and dub vinyl. I liked the name and took it as another song title. With hindsight, I think some of my writing was about me clearing the decks of all the headaches of the Pistols time, and the lyric to 'Burning Sounds' was another rumination on my feelings about what had happened with the band. I think, even then, my tenure in the Pistols was casting a long shadow over what was going on in my life. The point of 'Burning Sounds' was to say I didn't want any of the bread and circuses shit; I just wanted to be a musician and to write songs: 'Cos all you want is burning sounds that come from the heart.'

It's a song that I'm very proud of. When I took it in to Rob Dickins, who was handling the Rich Kids' publishing, he said it was one of the best things he'd heard, and later he lamented the fact that it had got kind of lost as an album track.

Once we'd assembled the demos, we went into the studio with Mike Thorne. The recordings sounded okay, but I felt we could do better. Mike was disappointed when I said I was thinking about maybe trying again with another producer, although I didn't have anyone specific in mind. The idea that Mick Ronson from the Spiders from Mars might end up working the console wasn't even a consideration. Mick getting involved was almost a pure fluke. I was hanging around my manager's office one day after the Mike Thorne sessions and the phone rang. I looked around and as there was no one to answer the call, I picked up the phone.

'Who's that?' I asked.

'This is Michael,' the fella said in this thick north-west accent that I recognised instantly.

'Mick Ronson?'

'Yes, who's that?'

'It's Glen,' I told him.

'Glen Matlock?'

'How do you know who I am?' I said, slightly defensively, I'll be honest.

'I've heard a lot about you,' he said, and when he asked what I was up to, I said we were about to record the album. I dropped into the conversation that we were looking for a producer and maybe he could come down to our rehearsals. *Nothing ventured*, I thought, *nothing gained*. I was beside myself when he said he'd come along and check us out.

'Bring your guitar,' I told him, and that was that. Mick turned up for rehearsals the next day. It was a pinch-yourself moment. He just strolled in, said hi to everyone and in no time flat, we all got to work. We got through two songs and went across the road to the pub. Completely out of the blue, we had Mick Ronson producing our record. I was completely starstruck, but we got along great. He clocked that he and Steve New were kindred spirits and immediately took him under his wing. Mick even gifted Steve his Spiders from Mars stage outfit, with the knickerbocker trousers and the jacket with the glittery lapels.

It probably goes without saying that Mick was a great musician, and because he was on the same wavelength as the rest of us, the sessions were a lot of fun. He was such an innovator in the studio, and he knew so much about the technical aspects of recording, so it was a real learning experience for all of us. He wasn't precious about his own work either. One day, he played back a recording of a guitar overdub that I didn't think worked. He just agreed that it was shit and wiped it from the tape. You would have thought that he would have acted like a star, but he was completely grounded and slotted into our set-up as if he was just another member of the band. One night I went along to the Vortex club with him and we hung out for the evening surrounded by gobsmacked punk kids. As we left, we saw the doorman[2] haranguing a hippy-type couple at the front of the queue.

'I don't care who you are,' he told them. 'You're not getting in.'

As we edged past the scene, both Mick and I laughed when we realised the hippy couple was Cher and Greg Allman of the Allman Brothers, desperate to get in to see what all this punk rock business was about. Because I was hanging around with Mick at the time, I got to work on Ian Hunter from Mott the Hoople's solo album, *You're Never Alone with a Schizophrenic*, and a

---

[2] I knew the Vortex doorman. He was a guy called John Miller and he was the Sensational Alex Harvey Band's tour manager for a while. A couple of years after the Cher and Greg Allman incident, John was part of the gang who kidnapped Ronnie Biggs in the Bahamas and attempted to bring the Great Train Robber back to England to face justice. The kidnap was bank-rolled by *The Sun*.

couple of years later, Mick sounded me out about joining a band he was putting together. Nothing came of it, but just the fact that he called me and asked if I fancied playing bass in his band meant a lot. It was a fun time. But I was also burning the candle at both ends – out most nights, getting smashed and then working hard in the studio the next day.

We were fine-tuning a track one day, 'Cheap Emotions', and I felt that it just needed something else. Mick called Ian McLagan from the Faces, and Mac came down to the studio and played for us. It was a thrill to meet him. He liked us and played at a few of our shows when we went on tour. His playing really filled out our sound. Once Mac came on board, we became firm friends, which is shorthand for drinking buddies. Mac was a funny London guy, with Irish roots and the proverbial heart of gold. Having said that, you didn't want to get on the wrong side of him. For my money, he's right up there with Booker T. Jones as one of the all-time great keyboard players. I even asked if he'd like to join the Rich Kids on a permanent basis. He said it was an honour to be asked, but apparently, he had another session job lined up in Paris with the Stones.[3] Still, I was taken aback to be playing with these guys I used to idolise, and I wouldn't have had it any other way, even if it didn't do much for my punk credentials.

---

[3] This was the first of two occasions the Rolling Stones put a spoke in the wheels and deprived me of a band member. The second was Ronnie Wood being called back into service by Mick and Keith while we were touring with the re-formed Faces.

All the music papers were talking about 1976 being year zero in punk terms. I think my problem, if it is in fact a problem, is that I've always worn my influences on my sleeve. Steve Jones told me recently that he quite likes the Beatles and even a few hair metal bands like Rainbow, but he would never have dreamed of letting that cat out of the bag in 1977. When the Sex Pistols were nominated for entry into the Rock 'n' Roll Hall of Fame, he had an answering-machine message left by Cliff Richard, singing 'Congratulations', and Steve was beside himself. He didn't mind a bit of Cliff. In fact, on one of our later tours, we were pulling out of LA on the tour bus and the bus was surrounded by an army of cheering punks while we were watching Steve's DVD of 'Summer Holiday'. We'd all grown up with the Shadows and Cliff, as well as all that end-of-the-pier British humour, so why deny yourself those pleasures at the risk of being deemed 'uncool'? The Pistols was a very rich broth of different influences. Our trick was to translate those influences into what we did. It doesn't mean you'll hear it in every song, and some are practically invisible, but each of those distinct influences on our lives are part of the stock. According to some writers at the time, all the groups from the old guard were anathema to the punk scene. I don't think I got the memo, but we were all meant to burn our old records and start over, but they forget that Steve, Paul and I first got together because of a shared love of the Faces.

Either way, the Rich Kids' journey from flavour of the month to backlash was sickeningly quick. Some people felt that we'd been overhyped, and I guess there's something in that. The press, who had been on-side when we started out, quickly decided to turn. Once the hype began to fade, we were plugging away, but we were swimming against the tide. There was one particular show that we played in the Midlands, I remember, that wasn't exactly standing room only. When the show was reviewed in one of the music papers, the headline read, 'Anarchy in the UK . . . Apathy in Wolverhampton'. This was the same paper that had been treating us as if we were the Second Coming a few months earlier. It really did turn that quickly.

In certain respects, we were also the architects of our own downfall. First things first, we should have taken more time over everything. The Rich Kids' album is a good record, but I would have liked it to have been perfect. We didn't always make the right choices. Although it was my band, I always wanted to treat the Rich Kids as a democracy, so I tried to give everyone a fair crack of the whip. So, for our second single, we went with one of Midge's songs, 'Marching Men'. At the time, I figured it was right to share the spoils. Partly that was down to politics, to keep Midge in the band. I'd already written the first single, so it seemed only fair to give Midge a break. Ultimately, however, it didn't help our progress. Maybe it was a little naïve lyrically, but I like the sentiment of the song. It wasn't a bad tune by any stretch, but it stalled outside the top forty and suddenly momentum was lost; the eyes of the British public were being drawn elsewhere. In a band, sometimes being too democratic can be a disadvantage. We'd been flavour of the month after 'Rich Kids', but the relative failure of 'Marching Men' marked the end of that. It was frustrating because I'd desperately wanted 'Ghosts of Princes in Towers' to come out and to follow up on the groundswell of enthusiasm after 'Rich Kids' went top thirty. There's no way to tell if it would have fared better in the charts, but personally I think it would have set us apart from the second-division punks that were popping out of the woodwork and denting the top thirty.

I had a conversation with Bob Geldof a few years after the Rich Kids had split. He agreed that our undoing was the choice of second single. If we'd released 'Ghosts of Princes in Towers', there's a good chance our story might have had a tidier ending. Instead, we were already on the back foot, and by the time we released it, the music press had moved on. It felt like a case of right song, wrong time. It was quite dispiriting. We were already demoing some tracks for a second album, working on our own songs separately, which is never a good sign, but really, we had run out of road. Already. We just hadn't realised it yet.

I always try to look at the road ahead, rather than where I've been, so I didn't spend for ever gazing at my navel, wondering what had happened and trying to unpick the past. The album we made showed a lot of promise and I know the second would have been the real deal, had we gotten around to making it. I didn't analyse how things went sideways, but I got an interesting insight into what might have happened from an unlikely source.

A year or so later, in 1979, I'd just played a show at Théâtre le Palace in Paris with Iggy Pop, and the record company in France were laying on a swish dinner for us after the show. Malcolm McLaren, who was in town, had somehow gatecrashed his way into our party, so I wasn't exactly thrilled to have him tagging along. I persuaded Iggy that we should go to a brasserie

I'd read about, La Coupole in Montparnasse. It was a bit of a hike, but La Coupole was a cool place and had been the hub of the artistic and literary crowd in the 1930s. The walls there are lined with Picassos and artworks by all these starving painters who'd had lunch there over the years and paid with their talent when cash was short. Hemingway used to dine there when he was in Paris and Jean Paul-Sartre had his own regular table. Malcolm came along and freeloaded the meal. I wasn't thrilled and I said something to Iggy.

'Well, he's here now,' he said. 'Sorry, Glen. I didn't realise.'

In the end, despite my feeling prickly, I was glad Malcolm came along. Considering how much time we'd spent in one another's pockets, it was one of the last times he and I spoke. We chatted a while and broke the ice. I was still sore about the Beatles telegram, so I was a bit guarded. I'd assumed he hadn't been paying attention to what I'd been doing after I walked out of the Pistols, but we talked a while about the Rich Kids, and his comments were quite insightful.

'Where you went wrong with the Rich Kids was you started to move forward too quickly,' he explained. 'That might have been cool in London, where people are more hip, but you were moving on, and from the perspective of the kids out in the provinces, the punk thing was only just arriving. It might have been old hat to you, but to them it was still brand new. It's as if you were trying to take away this thing of theirs, and so they became less receptive to you.'

I hadn't really considered that, and I think possibly there was something in Malcolm's theory. Maybe if we'd taken a bit of time, stopped and smelled the roses, we might have found a way, but who's to say?

There's a lot of love still for the Rich Kids and what we tried to do, and that is always nice to hear. Looking back, because we positioned ourselves outside of punk and tried to progress our sound into something more melodic, we created a kind of bridgehead from New Wave to the New Romantic movement that was going to define the start of the next decade. The show we played at Barbarella's in the summer of 1978 was attended by the kids who went on to form Duran Duran. I heard at some point, they even tried to get Steve New to join them on guitar. Spandau Ballet's Gary Kemp was a big fan and used to come along to our London shows. Gary even appeared on stage as a guest when we re-formed for a benefit for Steve New in 2010. Later, in 2016, when we got back together for a couple of shows, Gary took over lead guitar duties and played the whole set. Naturally, I announced him onstage as 'Gary Kemp: a real rich kid'. In those first rehearsals he'd often turn to me, grinning from ear to ear. He started telling me about the shows he'd come to see us play at the Nashville when we were starting out and how important we were to him.

'Me doing this,' he said, 'this must be what it felt like for you when you played with the Faces.' He didn't have to say that, but he was sincere, and I really appreciated that. It's easy to forget that amid all the sniping you sometimes get, there's a lot of bonhomie between people in bands.

28

NEW VALUES

In 1979, I made the decision to split the Rich Kids up. In hindsight, it was a tricky moment. The Rich Kids were still contracted to record a second album for EMI, but it soon became clear that was going to be impossible. It's a rock 'n' roll cliché I suppose, but the dreaded 'musical differences' had started to bubble up between us. It was a blow, but as a group we were heading in a different direction from how I originally saw the band. You can spend a lifetime trying to analyse these things, but essentially, Midge and Rusty had a different vision to mine and consequently, the band began to teeter.

I'd introduced Midge and Rusty to Steve Strange and they started working together on Visage. Initially it was a side project, but it started to take off for them. Over the past year or so, they'd become more interested in electronic music, synthesisers and drum machines etc., and I didn't really see the Rich Kids heading down that path. It was slightly ironic, because when we'd signed for EMI, I'd gotten the label to give all the band members complete back catalogues of all those Krautrock bands as a kind of welcome gift. Ultimately, it drove a wedge between the band, so I did what was necessary and we parted ways.

Credit where it's due, however, along with the late Steve Strange, they really started the ball rolling on that whole scene – a scene I just knew intuitively wasn't for me. I felt bad for Steve New mainly. He was always a bit of a wayward spirit. That didn't show itself so much when he was with me in the Rich Kids, but I don't think that my splitting the Rich Kids did him a lot of good in the long run. He was led astray by certain individuals. Obviously, he had some substance abuse issues, but I think a lot of that stemmed from frustration. There was no bitterness, but still, it was a wrench for him.

So, for the first time since before the Pistols, I found myself sitting around at home wondering what on earth I was going to do, wondering if the phone was ever going to ring.

It rang.

'Is Glen Matlock there?' I didn't know the voice, but he had an English accent.

'Yeah, this is Glen,' I said. 'Who's that?'

'Hello, Glen,' he said. 'My name is Peter Davies. You won't know me, but I manage Iggy Pop.' My ears pricked up immediately. 'We're over in London, and Jim would like to meet you,' he told me. 'Are you free to come for a drink?'

'Who's paying?' I said, because it's always worth checking. I went down to their hotel in Piccadilly to meet them later the same day. Iggy and Peter were staying at the Athenaeum, a plush five-star joint overlooking Green Park.

From that first meeting, I have to say, we got along famously. It was easy to identify them in the lobby. Iggy was, well, unmistakably Iggy, but I realised I knew Peter Davies from somewhere, too. It transpired that, as a younger man, he'd appeared in an advert for Ski yoghurt. I said hi to Peter and Iggy leaned across the table to shake my hand. He was tall and tanned, smiling.

'Hi. I'm Jim,' he said.

I don't know what I was expecting from him, but he was extremely well-mannered, polite to a fault, as is often the way with Americans abroad. It was kind of sweet. If someone at a nearby table dropped a napkin or if their coat slipped off the back of a chair or something, he'd pick it up and tap them on the shoulder.

'Excuse me, ma'am, you left your purse on the floor.'

It was disarming. He defied all your expectations of him.

Iggy – or Jim Osterberg, if you want to be formal – had recently made his album *New Values* for Arista Records. Jackie Clark, the guy who played bass on the album, was switching to second guitar for the tour and that had opened the bass spot for someone else. I think what had happened was that John Giddings, our mutual agent, had heard that the Rich Kids were splitting, and he'd thrown my hat into the ring for the Iggy gig.

As with a lot of these meetings, I think it was more to see if Jim and I got along as people. Luckily enough, we clicked right away. I tend to get along with most people, but I think if we hadn't got on, I wouldn't have got the gig. I was happy I was around to take the call, but it was a mutually beneficial arrangement; good for me, but with Jim being kind of a Godfather of the punk thing, it would have been quite a feather in his cap to have a former Sex Pistol in his band, too. Anyway, as I mentioned, Peter was paying, so I took full advantage of their tab and drank a skinful. I was in.

Whenever people ask me what was it like working with Iggy, I always say that he was very professional. That seems a strange thing to say maybe, but that time was a real eye-opener for me. You must remember that everything I'd done up until that point, be it the Pistols or the Rich Kids, had all been done almost on a wing and a prayer. You'd rope your mates in to be roadies and generally they didn't know which ends of which plug went into which socket. Everything was ramshackle. Iggy, on the other hand, had been touring for years at this point, so suddenly I was working in this very slick operation. A well-oiled machine. Managers and assistants and people who knew what they were doing, telling you where you had to be and at what time. Instead of rolling around in a knackered van, I got to fly everywhere. It was a sweet deal. All I ever had to do was arrive on time, know what I was playing and make sure the drink I wanted was on top of my amp when the show started.

After our initial meeting, we started work quite quickly in London at a rehearsal place in Vauxhall called Vanilla, where I met the other guys who were on the tour with Iggy: Klaus Krüger on drums, who'd played with Tangerine Dream, Scott Thurston of the Stooges (and later Tom Petty and the Heartbreakers) on lead guitar and Jackie Clark on rhythm guitar.

Jackie Clark used to play with Ike and Tina Turner, among others, and on stage he wore a Stetson hat and a Nudie Suit – one of those Rhinestone-covered Grand Ole Opry-type affairs from back in the day. With Iggy up front, we made a terrific five-piece. I do remember, however, there was one song in particular, 'Billy Is a Runaway', from the *New Values* LP, and the bass part is kind of a 'slap bass' thing, which is a style of playing I'd never had to do before, and initially I struggled a little with that. When everyone went to lunch, I took some time to practise on my own until I had the technique down. I was just getting the part together when the studio doors swung open and Jim came back from lunch with one of his mates. You get used to people strolling in for a chat when you're in a band, but Iggy Pop's mate was David Bowie, which would have been enough to throw even the most seasoned professional. When I looked up to see Bowie, my heart kind of stopped and all the notes just fell off the fretboard and onto the floor.

'Hello,' he introduced himself. 'I'm David.'

'I know who you are,' I laughed.

'You're Glen, aren't you? The Sex Pistol?'

'Yeah, that's right.'

'Ah, the Noble Savage,' he said, and he waved his hand dismissively.

It wasn't an out-and-out compliment, let's be honest. To be fair, the noble savage dig was the only time that David was ever high and mighty with me. Given it was our first meeting, we didn't exactly get off on the right foot, but we were always fine after that. Whenever I met him, he was always genuinely interested in what I had to say. He always made you feel that you were of consequence. Everyone has their own particular take on what Bowie was like, but to me, he was always a regular bloke. Even so, I was a little irked by his noble savage comment and couldn't resist having a gentle prod back.

'Do you remember your microphones and cymbals that went missing from the Hammersmith Odeon?'

'Yes,' he said, suddenly guarded.

'Well, they didn't half come in handy when we were recording our demos.'

'What do you mean?'

'Steve stole them from the Hammersmith Odeon.' I grinned. Suddenly Bowie didn't seem so sure of himself. 'How does it go, David? The bitter comes out better on a stolen guitar?' It was a line from his song, 'Hang On to Yourself'.

Bowie was flabbergasted to learn that Steve Jones was the notorious 'Phantom of the Odeon' who had stolen his gear in 1973, but he took it in good humour. We always got along famously after that.

29

HEROES

We headed out on the New Values tour in April, with the original, pre-global-fame line-up of the Human League as our support, following us in their transit van. We played up and down the UK for two or three weeks, appeared on *The Old Grey Whistle Test*, then went over to the Continent for shows in France, Spain, Italy, Belgium and Germany, before heading back across the Channel. The tour was a massive success. Over the course of a few days in London, we played sold-out shows at the Hammersmith Odeon, the Lyceum and the old Music Machine in Camden. All the shows sold out in one week. Even if I was only the gun for hire, it felt good to be wanted.

Even though flying was still something of a novelty for me, I wasn't a big fan of air travel back then, so I swapped my flight with one of the roadies and a couple of us drove into Berlin. There was a real sense that you were right on the edge of the western world. Not only did I visit Checkpoint Charlie, but I saw it back when the East German guards still had their guns trained on you. Driving from East to West through the Berlin Wall, the authorities would time-stamp your passport, and you were given a certain amount of time to travel into the rest of West Germany. If you didn't make the journey within the allotted time, there would be serious questions. It felt like Richard Burton's character in *The Spy Who Came in from the Cold*. I saw that film when I was a kid. I went with my aunt and uncle, back when they were giving the idea of having kids a trial run. I think that may have been one of the first movies I ever watched from beginning to end, so it was a strange experience to see that place, where East meets West up close. Bowie's 'Heroes' – recorded at Berlin's legendary Hansa and a chronicle of his observations looking out at the Wall from the sanctity of the studio – started to make much more sense.

One night in Berlin, I went back to my hotel a little worse for wear. I had the hump about something. It was a shitty hotel, coming apart at the seams. I don't think I was really used to touring on that scale before and I'd probably overdone it. Somebody had given me a bottle of champagne and as I went into my room and closed the door behind me, I stubbed my toe on the knackered carpet runner, tripped slightly, and the bottle went flying. It hit the wall and, as if I was in a *Laurel and Hardy* film, all the plaster fell off in one giant sheet and onto the bed. This didn't help my mood at all. I just wanted to get the hell out of there and go home. At 4 a.m., I found myself out in the street trying to flag down a cab to take me to the airport. Of course, no one's going to stop to pick up a drunken Englishman at the crack of dawn, so I don't know what was going on in my head there, to say nothing of the gigs I was contractually obliged to perform. Eventually the tour manager's assistant came out and she took me to another hotel where all the management were staying. I'd calmed down a little and a room was found for me.

When I woke up around three or four o'clock in the afternoon, I had no idea where I was or how I'd got there, so I went down to reception. It was one of those old-fashioned foyers – wrought-iron staircases, ornate ceilings and bellboys rushing around. I walked through reception and found the restaurant and bar and ordered myself a boiled egg and a stein of lager. On the other side of the restaurant, there was a gathering of old German ladies in old-lady-style hats enjoying a very civilised afternoon tea: little triangular cucumber sandwiches and fancy cakes and pastries on a three-tier cake stand. They were all aghast, clutching their pro-verbial and literal pearls over the notion that a hungover punk like me was dragging the class of the place down by several notches. When they started mumbling and complaining to the waiters, the owner of the hotel marched in, clapping his hands furiously.

'Ladies! How dare you?!' he barked. 'Do not be so rude to our guest!' The restaurant fell silent. 'Have you never seen a man eating his breakfast before?'

It turned out that the man who owned the hotel was friends with Iggy Pop's manager, so after I finished my egg and my stein of beer, he came over to my table and asked me to follow him to an adjacent room. He said he had something that might interest me. The room was dark, but when he flicked the light switch,

there were rows of Stockman's tailor's dummies and manne-
quins, and they were all dressed to the nines in these elaborate
costumes. It was like something out of a dream. Or maybe I was
still drunk from the previous night? The owner of the hotel had
been friends with the film director Federico Fellini, and they had
all the old costumes from *Satyricon*, *8½* and *La Dolce Vita* just sitting there in this secret room. It was incredible. I wonder sometimes if that place is still there. This was before the Wall came
down, obviously, so I imagine a lot has changed. I've been back
to Berlin many times, but since the two halves of Berlin became
one, I've never been able to find that place again. It was the
strangest on-tour breakfast I've ever had.

One night after our show at the Neue Welt, I saw another side
of the city. Iggy had an apartment with the girl he was seeing at
the time, but for some reason, he'd had a falling out with the girl,
and she buggered off with the keys. He didn't have a hotel room,
so Iggy decided to cut his losses and suggested we go out after
the show. Iggy knew Berlin backwards from his time there with
Bowie and he took me to this incredible after-hours place. Compared to how drab some towns or cities can be, Berlin was so
vibrant. We finished our show at around 11 and turned up at this
club just before midnight. It was everything you could want from
a night in Berlin: a lavish floor show, glamorous women doing
trapeze acts, and singers performing these old torch songs. It was
like the Bob Fosse movie *Cabaret*, but in real life. As the place was
getting set to close for the night, the woman who ran the cabaret
and a friend of Jim's came over and joined us for a few drinks.
She was a glorious-looking redhead by the name of Romy Haag,

and she accompanied us as we moved on to another club, then another, then another. We were driving around Berlin as the sun came up in this open-topped VW Beetle, me and Romy in the back seat, with Iggy Pop up front with Romy's minder, Sugar.

Romy was an old flame of Bowie's. She was also a famed singer and a trans woman. Romy was very upfront and had spent practically the whole night telling me in minute detail about the surgical procedures she'd undertaken during her transition. Now, if I hadn't had a few drinks and I had taken the trouble to write it down, I think there was enough detail in her description for me to have become a gynaecologist. We had worked our way through most of Berlin's nightlife, and at around 9 a.m. we stopped at one last place for a nightcap. Romy and I were clicking, I thought, so I decided to make a pass at her. At the time, it seemed like the gentlemanly thing to do. So I moved towards her and asked if she was a natural redhead. She looked at me sternly and rose to her feet.

'Glen! How dare you insult a lady and ask such an intimate question!' she said, and promptly stormed off.

Given the gynaecological detail she'd gone into earlier, I didn't think it was such an intimate thing to ask, but there you go. Lesson learned. Iggy moved over to console me. He'd been around a lot longer than I had and no doubt had seen more of life. He said I'd gotten off lightly and started laughing like a drain. West Berlin was a long way from the world I knew. It was a whole world of experience all in one night – all courtesy of Iggy Pop's girlfriend locking him out of their apartment.

30

AMBITION

Iggy was due to record another album, which was a quick turn-around, considering *New Values* was still so fresh in people's minds, but an album a year wasn't unheard of back in the late 1970s. Arista MD Charles Levison was keen to have a new Iggy Pop record in stores ASAP and wanted to strike while the iron was still hot from the tour. Levison was a former lawyer and, for a lawyer, he was quite a cool guy. I understand that he'd funded the sessions for *New Values* out of his own pocket. Jim asked me to work on the album, and following the European leg of the tour, I was delighted to step up to the plate. So, when the tour wound down, we immediately started rehearsing and knocking around new material for the new record. Iggy had a few song ideas and he asked if I had anything that might work. I had a few ideas, some that I'd been considering for the second Rich Kids album that we didn't get around to making. One tune, which was finished by this point, was the song 'Ambition'. Originally, I saw the song as an epic ballad. I wrote 'Ambition' for Celia, my girlfriend at the time. She was a fashion designer and was feeling a bit flat about the direction her career was heading. We were both pursuing similar artistic endeavours and in the long run, we didn't work out, but the song was my way of giving her a little bit of encouragement: 'She's the kind of girl / Who wants that whole wide world.'

I originally demoed the song with the Rich Kids, but we split before we got around to recording it, so I took it to Jim, and he really liked it. Aside from the odd cover of a Bo Diddley[1] song maybe, I don't think Jim had ever recorded someone else's lyrics before then, so it was a cool moment for me. I wrote the song in 4/4 time, but in later years, I've realised the song works better as a blues in 6/8, and that's how I play it live.

---

[1] While we were all hanging out in London between Iggy shows, I went to see Bo Diddley play a show at the Lyceum. After the gig, an *NME* journalist buttonholed me and asked me what I thought of him.

'Pretty good,' I told the journo. 'But I don't know what people would think, or how well it would go down with the audience, if I just sang "Hey Glen Matlock" all night long.'

They printed the quote in the 'Teasers' column they used to run at the back of the paper every week. It was basically a tongue-in-cheek take on the past week's news in rock. When Iggy read the story, he thought it was really funny. According to Iggy, Diddley may have had the Bo Diddley beat – that 'Shave-and-a-Haircut', 'two-bits' beat that originated in some commercial in the States – but maybe he didn't have the greatest songs. Iggy thought Diddley was important, but he wasn't as important as Elvis, because 'Elvis didn't walk around wearing a 10-gallon hat with a "Kiss-Me-Quick" badge on the front'.

Rehearsals for the new album, *Soldier*, took place in Borough, south-east London. The rehearsal studios were in these old, converted alms houses, laid out in a crescent shape, with a communal grass area out front. There are worse places you can spend your time. While we were there rehearsing, I bumped into Andy Anderson, this drummer I knew from around Maida Vale. He was working in one of the other rooms on another project. I'd heard he'd been playing with Nik Turner from Hawkwind, but over the years, Andy played with practically everyone. He had a stint as drummer with the Cure for a while, but his résumé is basically a roll call of interesting people and punk and post-punk luminaries.

'What are you doing round here?' I asked.

'I'm drumming for this bloke,' he shrugged. 'Why don't you pop in and see us when you've finished.'

Later, when we were on a break, I went by his studio and tapped on the door, but no one answered. From the other side of the door, all I could hear was hammering and the grind and buzz of electrical tools. It was 1979, so naturally I assumed Andy was playing in some German Avant Garde, Einstürzende Neubauten-type band and I'd caught them in the middle of laying down some industrial noise for a track. *That's interesting*, I thought, and I knocked again. There was still no reply, so I opened the door a crack and had a peek inside. They weren't creating an industrial noise scape at all, but it was a hive of industry, nonetheless. Dozens of people in crotchet shirts and batik tie-dye garb were scurrying about the place. They weren't creating an experimental Krautrock masterpiece; they were building a PA system. It turned out that Andy was playing with Steve Hillage and I'd just caught a glimpse of a day in the life of Gong. Andy introduced me to Steve, and later that day, I introduced Steve to Iggy, and because it was a nice day, we all decamped to the lawn out front. It was a real, strange bedfellows' scenario: Iggy Pop, Steve Hillage and me, sitting on the grass, smoking some grass.

The whole vibe of the place was quite relaxed, but one day it occurred to Iggy that whenever we were rehearsing, at any given moment, it always seemed that somebody had gone missing from the room. Someone was always sloping off for some reason or another. The assumption was that these musicians were sneaking off for a spot of 'refreshment', so Iggy had a word with the roadie, Henry McGroggan, who is Iggy's co-manager these days and had worked with me during the Rich Kids days. Iggy sent Henry out to get a big plastic dustbin, fill it to the brim with ice and then keep it stocked with beer, wine, vodka, the whole shebang, to keep everybody in the room while we were working.

During rehearsals, at my suggestion, Iggy brought in Barry Andrews from XTC to play keys. It was a weird situation because, when we rehearsed, no one saw Barry playing a single note. Not one. After a while, everyone picked up on it and, because I'd personally vouched for Barry's playing, Jim took me to one side.

'Are you sure about this guy?' he said.

I assured him that Barry was great, and we went back to rehearsals, but all through, Barry didn't play at all. He was just listening intently to the rest of us play. It was kind of odd, but when we finally decamped to Rockfield Studios in Wales to record the album, Barry had all his keyboard lines fully prepared. On the track, 'Loco Mosquito', he created these fan-tastic fairground-style piano runs. It sounds great on the record, but it still rankles slightly that he didn't play one of those notes while we were rehearsing. It was an odd process.

At Rockfield, Iggy was ensconced in his room a lot of the time, writing lyrics for the new songs. He wasn't at all starry, but it was always clear that this was his show. I think sometimes I had to tap-dance around him a little bit, but perhaps he may have felt the same about me. I had a tune I was working on that had the working title 'Forget Me Not'. Iggy liked the song, but I wanted a better title, so Iggy came up with 'Take Care of Me'. The words are great: 'I need somebody to pull me out / I'm sinking like crazy in my sauerkraut.'

David Bowie came along to provide some backing vocals and moral support for his friend. Ivan Král from the Patti Smith Group came down and laid down some guitars and keyboards for the album and I called up Steve New from the Rich Kids to come along and play on the record, although you won't find his name in the credits. With good reason. I'd already recorded my bass parts for the album, so had gone back to London to do a couple of things. When I returned, not long after David Bowie's arrival, James Williamson had walked out of the sessions. He and David had some dispute over the way the album was being recorded, there was a clash of personalities and James felt that Iggy and David had ganged up on him. After that, James stepped away from the music business for the next thirty years, until he got the call to re-form the Stooges. After James walked, all hell broke loose.

Rockfield is situated right in the middle of nowhere, and outside of recording, there is nowhere to go and less than nothing to do, so Steve had called his girlfriend, Patti Palladin, to swing by and keep him company during the sessions. In fact, Patti, a red-lipped, raven-haired US punk who sang with Snatch and had worked with Johnny Thunders, sang backing vocals on the track 'Play It Safe'. They were recording late into the night and apparently, they ran out of cigarettes. Patti went up to hers and Steve's room and Bowie, liberally refreshed at this point, assumed Patti had gone to retrieve some cigarettes secretly stashed somewhere upstairs. Steve New followed and, at the top of the stairs, he saw Bowie being all David Bowie, casually leaning against the door in a coquettish fashion, chatting to Patti. Steve assumed that Bowie was hitting on Patti, which in a way he was, but only to get one of the Marlboro Reds he thought she had in her luggage. He wasn't flirting exactly; he was just turning on that old Bowie charm. Steve, who had not been getting on well with David from the outset, apparently launched himself at Bowie. He landed a punch and the two of them came crashing down the stairs in an angry heap. Consequently, Steve didn't go on the upcoming US tour because he thought Iggy was angry with him, but Iggy just found the whole thing amusing and thought Bowie probably deserved it. It was unfortunate, because when Steve pulled out of the US tour at the last minute, that *did* annoy Iggy, and because I'd brought Steve into the fold, that didn't reflect too well on me. Iggy summoned Brian James from the Damned to cover for Steve, but the consequences of his cancellation were still waiting for me. When the album was mixed in New York, the big guitar riff that Steve played on my song 'Ambition' was taken out of the mix entirely, seemingly because Iggy was still angry with Steve. Unfortunately, the riff Steve played was the hook to my song. I was annoyed when I finally heard the finished mix. The whole character of the song was different and not what I'd intended when I wrote it. A lot of work had been undone, and I had no control over the outcome.

Possibly I could have stayed in the Iggy set-up a while longer. The band was decent and mostly I was enjoying life on the road as part of a professional organisation. There's a lot to be said for having someone on hand to make sure you make the flight on time, booking your hotels and seeing that you hit your marks every night. I think I was just feeling restless. I still think Iggy is great, but I was a bit disgruntled about the way 'Ambition' had been mixed without letting me know. Additionally, and I think uniquely to this situation, I was getting bored of Iggy exposing himself on stage every night. I mean, I guess that's fine, but the thing no one tells you about getting your dick out night after night, is that the dick must be properly 'prepared' before being exposed. That's not in the handbook. And Iggy always seemed determined to 'prepare' his dick right in front of me.

31

LUST FOR LIFE

The US tour that followed the recording of Iggy's *Soldier* album was a very exciting time. On my first ever trip to New York, we played the Palladium on Canal Street. Sadly, the venue isn't there any more, but on Halloween night, we played to more than 3,000 fans. In England, unless you hailed from some little village in Dorset, nobody celebrated Halloween, so to see an entire NYC crowd all decked out in Halloween costumes was something else. We had the Cramps as support and Debbie Harry was hanging around backstage dressed as a witch. We chatted for a while, and she gave me a little peck on the cheek before the show. I was twenty-three, in New York for the first time, playing to a baying crowd and Debbie Harry gave me a kiss, so I had no complaints about how things were going. It was very cool.

I enjoyed hanging out in Manhattan. I stayed a few nights at the Iroquois hotel and there were bands coming over all the time. It was the dawn of the standby fare, so everyone was taking up Freddie Laker's £59 flights from London to New York. British Airways and the other airlines were forced to slash the price of transatlantic flights to win back customers. The upshot was, everyone could afford to fly to New York, so for a while there, it was like a transatlantic bridge. Suddenly, New York was full of English people and London was full of New Yorkers because the fares were so affordable. There was a kind of two-way exodus taking place, and there was a lot of cross-fertilisation between the London and New York scenes. It was a lot of fun. The Slits were in NYC for a while. Chrissie Hynde, my friend from the shop days, was over doing something with the Pretenders, and I got to introduce her to Iggy in McGillicuddy's, an Irish bar that was downstairs from the hotel.

When I had a night off in New York, I went to this place called the Mudd Club. The Mudd Club was a nightclub in the Tribeca neighbourhood of Lower Manhattan and became a kind of post-punk mecca around that time. Even though it was a Monday night, there was still a long queue outside and red velvet rope at the door. I stood outside for a minute and a guy on the door recognised me. He pulled me out of the line and ushered me in past the lines of people waiting to go inside.

'Glen,' he said. 'You don't wait in line in New York.'

I went inside and the Cramps were playing to a packed club. While I was standing at the bar waiting for a drink, taking it all in, I caught sight of a familiar face. It was Frank Zappa. I gave him a nod and we both said hi.

'You want a drink?' I asked.

'Sure,' he said. 'I'll have an orange juice.'

'Come on,' I said. 'Have a drink.' Meaning, have a *real* drink. Back in those days, I was still drinking beer, or if I was in the mood, I'd take a Boilermaker, which was a shot of Bourbon with a beer chaser.

'Just an orange juice, thanks,' he said. 'I'm Frank, by the way,' he added, by way of an introduction, and he reached out to shake my hand.

'Yeah, I know who you are.' I laughed. 'I'm Glen.'

'I know who you are, Glen.'

I tried to not look too happy, but obviously I was chuffed that Frank Zappa knew who I was.

'I'm friends with Jim and he's told me all about you.' As he was talking, he signed an autograph for one of the other hip people in the club. He had to sign a lot of autographs, I noticed.

'Doesn't that get on your nerves?' I said as he signed yet another. 'Coming out and signing autographs all night?'

Frank took a long sip of his orange juice and shook his head. 'It's the only reason I come out on a Monday night,' he said.

As a postscript to the Iggy Pop story, or my part in it, in 2023 I was asked to join a tribute tour to mark the forty-fifth anniversary of Iggy's album, *Lust for Life*. As is sometimes the case, it was quite a last-minute thing. Tony Sales, who played in Tin Machine with Bowie, unexpectedly dropped out of the UK leg of the tour and they were stuck. I got the call from Tom Wilcox, the guy who was putting the tour together, to see if I'd be able to bail them out. The band is Clem Burke from Blondie, Iggy and Bowie collaborator Kevin Armstrong on guitar, Luis Correia, who plays with my mate Earl Slick, Florence Sabeva on keys, and TV presenter and author Katie Puckrik on vocals. We've been playing the whole album, plus songs from everyone's back catalogues, across the length and breadth of the country and it's been a lot of fun. They're all good people, the songs are great, and I always enjoy playing and hanging out with Clem. A lot of these tributes can fall flat, because they are too reverential, I think, and you wind up with a poor man's version of the original. Because Katie's brings a female perspective to the songs, and has bags of charisma, we don't have that problem. It's a pleasure to play those songs, particularly 'Lust for Life', which captures Iggy's searching spirit perfectly. And there's the added bonus that nobody needs to 'prepare' their penis in front of me before we take to the stage.

32

WHITE RABBIT

I have a motto: doff the cap to what's gone before, but always look forward. I don't want to project myself as someone who is consumed with angst, holding onto any bitterness from incidents past, because that's not how I see myself. I'm not a tortured artist, but that's not to say there haven't been ups and downs along the way.

It wasn't immediate, but for a time in the 1980s I went off the boil. I don't think that's too uncommon. With hindsight, I realise that everyone has their moments in life when things aren't working, but I don't know if I could see it when I was right in the middle of it. It was a surreal time, nonetheless. I was never a druggie, but over the course of a few short years, I'd gone from enjoying a drink to being known about town as someone who was more than just a boozer. It didn't take all that long to make the leap from sociable, albeit frequent, drinker to my having a full-blown alcohol problem.

It's a cliché, I know, but when people say it's a slippery slope, I can really relate to that. I had found myself in a place where I couldn't have 'just the one' because I couldn't control my intake. It wasn't even a guilty secret, something confined to the four walls around me, because everyone seemed to know about it. Consequently, I earned myself a bit of a reputation. Very noticeably, the phone wasn't ringing any more. I would say I couldn't get arrested, but as you will see, that's not strictly true. Still, no one was calling, and that was because I was drinking so much, and that got so bad that I'd go out drinking *because* the phone hadn't rung. It became quite a grim cycle. From my experience, it felt more likely that I would perpetuate the cycle, rather than end it. And that's kind of what happened for a while. Everywhere I went, I was Glen Matlock, the guy from the Sex Pistols, then I was the guy who was thrown out of the Sex Pistols, then I was Glen Matlock, the drunk guy who used to be in the Sex Pistols. It was frustrating that people didn't see my value, but at the same time, I wasn't exactly making my life easier by continuing to drink.

Despite the drinking, I was still a grafter. I carried on working as and when opportunities arose for me. I did some work with Patti Palladin, and I played with Johnny Thunders in Japan, Australia and Europe. I did some production work with the London Cowboys, a band I knew, but maybe I was treading water a little. I sometimes think I should have upped sticks and moved to the US, but I'd had a couple of bad flights and I think I had talked myself out of ever getting on a plane again at that point in time. Creatively, I had slowed down, but I didn't lose the desire. I wasn't experiencing writer's block. It's never been an issue for me, as I've never had a record label breathing down my neck, so I've never been subject to deadlines. I was still writing. If I got an idea that stuck in my head, I'd get out the guitar and work on it. A lot of songs or song fragments from that time I held onto and worked into my later records. That's one of the neat tricks to writing a song. Often you have something that's a missing an element and you suddenly remember a middle-eight or a chorus from something you were working on twelve years ago that dovetails nicely into the new song.

One of my usual haunts was a pub called the Bridge House in Little Venice, near where I live. It was a lively establishment that used to put bands on. Back in the day, it was a good place for a lock-in, and all sorts went on in there. David Gilmour, who used to live around the corner, would sometimes turn up and play. It was all bar band-type fare, with food and drink laid on by the pub. You sat at the bar, you ate your meal, drank your beer, and then got back on stage with whoever was still playing. I played there one night with the 1960s R&B group the Pretty Things. I remember their regular drummer wasn't available, so they got their mate from the US, Richie Haywood from Little Feat, to sit in with us. I must have drunk a skinful, because I staggered out at the end of the night and spotted a minicab parked up by the canal near me. I climbed in the back and was about to ask the driver to take me home. When I looked up, there were two police officers looking back at me from the front seats.

'Hello, Glen,' the first officer said, while his partner tried his best not to laugh.

After spending the night in the cells, I began to realise I couldn't keep living life that way. With hindsight, it was an amusing mix-up, and it should have felt like a moment to reflect on. But I just wasn't quite there yet.

Signs, as they say, are always there if you need them, although the signs for me were like something out of a French surrealist movie. Drinking had become such a routine for me that I used to roll out of bed in the morning needing a drink. One morning, I remember heading out of the house and walking up the road to have a straightener. I was at the pub when it opened at 11 a.m. for that first drink of the day, to calm my nerves and stop the shakes. As I was waiting for the doors to open, I realised how daft it was to keep doing this. Standing outside on the pavement, waiting to get a drink on an empty stomach. I had no appetite – I never had any appetite at that point – but I decided to at least try to eat something before I had a drink, so I went and bought myself a packet of crisps from the local shop.

I opened the pack and started eating. I was so jittery with the DTs that when a rubbish truck noisily wheeled past me on the road, I fumbled and dropped the pack of crisps on the pavement. Still shaking, I bent over and picked them up, sat on a wall and started to inspect the crips to see if they were still fit for human consumption. I ate a couple, discarded a couple that looked like they were a bit worse for wear, and then I noticed some words printed on the inside of the pack. I peered inside the bag and read what it said. It said – and I can confirm this was not an alcohol withdrawal fever dream – 'Glen Matlock'. If I was shaking before, I was all over the place now. I stared at the inside of the pack in complete disbelief. They'd even spelt my name correctly – Glen with one 'n', not two. I dropped the pack of crisps again. I genuinely felt like I was going to have a coronary. I clambered down off the wall and waited for my breathing to level out and for my heart to stop pounding, then picked up the packet. Only then did I see the outside of the pack, on which there was a quiz question: 'Who did Sid Vicious replace in the Sex Pistols? See inside pack for answer.'

When I'd composed myself, I walked back across the road to the pub and walked in. The place was completely deserted, but there was a live rabbit sitting on the bar. *Jesus*, I thought. *Now I'm seeing rabbits, like in* Harvey, *the Jimmy Stewart movie.* I walked straight back out and paced around the block, telling myself that I didn't see what I thought I'd just seen. When I returned a few minutes later, the rabbit was still there. Turns out one of the barmaids had brought her new pet rabbit in to show to her colleague, but for ten minutes I thought I was genuinely hallucinating. When I walked in the first time, she must have ducked below the bar or something, but it had looked like I'd just wandered into this weird, dreamlike scene. Even so, just to be on the safe side, I stopped drinking.

I don't want to characterise my life as a tale of woe, or struggle, because I'm always looking for the positives. Life was changing. My time wasn't so much my own as it had been, so it was as good a time as any for me to ring the changes. In the early 1990s I became a father for the first time and my parents' health started to get a bit more precarious. I knew I had to take care of myself so I would still be around to take care of others. There were no months of self-loathing, and there was no intervention. All it finally took was me finding my name in a pack of cheese and onion crisps and thinking I was hallucinating a rabbit in a pub. How's that for a sign?

33

HUNGRY HEART

I'm not necessarily the world's biggest Bruce Springsteen fan, but I am someone who appreciates good writing. I feel much the same about Springsteen as I do about Bob Dylan; I'm an appreciator rather than a rabid fan. They've both written some pretty good songs, some classics obviously, but every now and again, there'll be one song that truly means something to me and gets me right where it hurts. 'Hungry Heart' is one of those songs: 'Got a wife and kids in Baltimore, Jack / I went out for a ride and I never went back.'

Now, at first glance, it's quite a specific lyric, but also, it's universal. I mean, I've been to Baltimore, but you don't need to have been there to connect with what he's singing. I have had a wife and I've had a family, but like in the song, sometimes it doesn't work out as you might have planned it.

I can hear echoes of my own experience in the words. I'm not sure whether it's something to be proud of but, being in the music business, travelling from city to city, the life of a troubadour doesn't always make for the most stable home environment. You can't be around all the time. I mean, over the years I've done a bit of both. I think I've lived quite a steady, regular life, for the most part. I don't have a Learjet or a chauffeur. I go to the corner shop when I'm running low on semi-skimmed. I've done the school run, and I enjoyed doing it very much. I've really loved being part and parcel of my kids' day-to-day lives whenever possible. We're going back a few years, so when I did those kinds of things, it was a little different. Most of the dads were at work, so it was a sea of mums, but if there was a gap between gigs or the projects I was working on, I really valued those moments. I couldn't always do it, of course, because I wasn't always around, and that was a wrench sometimes. Missing a parent–teacher evening or something like that, the mechanics of family life, were sometimes a challenge. On the other hand – because there's always another hand – both my kids got to come to Japan and see the Sex Pistols and hang out with their dad on tour. Not everyone's children get that opportunity. Hopefully that's the thing they'll remember.

One of my favourite family memories stems from the time I was playing with the Faces in 2011. We were booked to fly to Japan, and I was given a first-class business ticket, which I exchanged for two economy flights and took my son Louis along for the ride. We played the Fuji Rock Festival and he got to hang out with us the whole time we were there. Not long before, he'd shown an interest in photography. So I'd bought him a camera and he brought it along with him to the photographer's pit at the front of the stage. Normally, the pit photographers are only allowed to take a handful of pictures at the start of the show and then have to bugger off, so their flash photography doesn't distract the performers or spoil the show for the audience. This night, as we were playing away, really enjoying ourselves, Ronnie Wood sidled across the stage to me and told me to look up. I was concentrating on my bass parts and hadn't really been paying attention to the flash bulb going off every now and then. There in the pit was Louis, on his own, in front of 50,000 people who'd come to see us, click-click-click, still taking photographs. It's not traditional parenting, I guess. It's not a school run or a parent teacher association meeting, but it's kind of a cool memory for us both. He took some great photographs, and they were used on the Faces website. I used to have the Faces poster from *A Nod Is As Good As a Wink* on my bedroom wall in Kensal Rise and here was my son taking their picture on stage.

I have a good relationship with my kids, so I know I'm lucky in that respect. They're both musicians and I think I've managed to instil the same kind of work ethic in them that I've had all my life. They're not spoiled kids who've had everything handed to them along the way. Just as an example, when Sam, my older son, decided he wanted a guitar for Christmas, I picked out one of my old guitars and said he could have it. It was a cheaper one, a Jedson Les Paul copy, but not a bad guitar by any stretch, and it was certainly good enough for a player who was just starting out. I said if he proved he was committed, that he'd apply himself, we'd look at getting him a better one down the line. To his credit, he did. He wound up getting a nice Gibson SG, a combined birthday and Christmas present. He appreciated it more, I think, because he had to work a little harder for it. He's doing so well with his band now he has a sponsorship deal with Gibson.

More recently, Sam landed a role in the Danny Boyle *Pistol* series. With the Pistols, I sometimes get a feeling that I'm always the last to know anything, but a couple of years ago, I started to hear a few whispers that there was a show being made about the original punk scene. All the teenagers in London seemed to be attending auditions and I asked Sam if he'd heard anything about it. He was a bit cagey with me. He said it was just some punk thing that he'd tried out for. He quite fancied himself playing Billy Idol, he told me.

Eventually the Pistols management called me. As I said, always the last to know. It transpired that it wasn't just some punk-flavoured thing; it was a show about the Pistols. They were making a TV drama based on Steve Jones's memoir, *Lonely Boy*. Danny Boyle was directing and I was invited to meet with him a couple of times. I told Danny I had some fears about the project I wanted addressed before I signed anything, but he assured me it was going to be the real deal and I didn't need to worry. Having had my fears assuaged by Danny, I signed off on the project because I thought Steve, the one who'd formed the band, should have the right to tell his story his way. I signed off, Paul Cook signed off, but there was a major brouhaha when John brought about a legal challenge when he got wind of the production.

He felt it should be a unanimous agreement across the band, so he took it to the high court and lost badly. In a way, I think that legal defeat for John was the final death knell for any chance of a Pistols reunion, but I don't personally see myself playing on stage with someone in a MAGA hat anyway. It was a painful, expensive loss, I imagine, but he had bad advice. John lost his wife Nora soon after the case, so my heart goes out to him. I knew Nora a little over the years and she was a great person. Unfortunately, so much water has passed under the bridge, I don't think John and I will ever be reconciled. I speak to Paul and Steve regularly, and if we're in the same part of the world, we see each other, but John isn't interested. He has my number. He can call me any time and I'd have a civilised chat with the guy. But in all the years we've known each other, even when the band reunited in 1996 and 2007, he never has. Not once.

By the time I had the meeting with Danny about the production, Sam had cooled on the idea of being involved, but when we spoke, Danny was enthusiastic about his audition.

'Oh, I remember Sam,' he told me. 'We were very interested in him but he kind of removed himself.'

'Removed himself? Who did you want him to play?' I asked.

'Didn't he tell you? It was Johnny Rotten.'

Well, it was no wonder he'd been so cagey when I asked him about it, I thought. Anyway, Sam wound up taking a small role, playing Danny Kleinman, the singer with Bazooka Joe. Props to him, because he's very good. To be honest, I think he's one of the only good things in it. I don't want to open a whole can of worms, but it was a mess. I was given a personal screening at the film company and invited a couple of friends along. I genuinely couldn't believe what I was seeing. It was all bullshit. Afterwards, I was on tour in the US with Blondie, so I attended a red-carpet event in Hollywood. Steve was there, and so was Sam. Steve asked me what I thought, and I told him he had a shocking memory. When I saw Danny Boyle, I was a bit more forthright.

'Danny, you're a cunt,' I said. 'I would never have signed up if I'd seen the script.'

Steve Jones might be the beating heart of the Pistols, but he has the worst recall of anyone I've ever met. I didn't understand how a multi-million-dollar project got off the ground without anyone doing any proper research beforehand. I was assured my concerns would be addressed but, ultimately, they were ignored. In the end I think they just wanted me for a few red-carpet events, to bring a bit more cachet to the project. I was pissed off about the whole thing.

My kids are doing alright, so everything has worked out on that front, but sometimes, I still feel like my heart is on the road and that it's almost impossible to settle, to accept a kind of blissful domesticity. I've shared my life with some people who don't see the world like that. It's not nasty, I think, but sometimes it feels difficult to reconcile this life with someone whose hopes and dreams conflict with my instincts to keep playing. Living as a musician – or as any kind of artist – isn't a conventional job. I think that's half of the appeal. I don't think that makes you cold-hearted; it's just that your mind is often racing with a thousand ideas. Part of being a songwriter, it seems, is that your mind is almost permanently distracted.

There's always a song idea floating around somewhere in the back of your mind, tugging at your coattails. It's a difficult situation to navigate sometimes. I remember from my time working with Iggy, a lot of his songs were about that kind of hunger; he was hungry as a horse, hungry for love, hungry for you or whatever. Now, personally, I've never been *that* hungry in my life, but I understand what it's like to have a hungry heart. To have something not work out, or maybe you make the decision yourself that it's time to move on. I think that's what the song says to me personally. You're always searching for that something else that's just out of reach, whatever that may be.

I've heard it said that you should never go out with a musician. My answer to them is that it's probably better than going out with a drummer.

34

FILTHY LUCRE

A couple of weeks after I walked out on the Pistols, and Malcolm had sent the telegram to the *NME*, he called me up out of the blue and asked if we could meet up. I was still pissed off, but I deigned to meet up for a drink at the Blue Post pub behind the 100 Club. He didn't mess around with any preamble. He got straight to the point and asked me to rejoin the band.

'It's not working out with Sid,' he told me. He wanted me to come back, kick down a few doors, that kind of thing. Be more of a larger-than-life character within the group. Essentially, he wanted me to behave more like Sid, but play better and, maybe most importantly, continue chipping in with the songs. I'm quite a self-aware person. I knew full well, possibly because I was younger than the other guys, that I wasn't as self-assured as the rest of the band. I wasn't a wallflower, by any means, and I had come out of myself, but it's difficult to be as confident as someone like Steve Jones, who was a right likely lad and essentially spent his formative years living on the streets. I wasn't going to pretend to be something that I'm not. I thought that was the whole point of punk. I could have gone back, but it felt like more trouble than it was worth. I'd been wounded and I'd genuinely lost interest pretty quickly. Call it self-preservation if you want. I don't know if it was the right move. I can say that maybe we might have weathered the storm a while and possibly kept it together long enough to make a couple of albums, but it seems obvious we weren't going to be around for decades and have a massive back catalogue. Given everything that had happened, I declined. I had my own ideas. Malcolm and the rest of the band had said so much shit about me in the intervening weeks, I thought he had a bloody nerve to ask. I considered his proposal for a minute and then I told him to fuck off.

There'd been whispers of a Sex Pistols reunion before 1996. Anyone who's ever been in a band has to get used to re-treading the same tired ground in every interview. You talk briefly about your new record or the show you're playing at the weekend, but they're always lying in wait with their 'will they/won't they?' questions. In the early 1980s, when the Rich Kids were done and dusted, and I'd finished my tour of duty with Iggy Pop, I heard the occasional rumour floating around that we were set to re-form. I understand Malcolm was looking to put the original line-up back on the road, and possibly back in the studio. No one contacted me directly, but it was out there on the grapevine. At the time I was probably drinking too much and from what

I can gather, Malcolm was preparing to send me to a drying-out clinic, but nothing came of it.

Any chance of Malcolm getting to step up and play Svengali again went up in smoke a few years later when John, Paul and Steve took him to court over unpaid royalties from the band. I wasn't party to that, but essentially Malcolm had sunk the band's money into *The Great Rock 'n' Roll Swindle* movie and the three of them weren't seeing any income at all. From the outset it looked like he wasn't going to win, so rather than be saddled with the court costs, Malcolm was forced to withdraw and settle out of court. I was still getting my 25 per cent of the songwriting, so financially I was ticking over okay, but John, Paul and Steve were getting nothing. I guess the court case marked the end of Malcolm's pipe dream of a reunion. There were occasional rumours that maybe there were plans afoot without McClaren's involvement, but that's all they were. I'd reconnected with Paul by this time, but I didn't see or speak with Steve and John until that day in Los Angeles almost ten years later. In the meantime, no one called me. And I didn't really expect them to. I imagined if the band ever did try to get back together that they'd have their pick of bassists, but I think it says a lot that when talk of the Filthy Lucre tour began to circulate, I was the man they turned to.

Given how small the crowds were during our 1976 heyday, the reunion was a major event. We spent six months on the road and brought the show to six continents – we gave Antarctica a miss. We played seventy-two dates, all told. A further six were cancelled by the authorities. *Plus ça change*. We played to 115,000 fans at the Roskilde festival in Denmark. The London show in Finsbury Park was a highlight, playing right at the height of the Euro '96 tournament. That felt especially good because the first couple of shows of the tour were a bit cagey. We were jetlagged, and I wasn't sure it was working. But at Finsbury Park, I felt as if we'd really hit our stride. I don't know where they'd been hiding all these years, but the whole crowd was a sea of punks and Mohican hairstyles. England players Gareth Southgate and Stuart Pierce, who was a big punk fan, introduced us onstage. After that, I think we brought our A-game to every city we played.

I don't want to be vulgar, but we made a few quid. We mended some fences and built some bridges along the way, but some of the familiar tensions were still there. We have something in common that no one else on the planet can lay claim to: we are Sex Pistols, and I think that's something that should be celebrated. John said later that we got back together and suddenly remembered that we all hated each other. I don't know about that, but I think we eventually came to realise that John was still the same tricky character he'd always been, and maybe even more so. We re-formed for two further tours in 2002 and 2007, basically because the money on offer was too good to turn down.

The truth of the matter is, whether you're talking about John, Paul, Steve or myself, nothing any of us has ever done has eclipsed the Sex Pistols, and whatever we do in life will always be measured against that. I answer questions about the Sex Pistols every single day of my life. Like it or not, the Pistols are a big part of a lot of people's lives. People want it, so just give it to them. And we should be paid for that. Everyone else is making a mint off our name, so why not us? We worked hard, even if we didn't all get along, and ultimately, we found ways to make it work. On the later reunion tours, Steve had to suggest we travel in two separate tour buses to separate hotels. If we had to fly, we took different flights. I don't need to explain the tension, but put it this way: the people who played instruments ended up in one coach and hotel, and the people who didn't were in another. I said to Steve that this was costing us a fortune.

'But this way, we'll finish the tour,' he said. 'And we'll get paid.'

Ultimately, it was a case of 'too much too soon'. We wound up as four separate trains, on a collision course. It could have been so different. When we held our first tentative talks about the reunion, I'd suggested we write and record a bunch of new material. I thought it might add a sheen of credibility to our endeavour.

We rehearsed for probably six weeks in Los Angeles, in between a cycle of press conferences and interviews and promotional stuff. We tried a couple of things, but it was clear that John just wasn't interested. Somewhere there's a recording of me, Steve and Paul at Guns N' Roses' rehearsal place with Chris Thomas. We laid down a couple of tracks, one of Steve's and one of mine. Chris felt that if John wrote some lyrics, we had a hit on our hands, but John didn't want to play ball. There was a divide in the ranks over whether it should sound like the Pistols recordings of old, and John didn't want to be tied to the old sound. I didn't necessarily think it was regressive if we sounded like the Sex Pistols. What makes the song contemporary is the lyrics.

I can't put myself in the guy's shoes, but maybe John felt it was a backwards step. I don't know because none of us ever spoke to each other properly. That was always our problem in the Pistols. With the reunions, the problem was exacerbated by the fact that in dealing with John, you always had to go through a buffer. Over the years, John's built a wall of spiky, cantankerous middlemen around him. You never spoke with him one on one, so that made it even harder to try to convince him. My take was that if we weren't happy with the finished songs, we weren't under any obligation to release them.

I even pitched the idea of us writing and recording a rock opera, based on the life of Sid Vicious, called simply *Sidney*. We missed a trick there. I realise it would have been an outlandish move, but it could have been interesting. Even if it had been a swing and a miss, I like the idea that twenty-five years down the line, people would be saying, do you remember when the Pistols made a rock opera? It would have been a genuine curveball, and we could have had a lot of fun with the subject matter. People like to write their own history books, so it's always assumed that there was bad blood between Sid and myself, but my beef was with the rest of the guys and Malcolm. Sid and I weren't the best of friends, but we weren't enemies by any stretch. I always got on okay with him. We lived around the corner from each other in Maida Vale for a while, and after the Pistols spectacularly flamed out on that American tour in 1978, we used to bump into each other from time to time. I remember one occasion we were having a drink in my local.

'It's weird how people think we're enemies,' he said. 'But we're sitting in the pub together having a drink. How do you think we could prove it to people that we get along?'

I didn't think we needed to prove anything, but if he really needed to show people that we got on alright, I proposed we play a gig. It might even be a laugh, I said optimistically. I suggested getting Steve New from the Rich Kids on guitar and Rat Scabies on drums. Around that time, Rat had fallen out with the Damned and had another band called the White Cats. We took a bit from everyone's names and played as the Vicious White Kids. It was just something we did for fun, so it's always strange when it's written about as some kind of seismic moment in history or a punk supergroup. I do recall that when we sound-checked, Nancy Spungen, Sid's girlfriend, got up on stage to join us. I went over to the sound guy and before I even said a word, he told me, 'Don't worry. I've switched her mic off.'

Between Filthy Lucre shows in New York, Paul, Steve and I hung out for a while and took a bit of time to decompress. While we were there, we bumped into Clem Burke and he confided to me that Blondie also had plans to re-form, but not until they had written some new material and had a record in the can. A year or so later, they had a worldwide number-one with the song 'Maria', so it was clearly a decent plan. If anything, they showed us that we'd missed a real opportunity.

We took to the road a couple more times over the years, most recently the world tour of 2008. That year, after a show in Washington, we travelled overnight to New York for a spot on *The David Letterman Show*, which was recording the following morning. To kill time on the tour bus, Steve found a DVD of the Cheech & Chong stoner movie, *Up in Smoke*, to keep us amused on the drive. The next morning, while we were waiting in the green room at the Ed Sullivan Theater in midtown Manhattan, there came a knock on the door. I opened it and there was Cheech, standing outside. Or it could have been Chong, to be fair. Apparently, Cheech (or Chong)[1] shared a manager with John and just wanted to tell us to 'break a leg' before the show. From the *Letterman* performance, we hotfooted our way to soundcheck at our show at the Roseland Ballroom. John didn't like anyone being there when we did our soundcheck, but I did notice a couple of people lurking behind the PA stack. A little later, Steve introduced me to the pair. It was Uma Thurman and Steve's friend from AA, Dennis Hopper.

The last show we played together in 2008 was at the Azkena Rock Festival in Vitoria in Spain. Ray Davies from the Kinks was on the bill too, playing a solo show. I plucked up the courage and popped by Ray's dressing room after he'd finished his set. The dressing rooms were in this warehouse-type building, divided by these walls that didn't quite reach the top of the ceiling, so you could hear the people next door talking. I knew John had the next dressing room along from Ray's, so I was being careful with what I said, just in case he overheard and got the hump with me.

---

[1] Further research on this matter confirms that it was Cheech Marin, who was on the *Letterman* show with us that day.

Ray was having his dinner, but he asked me to stay and talk with him while he ate. He complimented me on all the songs I'd written. I explained that I'd done bits and pieces, but ultimately the Pistols were kind of a collective consciousness. Ray shook his head.

'Come off it, Glen,' he said. 'I used to take my songs into the Kinks, and we'd argue hammer and tongs about the arrangements. It used to get physical sometimes, but I always won because someone's got to be in charge.'

He started laughing while I desperately tried to shut him up for fear of incurring the wrath of a scowling Lydon on the other side of the inadequate partition wall.

35

OPEN MIND

The Filthy Lucre tour ended in early 1997 with a run of stadium dates in South America. I didn't return to England immediately because I wanted a bit of breathing space and to take stock. I came back a few months down the line to find the world had continued to turn in my absence. I wasn't exactly expecting a ticker tape parade on my return, but the world felt suddenly indifferent to me again. It was a bit of a wakeup call, to be honest. I realised I needed to get back to the routine I'd tried to establish before history came knocking on my door and the Pistols reunited. To some extent, I picked up where I'd left off with the *Who's He Think He Is When He's at Home?* album I'd released on Creation in 1996. The Pistols reunion had been lucrative, but it became clear once we'd re-formed that it wasn't going to be a case of together for ever. Then the old century ground to a close and the new millennium began. I'd become used to the Pistols money coming in, but now I realised I'd have to go back to cutting my cloth according to my means.

There was a lot going on in my life at the time. The relationship I was in was on the wane, so although I'd been in worse headspaces, I found that I still had a lot to get off my chest. The Y2K bug didn't get me, I'd survived six continents with the Pistols, and I had a few songs rattling around in the back of my mind. I felt it was important that I keep my hand in, keep honing my art. The old adage about inspiration vs perspiration is worth bearing in mind. Inspiration does come, but it's crucial that you work at it. It's part and parcel of the craft of songwriting. If you're like me, you come to see the flaws in your work much more clearly than your worst critic, but looking back on the album I made next, I do think there are a dozen good songs and no filler.

The album was called *Open Mind* and came out under the banner 'Glen Matlock and the Philistines'. I wanted to name the band the Philistines because it seemed a nice, self-effacing moniker, in the same way that Ian Dury had his Blockheads. You'll note that it's *and* the Philistines. *They're* the Philistines, not me. The Philistines were a loose conglomeration of mates who could play a bit and who were around at the time and fancied doing something together. I always figured that when we scored enough hits, I could release a 'best of' album under the title *Complete and Utter Philistines*, but it didn't work out like that. Because we didn't have decent promotion behind us, we'd arrive at the venue and most of the time, the posters wouldn't mention the Philistines at all. They generally always read,

'Ex-Sex Pistol Glen Matlock'. It was kind of disappointing. I have a theory that practically anyone with some degree of musical aplomb can make a record, but if there's no promotion behind it, it's hard to break through the noise of all the other stuff that's going on in the world. It can be a galling experience if people don't like your record, but it can be heartbreaking if they don't even know you made it. And that's the fate that befell *Open Mind*. I have a soft spot for the title track particularly, which was a meditation on my own experience when all anyone wanted to talk about was my past and I felt like I couldn't get arrested in the present day.

There are a lot of links to my past littered across the whole album. Not least the personnel. Steve New, my old brother in arms, plays on a few tracks. Mike Peters from the Alarm is there. I wrote a song with Patti Palladin, and Mick Jones even turned out for one of the sessions. He's credited on a track, at least. He came down to the studio, a little stoned, and jammed along on the tune, but none of it was particularly useable, so we had to fiddle around with Mick's guitar part. Still, when I played the tune back to him, he seemed impressed with his own contribution.

'Sounds pretty good,' he said. 'Are you sure it's me?'

In 2004, I released the album *On Something*. I don't know if it's still in everyday use, but I always associate the phrase 'on something' with the older generation. When I was a kid and there was a news report on the TV about someone doing something a bit wild, my mum would always say, 'Oh, he must be on something.' If ever there was a spot of bother at a discotheque or in a town centre, it was always the same. *They must be on something.*

When I started putting the lyrics down, I think I was harking back to my drinking days. Or, rather, the days since I packed it in. There's something that doesn't get talked about too often when you've been on the wagon for a few years, and it's that sense that life is all very one-paced. No peaks or troughs, just a bit . . . flat. My drinking days were a few years in the past, and I certainly didn't miss the chaos or waking up feeling dreadful, but one of the things I found after my recovery was that everything was always on the same level. Always fair to middling. Obviously, it's a good thing that there were no more crushing lows, but there were no dizzying highs either, and I'll be honest, I kind of missed them.

I'd gone from leading this charmed, chaotic life to a life of no ups and no downs. Deep down, I absolutely understood that I didn't want to go back, but I missed that sense of excitement in my life. There was a nagging voice in the back of my mind telling me I could take a little tipple and not backslide into drinking. But I knew that was rubbish. I know it's a destructive impulse, but in a way, my getting over the drink left me feeling rudderless. I wasn't living my life by the bottle any more but, in the parlance of my mum, a small part of me kind of wished sometimes that I was on something. I think on some level, I wanted just a momentary respite from middle-aged torpor. 'On Something' is me acknowledging that frustration. You don't want to lose what you've got, but equally you maybe feel like there's something missing.

As I've mentioned, usually I prefer to look at life from a more positive viewpoint, but although the song has some regret about losing one aspect of my life, it's also me saying, *I can't afford to go back to it because I have too much to lose.* However tempting it might be to experience that feeling of being *on something* again, I know it wouldn't end well.

The album, my second record under the Glen Matlock and the Philistines banner, came out of Liberty, which is part of EMI Records, but it wasn't like a 'conquering hero returns' moment. The music business had moved on in the early 2000s and I don't think the people there really understood what I was about. We recorded the album and shopped it around, and ended up at Liberty, but in truth, the record could have come out on any label. All the old guard of the music business I used to know had moved up – or on – and I was just dealing with the new breed of record executive, who were happy to have a Sex Pistol come by for a meeting because it's something to tell the wife and kids. But when push comes to shove, they really didn't know what to do with your records and they didn't take your calls once they'd ushered you out of meeting room two. It's not just me; it's a generational thing to some extent I'm sure. But you keep plugging away and you hope that someday, you do make the right connection.

36

TOMORROW ZERO

I loved Steve New. He had such fantastic ability, but he got lost somehow. He kind of slipped between the cracks, but given the breaks his talent deserved, the right band maybe, he would have been one of the greats. He was prodigiously talented, but he was also a real laugh to be around. He was the Jack Benny of the Rich Kids. Always there with a ready quip or one-liner. He was such a big part of my life.

After the Rich Kids, Steve put himself out there and did some interesting work. He toured with Johnny Thunders for a while, as well as Patti Palladin and Wasted Youth, among others. He played guitar on the Generation X track 'Dancing with Myself'. I heard that prior to getting Steve in the studio, they'd tried every guitarist in London. Generation X's Derwood Andrews, Steve Jones and Danny Kustow all got the call, and while each of them had a crack, no one could get it right. Steve came along and just nailed it. Like most of us, he did everything to the best of his abilities, but he always managed to add his own flourish. He also penned a few terrific songs, but they're kind of unheralded. One was called 'Forever and Ever', which alluded to Midge's number-one hit when he was in Slik, and there's another called 'Tomorrow Zero' which is genuinely great and makes me wish sometimes that we'd sorted out our differences and recorded that second Rich Kids album.

There were a lot of people who picked up a guitar for the first time after they heard 'Anarchy' on the radio or saw us on Grundy and treated it as a call to arms. There were a lot of two- and three-chord wonders on the scene, but Steve New had been honing his craft for years. Before he auditioned for the Pistols, he was a member of the London Youth Jazz Orchestra – under the stewardship of my old French teacher from Danes – and had a wealth of influences from right across the spectrum. He worshipped Frank Zappa and had an encyclopaedic knowledge of every kind of music.

I remember once he took me to see a show at the 100 Club, by this avant-garde free jazz guitarist, Derek Bailey. He looked a bit like Jake Thackray, the poet and folk singer who used to be on TV when I was a kid. It was a jazz crowd, so a hundred miles away from some of the nights I'd seen at the 100 Club, but Steve was beside himself. He was always turning me on to new stuff. I have great memories of hanging out in his bedroom at his mum and dad's place and him playing me the Derek and Clive album and the pair of us rolling around in hysterics. He even joined John as a member of Public Image Limited for a while as a violinist. When I asked if he could play the violin, he said no, but how hard could it be? That was always his approach. He just had so much self-belief.

Steve always liked to dress up in frocks and outrage people. In his later years, he went by the name and persona Stella Nova. As he put it, he 'felt like he'd been a tranny since day one'. It wasn't something I was that aware of, but I've always been a live-and-let-live person. To me, he was this lovely, affable person, so whatever he wanted to do, or whoever he wanted to be, good for him. Over the years, he'd always dabbled in a bit of this and that, and there were also more serious substance addiction problems. And although I don't want to paint him as this kind of tortured artist, I do think he was a frustrated one. He knew, as we all did, that he was so much better than where he'd ended up. Then one day he started to get sick. By the time he was diagnosed with liver cancer, it was all a bit too late to do anything about it. The cancer wasn't related to his lifestyle; it was some hereditary thing. When he started to get ill, I got a call out of the blue from Midge asking if I'd heard the news about Steve. I'd heard a couple of things, but not in any detail. Midge told me and suggested we could do something for him.

'Perhaps we could do a testimonial,' he said. A testimonial used to be kind of a football club's parting gesture to an old player who was about to retire. Still, I knew what he meant. You probably need to know Midge to understand these little Glaswegian idiosyncrasies of his. It still makes me laugh that he used to refer to going to a gig as attending 'a function'.

We worked quickly and put together a Rich Kids reunion show at the Academy in Islington in January 2010. Because it was for Steve, everybody came out of the woodwork. Steve played a set with his band, Beastellabeast, a duo with Beatrice Brown, who was this cool bohemian singer he was working with. You could see he was sick by then. But he seemed so brave. I was so proud of him. I remember there was an issue with the sound and he was upset. From his perspective, it was his last big moment, and he'd wanted everything to be just so. In that sense, he was a perfectionist to the very end.

At the end of the night, the Rich Kids played and everyone who'd performed through the evening got up on stage. Mick Jones, Tony James, Viv Albertine and TV Smith all joined us, along with Steve. Gary Kemp, who'd followed us around our London shows in 1977 and 1978, got up and played a couple of songs. I like Gary a lot. When we were rehearsing, he was running around the stage, giving it all the rock-star poses.

'Calm down, mate,' I told him. 'The gig isn't until tomorrow.'

Steve was sick for about a year, but even so, it still felt a bit sudden when he passed. I was over on the Isle of Wight when he was taken into hospital and placed on life support. Everybody gathered at his bedside. Patti Palladin, his former flame, was there, along with all his ex-girlfriends who held vigil in Steve's hospital room. He was always very popular with the ladies, even to the end. There was always so much love and goodwill for him. Even after a relationship had run its course, he still had enough charm to keep them in his life. They put in a call to me on the Isle of Wight to tell me Steve was near the end, and I hotfooted it to the ferry. I think I'd been mentally preparing myself, but it still came as a shock. After we were about to pull into the mainland, the boat developed a mechanical issue, and we couldn't dock. I was frantic, stranded in the Solent, waiting for the ferry to be repaired, while in London they were waiting to turn off Steve's life support. It was just a dreadful moment. When we finally docked, I pulled off the ferry and sped up the A3. I got there just in time to spend a few short minutes at his bedside and to say my farewells before he finally slipped away. It's often said that your hearing is the last thing to go, so I like to think my words got through. It was so sad. He was always such an inspiring person to be around. When he answered our ad in 1975, he was every bit the Whizz Kid guitarist we were looking for, but he meant a lot more than that to me. Even if he didn't get that haircut.

When it came to Steve's funeral, I said I'd arrange the carriage that carried his casket. As the day of the funeral drew closer, I was struggling to find six men to carry his coffin. In the end, I found them, but in the meantime, Emma Boulting, the daughter of filmmaker John Boulting, one of the Boulting Brothers, came up with a poignant idea. Emma suggested we should have Steve's ex-girlfriends carry the casket. It was such a touching idea I regret not doing it. I know Steve would have found it funny.

37

BORN RUNNING

When I have something playing on my mind, writing a song is sometimes the best way to clear the decks and work out my feelings. The song 'Born Running' is a good case in point. It didn't work out, but I remember I was sweet on a girl at the time, and I was feeling frustrated with certain aspects of my life. Then I heard the horrible news about Steve New's health. When Steve had his cancer diagnosis, it struck me that right from the moment we're born, we're all running out of time. The clock is ticking from the second it starts. Time goes so quickly, but it goes even more quickly when you know you're nearing the end: 'But that wheel keeps on turning / There ain't no turning back.'

The album *Born Running* saw me back on an indie label, after the one-time album on Liberty Records. Again, it was an album that was practically complete before I signed the deal. Even so, it took the label the best part of a year to release the record, which was a little frustrating. I think sometimes when you work to other people's schedules, it can hamstring your progress. Possibly, I'm just not a great businessman. There's a chance that's true. Maybe I'm not as skilled at selling myself. I love writing, I love recording and playing live, but the constant need to keep hustling can be quite exhausting, both mentally and physically. I started out as a hustler, chasing all the early gigs with the Pistols, then putting the Rich Kids together, so I'm no stranger to putting myself out there, but all the hustling can be a massive drain. It eats away at your time. It reminds me of that Charlie Watts quote, when he was asked how he felt about his twenty-five years on the road with the Stones: 'Work five years and twenty years hanging around.'

Today it's probably about 90 per cent hustle and you're left with maybe 10 per cent to divide between being creative and trying to live your life. If you're lucky enough to have a runaway success, this is an easy business to work in. Suddenly you're in a position where everyone is chasing you and hanging on your every word. If, on the other hand, it's you that's doing the chasing, it becomes a whole different ball game. Besides anything else, I consider myself to be quite a laissez-faire sort of personality, so the idea that I'm meant to go around blowing my own trumpet is counter-intuitive to me. Possibly it's a hangover from the punk days when nobody wanted to be seen to be selling out. Possibly it's just that times have changed, and I need to develop a thicker skin. I'm not complaining because I appreciate my lot in life. I don't sit down and compare myself to other writers or my peers from the punk days and the breaks they might have got that I didn't. Maybe it's not for me anyway. I do realise I was always a bit of a square peg in a round hole. But I'd be lying if I said I wouldn't like to have had more success in my own right and on my own terms. It's not something that I've ever really experienced. But this is still the best living I know. And for that I'm grateful.

38

MY WAY

The last time I saw Malcolm was in 2009, a year before he died. I was hanging out in New York, staying at a friend's place. My career was on a bit of an upswing, and I felt like I was going places. I was strolling down University Place one day, just down from Washington Square. I had a nice tan going and was wearing a dapper suit when I spied a familiar face coming the other way. It was Malcolm.

He was deep in conversation with a woman, his agent. As they walked closer, it became clear he either hadn't noticed me coming, or he was making out that he hadn't seen me, so I flagged him down and gave him a cheery hello. I was looking and feeling good. So, I'll be honest, I wanted to make sure he saw me.

'Matlock?' he said. He looked as if he'd just seen a ghost. 'What . . . what are you doing here?'

'Everybody's got to be somewhere, Malcolm,' I said.

I tried to make chitchat for a couple of minutes, but it was clear from his demeanour he wanted to be somewhere else. He started making his excuses and the pair of them walked off in the opposite direction. He seemed a little subdued, not like himself at all, but he looked fine. Maybe a year later, I heard on the grapevine that he was gravely ill. He died in April 2010 from peritoneal mesothelioma, which is a particularly aggressive cancer that attacks the lining of the abdomen. He was only sixty-four years old, so you'd like to think he still had a few more years' worth of mischief left in him. It was a drag. I always thought that there might be some future in which we could bury the hatchet and, not reconcile exactly, but get over our differences. When he died, that window closed for ever.

I didn't go to the funeral, but there was a memorial service held at a deconsecrated church at the top of Great Portland Street. Paul Cook and I attended the memorial, but it turned into a bit of a pantomime, which I suppose was kind of fitting, given Malcolm's riotous life. Bernard Rhodes, who had finally mended his fences with Malcolm, was among the mourners, as well as Vivienne, and some other faces like Bob Geldof, Tracey Emin, Alan Yentob and Adam Ant, all gathered alongside the great and the good of the fashion world. Bernard had a minor spat with Vivienne. I think he was claiming that she'd made the whole memorial about herself, but of course by doing that, Bernard kind of made it about *him*. Steve was still in self-imposed exile in LA, but he did send a note, which Malcolm and Vivienne's son Joe Corré gave as a reading.

'Malcolm,' it read. 'Where's all the fuckin' money? Shall I bring a crowbar and open the coffin and see if you've taken it with you?'

He went on to say that Malcolm, his friend, had changed the world.

Malcolm's casket had been spray-painted with the legend 'Too Fast to Live, Too Young to Die', and he was laid to rest in Highgate Cemetery to the strains of Sid's version of 'My Way'. His headstone reads, 'Better a spectacular failure, than a benign success.'

I think Malcolm only tried to take the reins of the creative side once. One day, when John wasn't around for some reason, the remaining three of us were rehearsing on Denmark Street. While we were working, Malcolm said he'd try his hand at writing some lyrics. We left him to it. We'd worn ourselves out playing full tilt and went upstairs for a cup of tea and a breather, but when I came back down the stairs, I saw Malcolm. The floor around him was littered with little balls of screwed up paper.

'How's it going, Malcolm?' I laughed.

'It's hard,' was all he said.

Despite everything that went down between us, we shared a lot of history. None of it would have happened without Malcolm. He wasn't responsible for the music, but he was the catalyst, this pebble in the pool, sending out all these ripples. Malcolm was like the sun. Interesting people were always drawn into his orbit. I doubt anybody would have heard of the Sex Pistols without Malcolm. Possibly no one would have heard the name Malcolm McLaren without us, but as Steve pointed out, he did kind of change the world.

39

ALL OR NOTHING

I was ten years old in 1966. QPR were treading water in the old third division and England had just won the World Cup at Wembley. Harold Wilson was prime minister and London was swinging. Kensal Green wasn't all that swinging, but that was about the time I discovered the Small Faces, the much-loved darlings of Wapping Wharf launderette. At the end of that glorious summer, they ascended to the top of the hit parade with their tune 'All or Nothing', and I was a fan from the first moment I laid ears on them. Released on the Decca label, it was the culmination of a run of incredible, raw R&B pop numbers that have truly stood the test of time.

I first saw the Small Faces when they performed on *Ready Steady Go!* (or *RSG!*), a music show broadcast every Friday evening between 1963 and 1966 on ITV. If you want to see a snapshot of what the Swinging Sixties era was like, then you'd be hard pressed to find a better example. The top groups and singers from the UK and the USA, captured in grainy black-and-white action. They performed the top hits of the day, while swinging London teens in all their Carnabetian finery twisted and grooved in the audience. All the girls were swooning, sometimes screaming, at the boys in the band, while the lads were looking at Cathy McGowan, one of the real 'it' girls of the time, hoping she would look their way. As I said, I was only ten, but even I could see it looked like a happening place.

Steve Marriott was the real deal. No one could touch him in my opinion. In a previous life as a child actor, he'd been the original Artful Dodger in Lionel Bart's West End production of *Oliver!*, and he and the rest of the group seemed to embody that mischievous Artful Dodger spirit. By any measure, he lived a life and a half, but in the early '90s, Steve Marriott died tragically in a house fire. He was only forty-four. Such a wasted talent. Of course, it was Steve who left the Small Faces to form Humble Pie with Peter Frampton and the remaining three Faces, and we've spoken about the impact they've had on me already. The first time I saw them was when they played at the Rainbow in Finsbury Park in 1972.

They put on quite the show. There were even dancing girls. 'Stay with Me' had just been a big hit, so they were in their Imperial Phase at that point. Between songs, and sometimes during, Rod and the band would kick footballs around the stage and into the boisterous crowd. Normally, during Kenney's drum solo, you'd expect the rest of the band to nip offstage and grab a quick drink, but that night they had a bar set up at the side of the stage with a bartender serving them drinks throughout the show. Later, when I got to know Steve and Paul, I found out they'd been in the audience, too.

Later the same year I saw the Faces again, at the Empire Pool Wembley, now known as the Wembley Arena. It was a pivotal gig. That night, the Faces were supported by the Pink Fairies and the New York Dolls. It was the original line-up of the Dolls, before the first album even, with Billy Murcia on drums, less than a month before he died of a heroin overdose in London. He was only twenty-one. I remember their performance so clearly. It was like they'd been beamed down from outer space. Sylvain Sylvain did the whole show on roller skates and the band wore frilly blouses while cavorting around with extravagant stage gear. The music didn't sound like anything that was on the radio over here at the time. The Dolls looked like a glam band, to some extent, but sounded more like Iggy and the Stooges. They ended their set with a real *follow that* kind of flourish. The Faces were probably the only band on the planet at the time who could.

After Ian McLagan played with us on the Rich Kids tour, we lost contact for a few years. He'd moved to Austin, Texas by then. He was keeping his hand in, of course, and when-ever I heard he'd played on a record, I always made a point of seeking it out. One night, I was driving down to see family on the Isle of Wight, listening to the radio, when a familiar voice came over the airwaves. It was Mac. He was a guest on Greater London Radio. It was a round table kind of affair, where a panel of guests reviewed that week's new singles. It was great to hear his dulcet tones again, but I lost the signal as soon as I was south of the M25. Because I'd been on GLR a hundred times and knew the people at the radio station, I put a call in and asked them to give Mac my number. He called me as soon as he got out of the studio, and we met up for a drink a week or so later in town. It was great to catch up.

'Well,' he said, 'I did a few bits with Springsteen. That was alright. Money wasn't too bad. I did a bit with Dylan.' He was reeling off this list of achievements like it was a grocery list. 'Dylan. That was okay. Yeah, he called me, but I like a song with a beginning, middle and end, and they're all over the place.'

'Yeah, but it's Dylan, though. And Springsteen,' I said.

'Yeah,' Mac sighed. 'But what I'd really like to do is re-form the Faces,' he said.

Sadly, Ronnie Lane had passed away in 1997. He died from pneumonia, during the final stages of the multiple sclerosis that had beset his last years. When Mac mentioned that he was thinking about putting the Faces back together again, I made it abundantly clear that I was the man for the job if they were thinking about hiring a bass player.

'I learned to play with these songs. I know them all backwards,' I told him. I said if there were discussions, I wanted him to put a word in for me, and he agreed. A while later, I received a call from Mac. I'd got the gig.

And that's how I wound up touring with Mac, Kenney and Ronnie Wood in the Faces. It was a solid-gold, dream-come-true moment. Originally, the plan had been for Rod Stewart to take part, but apparently there were some management issues and he had to bow out. They tried to get Rod to come on board, and it looked like he was in for a while but, ultimately, he couldn't do it. Mac had tried for years to reunite with Stewart and re-form the original Faces for a tour. Rod kept knocking him back. I think he just got tired of waiting and decided to press ahead without him. I'd heard that Rod wasn't delighted that it went ahead. When he declined, the guys asked Mick Hucknall of Simply Red if he was interested. Mick is a great soul singer, and the Faces were always a great rock band with a great soul singer, so it was a good fit. Besides anything else, I would have given an arm to play with Kenney, Mac and Ronnie, so they didn't need to ask me twice. I didn't really care who was singing. Ronnie Wood is my favourite guitarist, and the Faces are still one of my favourite bands. We didn't play too many shows together, but it's a memory I'll always hold dear. I got to be mates with the band I loved as a kid.

One night after rehearsals for the tour, we all decamped to the Jazz Café in Camden to see Bobby Womack play a set. Ronnie had been out to dinner with Rod earlier and he brought him along for the show. Once he spotted us in the audience, Rod good-naturedly shouted across to Mick.

'Oi! Hucknall, you fucking kant! You nicked my job!'

Between 2010 and 2012, we played maybe a dozen shows around the world, culminating in a headline show at the Fuji festival in Japan. I must confess it was an emotional time for me. Original bassist Ronnie Lane was the reason I picked up that second-hand bass in the first place, so it was an honour and a privilege to stand in for him. Learning to play those songs again, I realised just how crucial his bass playing was to the Faces songs. In truth, I didn't really have to learn them. I practically knew them by heart already. Once rehearsals were over and we were on the road, we had so much fun. We even brought 'All or Nothing' into the set. To this day, if I'm playing a solo show, I'll often finish with that song. It always goes down well.

When I was knocking around with Mac and Kenney it occurred to me that they hadn't played a lot of those old Small Faces songs since the band split in the '60s, so we added it to the set. While we were rehearsing, Mac watched me play.

'What are you playing there?' He had his eyes fixed on the fret board.

'B minor.'

'Everybody thinks it's B minor.' He laughed. 'It's B major actually. More manly.'

I tried it again in B major, as Mac had suggested. And he was right. It *was* more 'manly'. We played the more manly B-major version when we headlined the main stage at the Bospop Festival in the Netherlands. We encored with 'All or Nothing' and 'Tin Soldier'. As we walked offstage, Ronnie tapped me on the shoulder.

'How about that, Glen.' He was grinning from ear to ear. 'We played two Small Faces songs with two original Small Faces, and we got 'em right!'

40

MONTAGUE TERRACE (IN BLUE)

I'm quite a fan of Scott Walker, although I had to take quite a circuitous route to find him. If I had to put my finger on it, I guess it all stemmed from discovering the songs of Jacques Brel. And possibly the first time I knowingly became aware of Jacques Brel's work was when I first heard Bowie's cover of 'My Death' and the Sensational Alex Harvey Band's incredible version of the song 'Next'! As I've said before, connections everywhere.

When you're a kid and you're saving up to buy an LP, you always try to get your money's worth from every album you buy. Singles are cheap, more disposable, and you play them to death. An album is a more considered purchase, so you take your time over every detail, savouring everything about it – the music, obviously, but the sleeve, the label, the track listing and the song credits. Who's who and who wrote what. In the case of 'Next' and 'My Death', I realised both songs were written by the same guy, Jacques Brel. I did a bit of digging and I learned that Brel was a Belgian chansonnier, and he was hugely popular all over the French-speaking world. I don't know how you'd classify Brel. It wasn't exactly pop music. It was poetry mixed with something darker and more theatrical. Whatever it was, it had a real impact on me.

The song, 'Next', that the Sensational Alex Harvey Band recorded sounded completely out of synch with what was going on at the time. For a start, it was a tango. I mean, who records a tango? Also, the lyrics are outrageous. The song is written from the point of view of a guy who has joined the French Foreign Legion. To keep the platoon happy, a mobile brothel is brought to their camp and the young soldier is standing in line, waiting for his turn with the next whore. As he does, he has all these thoughts passing through his head, wondering what awaits him. All the while he's standing naked in the queue, the lieutenant is ushering the next soldier into the mobile brothel with a slap on the arse: 'Next. Next!'

Considering it was from the early 1960s, to my ears, it was the most shocking lyric I'd ever heard. It's difficult to imagine an English or American songwriter getting away with something so forthright.

Sometime later, I found an album, *Scott Walker Sings Jacques Brel*, in a record store. I knew of Scott Walker from my days listening to pirate radio. He was a member of the 1960s pop vocal group the Walker Brothers, and had enjoyed quite a few big hits back in the day. After he went solo, Scott changed gears and started releasing these lush, orchestrated records, but they didn't sound anything like the crooners of the time. They sounded kind of weird and other-worldly. And he covered all those Jacques Brel songs. It's hard to imagine a modern-day equivalent. I couldn't picture Gary Barlow jumping ship from Take That and singing songs about mobile whorehouses and death.

The song, 'Montague Terrace (In Blue)', was a track on his debut solo album, released in 1967. Everyone was trying their hand at psychedelia around that time, but Scott seemed to be forging his own path, creating something a bit more baroque. When you listen to the lyrics, you realise 'Montague Terrace' could have been written about any place in the world. It's a catch-all term for a place we all lived at some point in our lives, a place that holds some meaning for us. It's universal. Whether you're on Sunset Strip or living on the Harrow Road, everybody has a place in the back of their mind that they can relate to, where something of consequence has happened in their lives – a place or a time when the slings and arrows of outrageous fortune forced you to move on, but you still hold those memories.

I learned to play it on my acoustic guitar and started to perform it at a few little gigs I was playing after the Dead Men Walking shows. I always had a penchant for a ballad singer, particularly Anthony Newley and things like 'What Kind of Fool Am I?'. I wonder sometimes if I shouldn't have been a balladeer. You can get a bit darker lyrically, but the darkness isn't necessarily right there on the surface, so it creeps up on you. The first few times I played it, I enjoyed seeing the audience's faces when I segued from a version of 'Anarchy in the UK' straight into 'Montague Terrace'. You had all these heavy-duty punks nodding their heads. They loved it.

Around that time, it felt good to put a smile on a few faces. The world seemed to feel like it had gotten skewed somehow and was slipping off its axis. The orange guy was in the White House and over here in Britain, everyone seemed to have lost their minds. We'd gone back a couple of generations in time almost and were back to doffing our caps to the lords of the manor and kidding ourselves into believing this procession of Eton ghouls we kept putting in No. 10 were our betters. Before the Brexit curtain was pulled shut, my band and I took a fling around Europe, touring with the Dropkick Murphys, the US punk band, thinking it might be the last chance to exercise our right to free movement.

I'd started work on a new album, *Good to Go*, with my friends Earl Slick, from David Bowie's band, and Slim Jim Phantom from the Stray Cats. I started seeing the Stray Cats when they first came to the UK, playing small pubs and clubs and then catching the public's imagination. I had a publicist at the time, and she shared an office with the publicist for the Stray Cats, so consequently I saw a lot of Jim and we became mates. Richard Branson, the Virgin chief, used to have a club around by Victoria called the Venue and they regularly had fantastic bands lined up to play. It was an American-style supper club, where you could dine while the bands played their show. Across a period of a couple of weeks, not only did I catch the Stray Cats, but I also saw Captain Beefheart and the Reverend Al Green. One time I went down, a little worse for wear during my chaotic spell, Jim came over to join me and I threw up all over his drape suit. I think he realised we'd all been in that same boat before, so I'm glad to say our friendship managed to weather that storm. We lost touch for a few years, but reconnected when I was in Los Angeles later with the Pistols, rehearsing for the Filthy Lucre tour. Chris Thomas, who was supposed to be recording the live album from the tour,[1] was over and we went to see Jarvis Cocker's band, Pulp, play a club show. When we arrived, it turned out Jim was running the club. We caught up again after I'd finished playing some shows with Dead Men Walking, with Kirk Brandon from Spear of Destiny, Pete Wylie from the Mighty Wah! and Mike Peters from the Alarm, kind of a British punk version of the Traveling Wilburys.

It was good timing for me. I wasn't having a crisis of confidence exactly, but I wasn't as sure of myself as a singer-songwriter as I am now. Originally they wanted me to play bass, but having played bass with a lot of bands and artists down the years, I felt I wanted to stretch myself a bit and sing live with an acoustic guitar. It was a good atmosphere, working with a few like-minded individuals, but it took a lot of work to make

---

[1] The live album that was eventually released was recorded at the Finsbury Park shows in London. Steve Jones had pitched the idea of *The Sex Pistols Live at Caesar's Palace* in Las Vegas. Approaches were made by our people to their people, but Vegas was still a mob town, and the idea was nixed. Someone probably still has the telegram from Caesar's Palace saying: 'We do not want you. And please do not recommend your friends to contact us either.'

the transition. I don't think anyone is born to be on stage and comes out of the womb with a neat line in on-stage patter, but I felt it in my water that if I didn't do something to address the situation, I was always going to be pegged as Glen Matlock, the bass player.

I don't think any of us would really consider Dead Men Walking to be a crowning achievement in our careers, but for me personally, as a singer-songwriter, it was a step towards me gaining more confidence in front of an audience and a better understanding of my craft. We all played our own little segments and told stories between songs, and over the course of those dates and a few solo acoustic shows I played, I slowly became more comfortable stepping into the limelight, and that led me to the point where I was ready to start work on a new record. I'd enjoyed the shows, so I felt like I wanted to try to make a more stripped-back record. Some accompaniment, but nothing too heavy. Enter Slim Jim and Earl Slick.

We recorded most of the album over the course of a week or so, in upstate New York, in a little town called Rhinebeck. It was a cool, relaxed vibe between us. One day Jim broke a skin on his snare drum, and while we waited for that to be repaired, I sat idly strumming the chords to 'Montague Terrace' and humming the melody. Originally we hadn't planned to include the song on the album, but when Jim heard me noodling around, he suggested we have a crack at it. While Jim's snare was being fixed, I'd noticed him eyeing a pair of great timpani, kind of large kettle drums, they had in the corner of the studio. I told him why not, and that's how we got that great, epic drum sound on the finished record. Considering we didn't have the budget for a seventy-piece orchestra, our version of 'Montague Terrace' is a real statement song on that album. It showed that I really did have the confidence to put myself out front and centre as a balladeer. Who knows? Maybe one day I will record that album of covers.

41

HANGING ON THE TELEPHONE

'Hanging on the Telephone' was the first Blondie song I really picked up on. It was a cover of a song by the Nerves, a short-lived US power pop trio led by Jack Lee, who wrote it. The original had come out a couple of years before, but it hadn't been a hit. Blondie's cover, on the other hand, was a worldwide smash, and it sounds just as fresh and exciting today as it did when I first heard it in 1978. The only difference is that, these days, you're just as likely to find me playing 'Hanging on the Telephone' as you would be to find me listening to it.

I can't put my finger on when I first met Blondie, but I guess I've known them all a little bit for a long time, long before Debbie Harry gave me a peck on the cheek that one Halloween. (Apologies for mentioning that a second time, but I imagine if it happened to you, you would mention it more than once, too.) I think, because we were all knocking around on similar tour schedules, I first met the guys and Debbie in 1978. I remember they came to the Roundhouse to see the Vicious White Kids show I played with Sid and Rat Scabies. That was how it was. If you were on tour and you had a night off in an unfamiliar town, you'd always check the listings to see if there was a band playing nearby.

Whenever I saw Blondie out on the town, they always seemed to travel in a unit, so if you saw Debbie, you saw Chris and Clem and Jimmy and everyone. Possibly because the Pistols didn't do anything like that – camaraderie wasn't our strongest suit – it always struck me as kind of sweet. That was how I got to know Clem Burke. I saw Blondie play one of their first shows in London at Dingwalls and I have a clear memory of Clem smashing up his drum kit that night. We became good friends around that time. Back in those days, Clem used to describe Blondie as a bubblegum pop band, but I think that was probably just false modesty. They were always much more than that.

Clem and I come from a similar working-class background, and like me, he doesn't have any brothers or sisters. Although Clem is from the US, he's a real Anglophile, so we both had similar musical interests and influences. I consider Clem to be an honorary Englishman. His musical hero is Keith Moon, and he keeps a little shrine to him in his dressing room, with a pair of Moon's stack-heeled boots (as well as a letter of authenticity from Keith's mother, 'Kit' Moon). Both our dads had Alzheimer's, so we'd both had similar experiences of that – including the heartbreak of finding yourself on tour and getting calls from the neighbours in the middle of the night telling you that your dad's walking down the street in his pyjamas. Clem and I have an open-door policy with each other. If ever I'm in LA for a few days, invariably Clem invites me to stay at his place. If he's in London, I'll return the favour and he'll stay in my spare room. It's great to have a place to crash and friends to hang out with. It can take away some of the pressure. Air travel isn't exactly cheap, so for me it's a real luxury to have a kind of home from home when I'm away working. Plus, from my perspective, there's the added bonus of being away from fucking Tory Britain for a while.

At the tail end of the pandemic, Clem called me up and mentioned that their bass player in their live set-up was a little under the weather. He said Blondie were going out on the road and into the studio again and he asked if I'd be interested in signing on for a tour of duty. I thought that sounded cool. Whenever I've been in the same city, Clem's always given me tickets, and consequently, Blondie is probably the band I've seen the most, and I guess that meant I already had a good working knowledge of their repertoire. Clem and I have been involved in several hairbrained projects together down the years and we've always got a kick out of playing together. We have an occasional side project called the International Swingers and he's played drums on a couple of tracks on my latest album.

'When do you need me?' I asked, thinking this was going to be a few months down the line.

'Next week,' he replied.

As I've gotten older, I've realised that it can be easy to sit at home, waiting for just the right phone call, but sometimes it doesn't pay to spend too much time weighing your options.

A lot of my fellow musicians can be a little like that. Often, they'll say no because they don't think something's right for them or it's outside their usual, familiar lane. From my experience, sitting at home waiting for the right call begets more sitting around waiting for the phone to ring. Saying yes, on the other hand, sometimes begets more offers of work, and a lot of the time, you find yourself having a lot more fun in life. Sometimes, as I had with Iggy Pop, you get to see the world on someone else's dime, and you get to play and hang out with some cool people. You can mull things over in your head a hundred times, work out all the pros and cons, but the truth is, I didn't think about the offer for too long. Blondie are a terrific band, Clem is a great mate and, importantly, I quite fancied the idea, so I told him yes.

Besides anything else, I had a nagging feeling that I'd missed the boat with Blondie when they re-formed in the late '90s. After the Pistols' Filthy Lucre tour, I decamped to Paris for a few months. It was the early days of mobile phones, so if you suddenly went off grid, you became difficult to track down. I later discovered that Clem was trying to contact me. He had left dozens of messages at my hotel, but I didn't realise until much later. When I found out he'd been trying to speak to me about joining the band, it was quite disappointing. I guess when he called this time, part of me was thinking that I didn't want to miss out again. Anyway, after I hung up the call from Clem, I took myself down to Denmark Street to buy the complete Blondie songbook. I caught the first flight to New York, rehearsed with the band for five days, and then we were soon on the road.

Blondie's management and road crew go way back together. I was sixty-five when I arrived on the tour, which is a funny age to find yourself as the new kid on the block. If I was feeling anxious, though, I needn't have been. Everyone in the Blondie organisation was very welcoming. To announce my arrival, Chris Stein, co-founder and former partner of Debbie Harry, posted a picture of me and him on social media. The picture dated back to 1979 and showed the two of us hanging out at the Mudd Club in New York. When the tour rolled around to Chicago, the date coincided with my birthday, and they projected the words 'Happy Birthday Glen' up on the big screen before presenting me with a birthday cake.

We played a bunch of shows in the UK and US, and we were greeted every night like conquering heroes. In San Diego, an outdoor show, the stage was surrounded by palm trees and overlooked the yacht club. The show was a complete sell-out, so looking out from the stage, you could see dozens of ticketless fans hanging onto paddleboards out in the bay and cheering us on. We played two homecoming shows in New York at the Rooftop at Pier 17, on the Manhattan side of the East River, overlooking the Brooklyn Bridge and the NYC skyline. We even played a few shows in South America, big festival appearances in Mexico City and Colombia. They could have played it safe, but even today, they're open to ideas and doing things a little differently. In Bogotá, a local group called Systema Solar joined us on stage for the song 'Sugar on the Side' after Chris Stein discovered their music online and reached out to them.

Those were big, big crowds, a real sight to behold. Thirty thousand people singing every word of every song when English isn't even their first language. I've realised now that if I can't play these massive shows with the Pistols any more, having Blondie up and running and playing similar-sized events is the next best thing in terms of that kind of audience reaction. It's raised my stock as a musician. Plus playing those shows with Blondie takes the pressure off having to answer questions about the Sex Pistols whenever someone sticks a microphone or an iPhone under my nose. Now, instead of fielding questions about what John's really like, reporters ask me what Debbie's like, and I much prefer saying something positive to something negative.

I went into the studio for ten days or so at the end of 2022 and recorded the bass parts for their new album. Bearing in mind it's someone else's band, they're still progressive and open to ideas. But in any case, just being invited along to join the party on stage and in the studio has been a real privilege.

Blondie mastered the three-minute pop song a long time ago. Three minutes has always been my personal yardstick. If you can say what you need to say in three minutes flat, you're probably doing something right. It goes without saying that their songbook is packed with these well-crafted punk-pop crossover classics, but there's always been more to Blondie than that. They came up with all the New York punk bands, but they were never constrained by the scene, which is kind of the thing I was aiming for when I started the Rich Kids. They have always had an art school edge. In fact, Chris Stein used to say Blondie isn't a band, it's an art project. Possibly that's a stretch, but I can see where he's coming from.

The band has gone through some line-up changes down the years. Chris doesn't come on the road these days, but he's still involved, masterminding the operation from afar. Jimmy Destri has also taken a back seat, but he's still involved in the organisation – he also wrote the Blondie comeback hit, 'Maria'. Essentially the heart and soul of the band is Debbie and Clem, so while they are there, it will always be Blondie. Recently, someone online popped their head above the parapet and had a dig at me for landing these kinds of gigs. He was harping on about how I'm an average bassist who just landed on my feet. I never pretended to anyone that I'm great, but in this case, I did reply.

'Sometimes, mate,' I said. 'You've just got to be the right guy.'

42

CONSEQUENCES COMING

In 1976, when the Pistols signed to EMI, we were asked along to do a photo call with the Esteemed Gentlemen of the Press. Even the *Daily Mail* sent a photographer along. The man from the *Mail* came down to EMI in Manchester Square and we were all sprawled across a sofa while the photographer was trying to arrange us, getting us to move closer together so we would all be in the shot. He was cheerful enough, old-school Fleet Street, trying to butter us up. It was all 'Alright lads?' while we jostled around and mugged for the camera. We were kids, having a laugh. We had probably drunk a few cans of beer before the session, so to someone of that generation, it probably seemed a bit chaotic. He was snapping away and, because the beer was gassy, I let out a noisy burp. Because my parents raised me right, I immediately covered my mouth and said pardon me. The next day, when they ran the story, it read, 'When asked to move, bassist Glen Matlock just belched.'

This was in the aftermath of Grundy, so I guess it was to be expected. It was a small thing, just a modest twist on the truth, but it was my first insight into how some elements of the media worked. Or, in this case, how they worked against you. They're happiest when they can put you in whatever box they assign to you. In the following months, on the Anarchy in the UK tour, the same 'gentlemen' hounded us across the country. We hardly got to play anywhere because of the media storm around us. The Bill Grundy appearance may have started the moral panic, but it was the press who were fanning the flames. We were touring in the north in an old-fashioned coach, and they literally tracked us backwards and forwards across the Pennines like we were the Great Train Robbers. Some of them were still wearing macs and trilby hats with a press card stuck into the band, like characters in an old black-and-white movie. Whenever we stopped to get a coffee or to have a pee at the services, we had to run a gauntlet of press people. After one show, I was at the front of the coach, a seat or two behind the driver near the window, and I could hear a couple of these guys talking.

'Fred, did you get the quote?'

'Nah,' came the reply from Fred. 'How about you, Bill?'

'Yeah, I got two fucks and a shit from Johnny Rotten.'

I was back on the promotional hamster wheel a lot in 2023, putting out the good word for my new album, *Consequences Coming*. Over the first week and a half of promo, I probably did somewhere between forty and fifty interviews. Every day there was a raft of telephone interviews; radio, TV, online with the States, different syndicated interviews that go out in all kinds of places that I wouldn't normally be able to get to. It's a lot of work and it can get a bit monotonous. Sometimes you can wind up feeling quite frazzled. You're on Sky News with Kay Burley one day and the next day you're up in Manchester for a BBC *Breakfast* interview. It's an objectively strange way to spend your life.

I wasn't ever given media training, in the way you might today, but I've picked up a few tricks on how to handle it. I was asked to give a talk once and turned to my old friend Midge Ure for some helpful advice. I explained that I didn't mind people asking me questions, but the idea of having to stand in front of a big room giving a talk can sometimes be a bit daunting. Midge had been doing some motivational speaking and told me his method of getting through it was to make out he was the person asking the questions and to repeat their question back as part of the answer. When you're facing the same questions, day in, day out, interview after interview, repeating the question back is a good way to keep your answers tight and keeps you on subject. When both my boys started out in bands and had coaching sessions on how to answer questions and how to conduct themselves, my only advice to them was to just be natural. Be honest and say what you genuinely think and then no one can pull you up on it. Be polite, speak your mind and stand your ground if you need to. And that's the approach I try to take myself.

The mechanics for these things are all broadly the same. If you have an appearance on the BBC *Breakfast* show for example, you tend to travel up on the train the night before. Cheap

Holiday Inn stayover. No expense spared. Once you've checked in, you do a few Zoom interviews from the hotel room, and then you have to cancel dinner with friends because you're booked to appear on the *Times* TV show, and you didn't see it on the schedule. If it's an early morning breakfast show, everything is geared to meeting a 6.30 a.m. call time, so you arrive bang on time and then hang around for an hour and a half in the green room. For a ten-minute TV spot, there's a lot of work going on just to get you on the studio floor and in front of the camera in the first place. With live TV, you get used to the delays – someone with a clipboard poking their head around the green room door, telling you something's come up, some breaking news or other, and would you mind hanging on a bit longer and can I get you another coffee, Glen? You get a little peeved sometimes, but you do your best to be all sweetness and light and finally someone comes along to wheel you into the studio. Ultimately, you have your record to promote, so you sit and paste on a smile while they ask you some not particularly probing questions and before you know it, your ten minutes is up.

It wasn't Bill Grundy by any stretch, but I went (semi) viral for a day recently following a BBC *Breakfast* interview. That was interesting. I took my seat on set, in front of a large projected image of Steve Jones and me on stage with the Pistols,[1] and Jon Kay, the presenter, asked me if I was still as angry at the world as I was in the Sex Pistols days.

---

[1] Keen-eyed *Breakfast* TV viewers will have noticed the word 'Slag' clearly emblazoned on Steve Jones's guitar strap.

'In a different way,' I told him. 'I'm not angry. I'm livid about the whole Brexit thing. As a musician, I'm livid about our loss of freedom of movement in twenty-seven countries and how it's hamstrung our chances of touring the way we used to be able to do. It's just needless really, especially when we were promised as musicians, we would still have a way of working. The EU offered the government a way around it, and our government turned it down.'

I remember I called the whole thing a cock-up and Jon Kay immediately tried to smooth things over in case anyone was spitting out their tea or choking on their cornflakes.

'We don't want to turn this into a political interview,' he said. 'But you'll be aware that it's three years to the day since we left the EU and you know that the supporters of Brexit will say, it will take time to settle down, we've had a pandemic in the meantime, but in the end, there will be advantages for all of us.'

'I can't see any. And lots of people can't see any.' I smiled. 'I know you're working for the BBC and you've got to push the government line a little bit, but there's a whole bunch of people that think it's the worst thing that's ever happened.'

Afterwards, someone at the BBC had to come out and defend the show, which is obviously ridiculous. Unfortunately, the BBC have been painted into a corner. There's this very disingenuous phrase they use at the BBC: 'For the sake of balance, we're just trying to show both sides of the argument,' they say. When I hear that I think, *Well, that's not true. You're just not allowed to voice certain opinions because this is the BBC.* Because they need to be seen to show balance in everything, someone will say it's raining, and they immediately counter that with another talking head telling you it's not raining at all. In fact, it's a heatwave. As a result, we have these right-wing nutjobs on TV and radio every day. It has normalised these lunatics and dragged the country to the right. Anyway, I was just trying to promote my record and maybe a little bit of sanity at the same time.

I received a lot of nice feedback from people, thanking me for saying what everyone else had been thinking. I'm glad it struck a chord with people.[2] What's been going on in this country since just prior to Brexit is scandalous. As I see it, it all started with the EU announcing they were going to target offshore banking and tax havens and the rich not paying their fair share. It's all self-serving nonsense. It's so sad because, before all this kicked off, the idea that being a part of Europe was doing us a disservice was such a minority view, it's just been this drip, drip, drip of poison being poured into everyone's ears over the past seven or eight years. I think it's essential, if you have a platform, to make a stand.

You only need to look at the knots the BBC tied themselves in with Gary Lineker recently. He didn't say anything that wasn't true, he didn't call anyone a Nazi, but there was a ridiculous,

---

[2] Most of the feedback I got after the BBC *Breakfast* appearance was positive. The people who follow me, or who are fans of what I do, usually get me. Some people don't like to hear an inconvenient truth. They don't like to have a mirror held up to them. Very occasionally, someone will try to shout me down for sticking my head above the parapet or tell me to stay in my lane. You see the odd message on Twitter saying, 'Glen, you don't under-stand. The right is the new left.' Mostly, when you click on their profile, you find that they're Public Image Ltd fans.

pearl-clutching uproar from the right-wing press. But, because he has this massive platform and he's witty and he's apposite, they just want him to stop showing them up. It's ironic really. Every day, they print these toxic, gaslighting headlines, calling anyone who doesn't follow the party line snowflakes, but you shine a light on their hypocrisy, and they have the nerve to cry foul! But I like Lineker. He has his principles and he adheres to them. I was playing a show the night they suspended Gary and we dedicated my song 'Head on a Stick' to him out of solidarity.

When I think of where we are now politically, I'm reminded of this guy, Marc Zermati. I met Marc on my first trip to Paris. This was when I was sixteen, so before the Pistols. Mark was kind of Monsieur Punk Rock in Paris. He had a record shop that barely had any records beyond Metallic K.O. by the Stooges and maybe a Flaming Groovies record or two. If ever anyone ventured in to browse through the racks and asked if he had any records by, say, James Taylor, he would angrily chase them out into the streets. He was friends with Iggy, but he also set up the Skydog record label in the early '70s – their claim to fame was that they put out 'T.V. Eye' by the Stooges. Mark was born in Algeria[3] and his family had been forced to leave when it all kicked off over there in the '50s.

---

[3] Incidentally, like most people of my generation, I saw that movie *The Battle of Algiers* (1966) years ago. It is quite a heavy and harrowing experience. Viv Albertine from the Slits said one of the reasons she always liked Mick Jones was because the first time they ever went for a date, Mick had taken her to see *The Battle of Algiers*. Obviously, it can pay dividends to be hip to politics.

'It was crazy,' he told me. 'Because the Algerians had fought in the Second World War on the same side as the French, we thought what we really wanted as a reward for playing our part was to become part of France. Then everything became factional and before long, everyone had taken up arms and were fighting among themselves. When I was leaving on the boat with my parents for France, there were literally bullets winging off the hull.'

I think the Tories are bonkers. But maybe that's too nice. They're inept, they're inadequate, but they're so factional, there's so much in-fighting, I think this is kind of what's happening to the Conservative Party now. It's as if they're re-enacting the Battle of Algiers among themselves. Fortunately for the rest of us, they just don't have guns. But that's what has brought us here. An internal squabble among Tories. And it's broken something fundamental in this country. It was a fucking disgrace in 2016 and, given what we now know, it's even more of a fucking disgrace today.

43

HEAD ON A STICK

I'm not a tubthumping political figure like Tariq Ali or Billy Bragg, but I do feel, as a songwriter, it's important to reflect what's going on around you. I guess, as a rule of thumb, people tend to drift to the right as they get older, but I'm happy it hasn't happened to me. I don't know if you'd call it activism, but in my own small way, I feel like I just want to say what's on my mind. I can't understand why people aren't doing it in a more forthright manner. I know lots of people would probably like to, but don't want to break cover. I'm too old now to worry about that kind of thing, but I can see how fear of a backlash is keeping some folk in their place.

When the Pistols sang 'God Save the Queen', we were speaking our minds and didn't want to be put in our place, and I feel much the same today as I did then. I still have a vehicle. Some people don't seem to like what I've been saying, and perhaps that's good. It's good to upset the applecart from time to time. We are living in dark times. Again. For one, racism has become more commonplace.

I've travelled widely over the years, to Russia, China, South America. You name the place and I've probably been there. And one thing I've learned is that wherever I go, people are essentially the same. Everybody's got the same ideals. They want to put food on their tables. They want to take care of their families. They want to be able to speak their minds and they want to be able to let off steam and have a laugh. Beyond our shores, people are seeing us now as a small, inconsequential country. Personally, I think it's a shame that some of the more insular people in the UK can't see the world that's outside their window. If they were sent on a modern-day equivalent of the grand tour and saw how the other half lived, I think they would have a different perspective on life. You would see less of this toxicity.

I may have done one or two Rock Against Racism things back in the day, but it's only these past few years that have made me more socially active. I've definitely become more politically engaged. Not long ago, I attended an assembly in Parliament Square for the Musician's Union. A bill had just been presented in support of the Agent of Change law, which supported live music venues across the country. Essentially, longstanding venues were in danger of closing after developers placed new-builds in the same area, and the existing venues were being targeted because of noise complaints from the residents. In some cases, the venues were forced to shut down. The bill meant that whichever party changed the environment, whoever was the Agent of

Change was responsible for soundproofing and protecting residents against noise pollution. I exchanged numbers and email addresses with Kevin Brennan, the Labour MP for Cardiff West, who was working on the bill. I mean, it stands to reason. If you move to Soho and don't like the noise, then maybe the fault lies with you?

That said, most of the marches I've attended have been against Brexit. I think sometimes it's important to stand up and be counted. It's a really unifying experience. I was on a march a few years ago, and I bumped into Kevin Rowland from Dexys Midnight Runners. There were pretty much a million people taking part in that protest, and it was almost totally ignored by the media. There were thousands of us sauntering down Piccadilly together, and one of the protesters had a ghetto blaster playing 'Let's Stick Together' by Bryan Ferry and I thought, what a fabulous place to have your song played. It was like an epiphany. I had to write a song like that, something just right for that scenario. That was the origin of 'Head on a Stick'.

Songwriting can be a funny process. It's a weird combination of instant inspiration and hard slog. When I write a song, it goes through many permutations. Mostly, I write of my own volition and usually that's when the idea for a song takes me. In this business these days, there are a lot of people who strike a rebellious stance, but what they say doesn't always amount to much. So I set about writing a proper protest song.

I wanted to write it because I feel so angry about where we find ourselves. I appreciate that I'm getting on a bit in age now and of course I don't fit in with what's happening in the charts, but that doesn't mean I shouldn't still express myself. Someone asked me recently how I would describe 'Head on a Stick' and I told them it's a 'spleen-venting toe-tapper'. It's hardly going to be rubbing shoulders with Sam Smith on the Radio 1 playlist, but I'm comfortable with that.

I feel like, as a society, we've been done over. What's been done to us, it feels like treason, so there should be consequences, right? I liked the idea of hundreds of thousands of people marching on parliament, demanding a few heads on sticks – metaphorically speaking, at least. The people who've brought us to this place are so brazen and should face some come-uppance. I don't want to wish anything bad on the people of Canvey Island, but if there was a particularly high tide coming down the Thames from the North Sea and the Thames Barrier were to fail, and these people happened to get a little wet, I don't think it would bother me particularly.

My latest album is called *Consequences Coming*, and that's how I feel. Consequences *are* coming for these people. I try to be opti-mistic, but ultimately, as I write this, I'm sixty-six years old, so I would like change to happen sooner rather than later. There's a whole house of cards that's just waiting to be brought down. This is the second Winter of Discontent I've lived through, and although people are suffering, part of me thinks maybe it's a good thing in a weird way. Winters of Discontent make people angry, and when people are angry enough, change is inevitable.

I would have liked to have heard 'Head on a Stick' playing as they dragged Trump out of the White House or when Johnson left No. 10 with his tail between his legs. The song was ready to go, but you can't always get your stuff out when you'd like. There's a long gestation period.

I've had moments when I've thought about leaving the country and obtaining settled status in the EU – I even had a flat lined up in Paris – but I missed the boat. Johnson was telling us – not just musicians, but anyone whose work meant they had a need to travel – things would be the same and we would be unaffected, so I was hanging on, expecting some kind of special dispensation. *Let them have their stupid Brexit*, I thought, *just so long as I can get on with my life*. But that didn't happen, and I missed the last helicopter out of Saigon.

I've reached an age where most of this crowd of politicians are younger than me. That means I'm old enough to remember what the UK was like before we joined the Common Market, as it used to be known. I don't want to rain on anyone's parade, but this country was a fucking dump. It's become a cliché, but we really were the sick man of Europe. Unfortunately, there's this toxic breed of politicians who are either too young to remember or they're just wilfully blind to reality. We're fast becoming the sick man of Europe all over again. Brexit is at the heart of everything that's gone wrong here. It's a huge backward step for all of us.

Despite what some might think of as its darker meanings, 'Head on a Stick' has a positive message. I want the song to be a call to arms, like a rallying cry. And it seems to have really struck a chord. It's worth reminding ourselves that they are terrified of us. When we appeared on the Bill Grundy show, we were public enemy number one according to all the red tops the next day.

Four blokes in a TV studio taking the mickey out of the older generation. What were they so scared of? I think it boils down to the fact that they know we're on to them. They've known all along, and they know one day, the tables will turn. In the meantime, we'll be here, sharpening our sticks.

EPILOGUE

When you walk out of Waterloo station, as you pass under the railway bridge across the Thames, you'll come across a line of arches. Last time I checked, someone had opened a wine bar and filled the place with thirsty commuters, but several years back, it was the site of an old artist's studio. It was open to passing trade, so you could float in off the street and have a nosey around if the mood took you. The place was kind of take-me-as-you-find-me and smelled of oil paint and linseed oil. The grey walls were lined with colourful oils and the paint-speckled floors were covered in stacks of unfinished or part-finished canvasses. The artist was a guy called Feliks Topolski, a twentieth-century expressionist painter who lived quite the life.

Topolski was a highly regarded draughtsman and became an official war artist during the Second World War. He was a Polish émigré who came to England in the 1930s and became a British citizen after the war, staying in London until his death in 1989. During his life, he travelled the world and became

303

this incredible witness to history. Topolski documented his life in a series of pencil-and-ink drawings and published them every fortnight from 1953 to 1979 in his *Chronicles*. I had some dealings with an expensive lawyer one time, and they had several Topolski pen-and-ink sketches displayed in their offices that I probably paid for. As I said, his art was superb, but that's not the thing I take away from Topolski. Not the main thing, anyway.

It's only when you see Topolski's work that you realise what good fortune he had. While he travelled the globe and went about the business of documenting his life, he was also creating a kind of illustrated history of the twentieth century. He had been in all the right places at all the right times and had watched all these seismic moments unfold first hand. Yet, as a Polish Jew, I doubt we would ever have heard of him if he hadn't come to London and gone on to live this incredible life. Obviously, I don't know what would have happened to Topolski if he had stayed in Poland, but I can take an educated guess. I don't mean to sound too highfalutin about things, but when I think about the weird confluence of events that took place in my life, all the interesting things I saw and people I encountered, I think about Feliks Topolski from time to time.

I've spoken a few times about serendipity, and the part it seems to play. How everything seems to dovetail together somehow. How if you pull on a strand here, it's attached to another, and if you tug hard enough, you see how some moment in time led to a moment of consequence. It feels like every important moment led seamlessly to the next and created an unrepeatable chain of events. Wherever I find myself now, I accept that a good deal of it is down to good fortune and being in the right place at the right time. I work hard and have done all my life, but I know that hard work isn't the be-all and end-all. I know that because I've been so fortunate, and I appreciate that. Without luck on my side, I could be in a different place altogether and my history would have to be rewritten accordingly.

Maybe if I hadn't stayed up all night watching those three-letter name bands under a starry Friday night sky, things might have worked out differently for me. I wouldn't have been half-asleep in the men's trouser department, and I would have stayed on at Whiteleys. It was just my good luck that I took those two buses from Kensal Green and found myself on the King's Road for the first time. It was pure chance that the shop with the brothel creepers had a vacancy the day I walked in, and I balked at the £12.50 price tag. Where would I be now if I'd missed that *Sliding Doors* moment in my life? Say, if they sold brothel creepers somewhere local and for half the price? The chain of events would have been entirely different. I wouldn't have taken the job at Let It Rock. I probably wouldn't have encountered Malcolm McLaren at all. There would have been no Vivienne Westwood in my life. I wouldn't have been told to keep an eye out for light-fingered lads who looked like refugees from *The Sweeney*. If I hadn't wanted to emulate Ronnie Lane, what would I have said when I overheard Fred and Barney discussing their need for a new bass player. It's like that poem: all for the want of a horseshoe nail, the kingdom was lost. Tiny decisions, leading to moments of real consequence in my life.

Unlike Topolski, I didn't bear witness to every key moment in twentieth-century history, but in my own way, I saw plenty. I stood witness to a moment, but it's a moment that resonates to this day. I walked away from and later returned to the most controversial band in pop history. Those songs, they have my handprint all over them, and I am proud of that. If I wasn't there, it's a fact that those songs wouldn't be there either. Maybe QT Jones and His Sex Pistols might have scored a record deal and had a couple of hits, with Steve singing a cover of a Love Affair tune. Who can say?

Beyond whatever I achieved with the Pistols, I've worked with some of the greats along the way: Iggy Pop, Mick Ronson, the Faces, Blondie. That's a decent résumé just on that front alone. But it's not just that. I'm still working my tail off, touring, hatching plans and finishing those half-written songs while I'm doing the ironing. Sometimes the song is fine, other times they come out perfect. Lyrics are just prose, a written-down conversation set to music, and yet somehow, when you get it right, there's more to it than the sum of its parts. I'll record a song, an album maybe. Perhaps I'll book a show in a town near you. I like a big theatre or arena occasionally, but I also like a small acoustic gig where I can see the audience. That intimacy. That connection. When you can feel – when you can *see* – that something you wrote decades ago has the power to reach out to people. That still spurs me on. My life in music.

I still get buttonholed wherever I go. Despite what you might have heard, people are generally nice. A kid came up to me in an airport recently and asked if I was Glen Matlock. I told him he was too young to know who Glen Matlock was and laughed. These things happen all the time, but it doesn't mean those people are going to buy tickets to see you play. I remember we gave an interview once, and some kid was saying our record changed his life.

Steve just said, 'Listen, mate, we just wanted to be in a rock 'n' roll band.'

History is just a matter of perspective, and we're each of us writing our own every day. There are a thousand different takes on what happened when and where. I remember when Jon Savage, the esteemed music writer, published his book, *England's Dreaming: The Sex Pistols and Punk Rock*, in the early 1990s. A mildly confused Paul Cook called me up after he'd read it.

'What's all this Situationist nonsense?' he said.

He was there and he didn't see it that way at all, but neither of them is wrong. As I said, it's perspective. What happened is what happened. Yes, we were different, but we were different for a whole bunch of reasons. There was a particular set of circumstances that brought us into being. That first time around, we were listening to the right kind of music – all these triggers – in an interesting place, hanging with unique people, and it was like some kind of magic formula if you like. Those moments could never be repeated because it needed all those ingredients for the spell to work.

I'm not a schizophrenic, but I'm aware there are two public Glen Matlocks. There's the ex-Sex Pistol, who every day answers a thousand questions about the same three-year period in history, and there's the second Glen who wants to be seen to be living in the present. He's the guy who's coming to a theatre or nightclub near you, and probably humping his own gear down to the venue. Or he's on tour with Blondie. Or he's writing a book. Or he's got a new idea for a song that he's singing while he makes a coffee. The second Glen is the one I'm rooting for. He's the reason I get up in the morning and put pen to paper. It's nice that it's going so well for him. He put in a lot of graft. Through diligence, hard work and application, there are more eyes on him now than there have been since the days of the Pistols. Maybe sometimes he wishes that had happened when he was a bit younger, but he's in a good place and he's not hung up on the past.

ACKNOWLEDGEMENTS

A special thanks to my publisher, Pete Selby, and his team at Bonnier Books UK. Thanks also to my agent, Adrian Sington, to Frank MacAweaney and to my collaborator, Peter Stoneman.

Finally, I want to thank you for taking time to read this book. I'd love to know what you think.

GLOSSARY

ACTION MAN The beloved British action figure equivalent to the American toy doll, *G.I. Joe*, created by Hasbro.

AIRFIX The premier British scale model-making kit company. Airfix models range from aircraft to military vehicles and were an inexpensive way to keep children quiet and busy in the dark days before the internet.

BARRACKING To shout someone down while they are speaking, without regard for what they might have to say.

BLAGGED To obtain something for nothing, often through charm or by other means.

BLUE BEAT The influential British record label, specializing in calypso, ska, reggae, and blues music. The Blue Beat label reached its zenith during the 1960s but continues to this day. "Bluebeat" was also a widely used term to describe what we now generally refer to as reggae.

BROTHEL CREEPERS A post-World War II British style of men's shoe. Brothel creepers, or simply "creepers," sport a thick, ridged crepe sole, with suede or leather uppers. It's thought they became known as creepers due to their association with the Creep dance craze.

BUDGIE The grimy 1970s British drama, set on the fringes of the London underworld. The eponymous Budgie, Ronald "Budgie" Bird, was played by 1960s cockney pop superstar, Adam Faith. The nickname "Budgie" is a derivation of the word budgerigar, a type of parakeet, commonly kept as pets in Britain.

BUNKED Avoiding an obligation. For example, "bunking" a train or a bus, is the practice of riding without a fare. It is also possible to "bunk off" school, which is the British equivalent to playing hooky.

BUTTER TOKENS A government assistance program introduced in the U.K. in 1973. In a similar vein but not identical to the U.S. food stamps program, recipients were able to exchange butter tokens for butter.

CANED A person who has smoked a whole joint with no assistance. This behavior is sometimes referred to as "bogarting" in U.S. circles.

CATHERINE WHEEL A firework, consisting of an angled rocket, mounted with a pin through its center. Once ignited, the energy of the firework causes the wheel to quickly rotate, creating a circular, spiral pattern of sparkling light. The Catherine wheel was so named after Saint Catherine of Alexandria, who was condemned to death by "breaking on the wheel", a form of torture and execution popularized in the Middle Ages. When Catherine touched the wheel, the wheel miraculously fell apart.

CHUFFED Being very pleased with oneself. If someone is extremely chuffed, they might describe themselves as being "chuffed to bits."

DANSETTE An extremely popular British brand of portable record players.

DROOG A violent young hooligan. Originally a Russian word, "droogs" was employed by British author Anthony Burgess to describe Alex's gang members in his famous dystopian novel, *A Clockwork Orange*, published in 1962.

GOT THE HUMP To be annoyed. If you have "got the hump," it's safe to say that you are not happy.

GRAFTED An informal way to describe working hard.

JACK-THE-LAD A cocky young man.

LEGLESS To be drunk e.g. I went out last night and got legless.

LOCK IN The illicit tradition of pubs staying open after hours for select customers to continue their revels beyond the legal licensed opening hours.

MAD KEEN To be enthusiastic. Extremely keen.

MODS Short for modernists, "mods" were a British youth culture tribe of the 1960s known for their affection for sharp Italian fashions, motor scooters, American R&B music, and amphetamines. Modernism was famously described by Peter Meaden, former publicist of the rock band The Who, as "clean living under difficult circumstances".

NAFF Someone or something that is uncool.

OFF THE BOIL To lose interest and subsequently become less vital.

PORTAKABINS A brand name for a portable, prefabricated building. Local school authorities in the U.K. still employ Portakabins as temporary classrooms and outbuildings at schools where space is at a premium.

PUB ROCK A short-lived but influential music movement in U.K. cities during the early 1970s and is often cited as a precursor to punk.

PUNT To gamble or wager.

RADIO CAROLINE The most infamous of the U.K.'s so-called "pirate" radio stations. In post-war Britain, the airwaves were strictly regulated, and licenses were not readily available. Therefore, "pirate" radio broadcasters circumvented the laws by broadcasting from outside British waters.

RUDE BOYS Jamaican street subculture. "Rude boys" (and "rude girls") helped popularize ska and reggae music in the U.K. in the 1960s and 1970s.

SKINFUL Excessive drinking. If you have drunk a skinful, it's safe to say, you have had more than enough to drink.

SKINT A lack of funds or reduced circumstances e.g. I would love to go out tonight, but I am skint.

SUEDEHEADS A British subculture that grew out of the skinhead youth tribe in the early 1970s, suedeheads wore their hair longer and adopted a more formal style. They favored button-down Ben Sherman shirts, loafers or brogues, as opposed to the heavy boots associated with the original skinhead style.

TEDDY BOYS Emerging as a post-war British youth culture tribe, stemming from the 1950s, Teddy Boys have roots dating back to the Edwardian era. "Teds" wore their hair greased back in a D.A. – duck's ass – style and donned drainpipe trousers, exposed socks, tailored drape jackets, button-down shirts, and the aforementioned brothel creeper shoes.

THREE-BAR FIRE An electric heater used in the U.K. with three power settings. Setting 1 will activate the first bar, setting 2 will activate the second, and so on.